Representing Translation

Representing Translation

The Representation of Translation and Translators in Contemporary Media

Edited by

Dror Abend-David

BLOOMSBURY ACADEMIC

NEW YORK • LONDON • OXFORD • NEW DELHI • SYDNEY

BLOOMSBURY ACADEMIC
Bloomsbury Publishing Inc
50 Bedford Square, London, WC1B 3DP, UK
1385 Broadway, New York, NY 10018, USA

BLOOMSBURY, BLOOMSBURY ACADEMIC and the Diana logo are trademarks
of Bloomsbury Publishing Plc

First published in the United States of America 2019

Cover image: Film: *The Railway Man*, 2014
Collection Christophel / Arena PAL

Bloomsbury Publishing Inc does not have any control over, or responsibility for, any
third-party websites referred to or in this book. All internet addresses given in this
book were correct at the time of going to press. The author and publisher regret
any inconvenience caused if addresses have changed or sites have ceased to
exist, but can accept no responsibility for any such changes.

A catalog record for this book is available from the Library of Congress.

ISBN: HB: 978-1-5013-3387-3
       ePDF: 978-1-5013-3389-7
       eBook: 978-1-5013-3388-0

Typeset by RefineCatch Limited, Bungay, Suffolk

To find out more about our authors and books visit www.bloomsbury.com
and sign up for our newsletters.

Contents

Editor's Note

Dror Abend-David
University of Florida

As Michael Cronin writes (2003: 68), translators in the twenty-first century have become important social and political agents. This fact has certainly been reflected in contemporary media. Who can forget the scene from Roberto Benigni's 1997 film, *La vita è bella* [*Life is Beautiful*], in which the hero volunteers to serve as an interpreter (despite the fact that he does not speak German) in order to spare his son from hearing the instructions of a Nazi officer? Those who do not speak Italian see this scene in (an additional) translation, rendering a translation-within-translation while representing the interpreter as an involved character (and, in this case, the protagonist). In this and other scenes like it, translation and translators become a part of the story and an inseparable part of a contemporary life that is increasingly multilingual, multiethnic, multinational, and socially diverse.

Consequently, media at the beginning of the twenty-first century presents a new trend in terms of the quantity, quality, and variety of foreign dialog. Moreover, such representation is often self-aware, ironic, and acutely conscious of the dramatic function of translation: not of transmitting content, but of infusing drama with social, political, and historical meaning.[1] Films such as Coppola's *Lost in Translation* (2003) and Pollack's *The Interpreter* (2005) reflect a number of theoretical issues that are discussed by translation scholars, presenting some thoughtful doubts and observations about the limits and potentials of translation (and interpretation). In television drama, translation and secondary languages can be ironic as well. One example might include the use in the drama, *Brothers & Sisters* (2006–2011), of Chinese (2008)[2] and of French (2009):[3] Chinese and French remain untranslated, highlighting the fact that Sarah (Rachel Griffiths) is ignorant of these languages, while the men that she is involved with speak them fluently. In *House M.D.* (2004–2012), the main character, Dr. Gregory House (Hugh Laurie), prefers the translation of an online Dutch stripper (2010)[4] to the services of a professional translator, an act that can be construed as a comment on the nature of translation as a profession . . . This trend does not skip the realm of online and offline commercials,[5] sometimes with surprising twists in plot. While it might not seem surprising that Japanese is used in a car commercial on prime-time television in the United States, it becomes quite a surprise when this is done to sell the Chrysler 200 (2014), an American car that is claimed to be (almost?) as good as a Japanese car. And translation is certainly made to steal the show in commercials such as those of Ukfoods (2008), in which actor Dennis Banks advertises imported food products that are brought from Britain to the United States. Although the commercial does not contain any languages other than English, translation is featured front-and-center as Banks talks of the imported products of Ukfoods in a local East London British slang, and his words are translated by subtitles into Standard English.

This phenomenon is a result of the fact that, even in the United States, foreign language, translation, and translators take an increasingly important role in everyday life. This is certainly reflected in the media: political drama, newscasts, thrillers, and comedies feature characters of translators and interpreters who often play an important role in the narrative. And even when translations and translators are not featured, contemporary media increasingly represent a multilingual, multicultural, and multinational reality. In the recent television series, *Mozart in the Jungle* (2014–2018), a New York-based opera company serves as a natural environment for the languages, identities, cultural references, foods, and traditions of a cosmopolitan city (often extended to exotic locations around the world). Beneath the surface, of course, such representation has an important political significance, oscillating between a diverse reality and the homogeneous political discourse that characterizes contemporary American politics.

Academically, the current collection, *Representing Translation: The Representation of Translation and Translators in Contemporary Media*, is a continuation of a previous collection: *Media and Translation: An Interdisciplinary Approach* (Bloomsbury, 2014; 2016). *Media and Translation* did not only contribute to the emerging field of Media and Translation, but was able to contextualize this field, highlighting the extent to which translation plays an increasingly significant social, political, commercial, and ethical role in the production of contemporary media. The current collection takes the next theoretical step to explore the manner in which translation has been moving from the background of media production, and made to serve as a captivating theme in film, television, commercials, online content, and other New Media. It addresses both the increasingly significant role that translation plays in a multilingual and global society—and the reflection of this role in contemporary media. Some themes that this collection addresses are: the role of translators and translation in drama (both in film and television); translators as protagonists; translators as agents, double agents, and negotiators; translation and translators in New Media; translation and global communication; the presentation of visual texts through alternative techniques (as in the cases of captioning and audio-description); translation within multilingual films; and translation in advertisements.

The purpose of the collection, among others, is to expand the view of translation beyond its utilitarian function, and present it as both performative and communicative. As Michael Raine (2014, 2016: 151) writes in *Media and Translation*: audiovisual translation is "a glaze that penetrates the surface of the film, making it transportable even [as it] change[s] it completely." In this collection, however, translation is not only seen as playing a significant role in the rendering of the text—but is, in fact, becoming a part of the story and an inseparable part of a contemporary life that is increasingly multilingual, multiethnic, multinational, and socially diverse.

It is of course in the nature of a collection of scholarly essays about translation that it presents a fascinating array of scholars from various nations who address different cultures and political realities, whether in Japan, China, South Africa, Poland, Italy, or the United States. Indeed, several months ago I knew very little about the differences between the Second Sino-Japanese War and the Pacific War between 1937 and 1945. Nor was I aware of the important difference between *lasagna* and *lasagne*. I did not know that the acronym, VIP, can stand for "Visually Impaired Person"; and I was not aware that the *TARDIS*, the translation device that is featured in the series, *Doctor Who* (1963–1989), is not a genderless machine, but rather a feminine and super intelligent bio-spaceship. I hope that the reader will enjoy as I have the diverse and enriching cultural landscape that the authors in this collection provide.

The collection also provides a wide interdisciplinary array, as it features scholars in Film Studies, New Media, Linguistics, Cultural Studies, and of course Translation Studies and Audiovisual Translation. Most of our participants wear more than a single disciplinary hat, and provide an erudite outlook that forces the reader out of a disciplinary, univocal, and entrenched academic agenda. Perhaps what is common to all the chapters in this collection is the realization that translation is never only about the transmission of a finite text, and that it always involves a complex and volatile cultural exchange.

The theoretical approaches in this collection can be roughly divided into two venues: the direct representation of translation and translators as events and characters within the narrative, and the indirect representation of translation, foreign language, and cultural exchange in films, television series, and commercials. In the latter, the realization that translation and secondary language within the text are almost never about transmitting content (or else that content could simply be rendered in the primary language), provides space for considering the diverse manners in which the dramatic function of translation is used in contemporary media.

Of the first group, Erga Heller presents an erudite and thoughtful discussion of the many translators and methods of translation that are presented in the science fiction series, *Doctor Who* and *Star Trek* from the 1960s to the present. This thought-provoking chapter discusses some of our fantasies, as well as our fears and suspicions of translators and translation. Among a number of highly contested topics in Translation Studies, Heller's discussion addresses the role of machine translation, the task of the translator as a mediator (and therefore as a human rather than a mechanical device), and the function of gender in determining both the image and the task of the translator. Kayoko Takeda presents a captivating discussion of the cinematic representation of interpreters who are involved in situations of war and violent conflict. Takeda raises a number of provocative ethical issues both about interpretation and translation as she examines the representation of different interpreters in very different situations. The discussion takes an unusual and unexpected approach to the ethics of translation, and is likely to cause the reader to re-examine some preconceived notions about the moral and professional obligations that translation involves. Delia Chiaro goes further to examine the representation of translation (and mistranslation) in the context of one of the more mysterious facets of human interaction: love. Is love truly universal? Can it be expressed, reciprocated, and maintained despite linguistic, cultural, and political barriers? Chiaro discusses films that feature lovers who are brought together by the lack of a common language as an effective humorous device. However, it turns out that there is trouble in paradise, and that the slippage from humor to ridicule and stereotype can bear testimony to an unequal relationship between lovers as well as between the national cultures that are represented on the screen. Love, and translation, are often more complicated than one tends to expect.

The second group discusses less direct, and sometime more complex facets of the representation of translation. Ying Xiao discusses the translation and adaptation of Shakespeare's *Hamlet* in the People's Republic of China during the second half of the twentieth century as an inclusive and holistic project that redefines translation as a cultural production that extends well beyond a single text or a single participant in the act of translation. Chiara Bucaria goes on to discuss a complete reversal as the act of translation replaces the narrative of the text as a topic of conversation among *Twitter*s. In "Talking about Dubbing," Bucaria discusses the reaction in social media to the adaptation of television programs, describing a new reality in which the target audience is at once familiar with the original text, critical of the process of translation and adaptation, and enabled—through social media—to react and to be an influential participant in the same process. Iwona Mazur introduces the reader to an innovative and theoretically exciting field of study: Media Access Services. She addresses the many ways in which audio descriptions have become an important part of the lives of visually impaired recipients, as well as a general audience, through audio guides, podcasts, audio books, and other materials. Mazur discusses an inclusive approach to environmental planning that strives to cater to the needs and expectations of as many users as possible. And, as the function of audio-description fulfills a great deal more than the mere transmission of context, the discussion hints at a new hierarchy between the translation and its original text. Zoë Pettit chooses the intricate linguistic landscape of South Africa to discuss a multilingual reality in which code-switching, code-mixing, and using different languages are indicative of a political, ethnic, social, and economic hierarchy. The discussion examines the creation of meaning through multilingualism in South African films, and translators' choices when adapting the same films in French, either by subtitles or by dubbing. Of course, the collection cannot be complete without an anti-thesis: in their discussion of the translation of advertisement from English to Chinese, Ying Cui and Yanli Zhao argue that when it comes to advertisement translation, the focus is on domestication (or rather, localization). On the other hand, translators are influenced by the original advertisement and certain features of the original language might "invade" the target language and provide the product with some exotic and prestigious appeal. It is therefore left to the reader to decide to what extent advertisement, while catering to its target audience, necessitates a certain representation of translation as well. Finally, I present my own chapter in which I explore the use of a reversed-translation and a "reversed-reversed translation" (when the translated scene is fitted with subtitles) in Joel and Ethan Coen's film, *A Serious Man*. I use this discussion to argue for an interdisciplinary study of multilingual films, calling for scholarship that includes a solid background in Film Studies, the languages that are used in the film, and the cultural and historical background that each language represents. This assertion is likely to anger some readers, as it sets a high bar for the exploration of multilingual films. But I hope that this discussion might encourage other readers to consider the intricate and highly demanding research that translation and the diverse use of languages in media necessitate. The best feature of this collection is that it includes very different, sometime even contradictory voices that explore very different facets of a single phenomenon: the increasingly active, reciprocal, engaged, emotional, ironic, volatile, creative, ethical, financial, and dramatic function of translation at the beginning of the twenty-first century.

Notes

1 The dramatic function of translation is discussed by Dirk Delabastita (2004), Dirk Delabastita and Rainier Grutman (2005), and Dirk Delabastita and Ton Hoenselaars (2015: 1–16).
2 Season 2, Episode 11; February 10, 2008.
3 Season 4, Episode 4; October 18, 2009.
4 Season 7, Episode 7; November 15, 2010.
5 See Wang and Zhao (2011).

References

2015 Chrysler 200 Commercial Japanese Quality (October 27, 2014), [Television Commercial] Produced by Wieden & Kennedy, USA: Wieden & Kennedy. Available online: https://www.youtube.com/watch?v=j1xBaMeOs-M (accessed May 9, 2015).
Abend-David, D., ed. (2014, 2016), *Media and Translation: An Interdisciplinary Approach*, 2nd edition 2016, New York: Bloomsbury.
Brothers & Sisters (2006–2011), [Television series] Creator: Jon Robin Baitz, USA: After Portsmouth et al.
Cronin, M. (2003), *Translation and Globalization*, New York: Routledge.
Delabastita, D. (2004), "If I Know the Letters and the Language: Translation as a Dramatic Device in Shakespeare's Plays," Ton Hoenselaars (ed.), *Shakespeare and the Language of Translation*, 31–52, London: Arden Shakespeare.
Delabastita D. and R. Grutman (2005), "Fictional representations of multilingualism and translation," *Linguistica Antverpiensia*, 4: 11–34.

Delabastita D. and T. Hoenselaars, eds. (2015), *Multilingualism in the Drama of Shakespeare and his Contemporaries*, The Netherlands: John Benjamins.

Doctor Who (1963–1989), [Television series] Creator: Sydney Newman, UK: British Broadcasting Corporation (BBC).

House M.D. (2004–2014), [Television series] Dir. David Shore, USA: Heel & Toe Films et al.

La vita è bella [*Life is Beautiful*] (1997), [Film] Dir. Roberto Benigni, Italy: Melampo Cinematografica.

Lost in Translation (2003), [Film] Dir. Sofia Coppola, USA: Focus Features.

Mozart in the Jungle (2014–2018), [Television series] Creators: Alex Timbers et al., USA: Amazon Studios.

Raine, M. (2014, 2016), "From Hybridity to Dispersion: Film Subtitling as an Adaptive Practice," Dror Abend-David (ed.), *Media and Translation: An Interdisciplinary Approach*, 151–172, New York: Bloomsbury.

Rhyming Slang Translation—Commercial (March 10, 2008), [Internet commercial] Uploaded to YouTube by ukgoods, USA: Ukfoods. Available online: http://www.youtube.com/watch?v=JzxttGuq1s4 (accessed November 7, 2011).

The Interpreter (2005), [Film] Dir. Sydney Irwin Pollack, USA: Universal Pictures.

Wang L. and G. Zhao (2011), "Function-oriented approaches in commercial advertisement translation," *Theory and Practice in Language Studies*, 1(15): 521–524.

1

Imagining Translation and Translators

Editor's Introductory Note

The first chapter in this collection introduces us to the manner in which translation is fictionalized in popular culture: the functions that it is imagined to have; the hopes that are attributed to translation as a mode of social and political communication; and the concerns that translation generates as a possible means of distortion and deception. In the context of science fiction in the English-speaking world during the 1960s and 1970s, the chapter examines two cult series that generated overwhelming viewership and critical reaction: *Doctor Who* and *Star Trek*. Beyond the anticipated realization that translation serves an important function in science fiction, the chapter highlights the extent to which popular culture precedes theorists of translation, much in the way that Jules Verne's novels predicted various scientific discoveries and inventions. Both *Doctor Who* and *Star Trek* envision machine translation to an extent that we are only beginning to imagine today. More importantly, at a time that Translation Theory still imagined translation as the exchange of "equivalencies," the two series already projected complex models of translation that involve cultural, political, social, and technical challenges. In addition, the two series envision gender as an important element, both in terms of the identity of the translator and of its role in determining a particular approach to translation. Overall, the chapter underscores the extent to which our future theoretical approach to translation can be found in our popular culture, and the ways in which fictional translation eventually influences translation in reality.

The Evolution of the "Universal Translator": Technical Device and Human Factor in *Doctor Who* and *Star Trek* from the 1960s to the Present

Erga Heller

What you want is irrelevant; what you have chosen is at hand.
Captain Spock, *Star Trek IV: The Undiscovered Country* (1991)

1. Introduction

Communication with "Other" was a main theme of Science Fiction (SF) in the English-speaking world during the 1960s and 1970s. Nevertheless, many SF writers intentionally avoided the question of "real" translation (Mossop 1996: 1–2). They did not use fictional human translators or other sorts of translation agents in order to transform a message in a source language (SL) into a message in a target language (TL). Instead, the writers preferred to elucidate the interpretive aspect within their narratives by telepathy, assimilated pan-communication features, or other non-human communication capacities in which all possible languages of the universe were easily processed by natural/automatic cognitive process. Because telepathy enables the brain to receive, to decipher, and to re-construct any message, the brain, literally, constructs a semantic meaning by its own terms, without a noticeable translation process. This literary solution for communication with aliens is easy to use in either simple or complicated narratives. In SF plots, communicating with an alien through telepathy is just a simple narrative "bypass," according to Brian Mossop (1996: 3). However, many SF heroes of the 1940s and the 1950s, such as Superman or other superheroes, have this ability (James and Mendlesohn 2003: 40).

In the 1950s, telepathy, as a potential way of communication, became a subject of an academic study, as in J.B. Rhine's lab at Duke University (James and Mendlesohn 2003: 228). Such studies legitimized and revived the SF concepts of communications with the "Other" through telepathy. Those concepts are the starting point for *Doctor Who*'s and *Star Trek*'s communication ideal of a Universal Translator.

Although the major part of stories about alien communication are based on telepathy, some stories suggest a different ideal. They are based on technological solutions, such as machine translation. These literary tendencies imply a sort of a universal axiom. Based on Noam Chomsky's theory of "Universal Grammar," which was first suggested in the 1950s (Chomsky 2006: 24; Chomsky 2009: 118), the new concept of a wide-rooted communication scheme was transformed to an idea of a utopian pan-communication potent scheme valid throughout the entire universe. Although Chomsky and other MIT bio-linguistics who studied the potential of universal extra-terrestrial communication for half a century do not know whether or not "Universal Grammar" can be found in other domains or organisms (Chomsky 2005: 2), Chomsky's theory has been adopted enthusiastically by many SF authors and screenwriters since the 1960s, and abandoned the former motif of pure telepathic communication. This new concept opens SF narratives to the question of translating extra-terrestrial languages into a terrestrial one (mostly English). In recent studies, as opposed to his extra-terrestrial aims that inspired many SF authors, Chomsky notes that language is "unique to humans" and "radically different from animal symbolic systems," yet he continues to argue for a "universal grammar" and that language is based on "conceptual structures" (Chomsky 2017: 200–201), two essential criteria for the creation of a Universal Translator in fantasy as well as in developing digital language tools and applications.

But even though the concept of universal communication is popular in SF productions, the question of the way translation acts in SF was hardly discussed; this field of SF translation was as neglected as the linguistic aspect of the entire genre (Wozniak 2014). In addition to the fact that there are few recent studies on the topic of translation acts in SF, such studies are generally occupied with technological aspects (Lasbury 2017) or discuss cross-lingual capacities as literary devices (Chapman 2014; Gonzalez 2017; Sandapen 2014).

This chapter focuses on the evolution of a new concept of automatic translation (AT), referred to as a Universal Translator, in two innovative SF television series. It depicts its transformation from a technical device to a human interpreter or meditator through the last half a century in relation with actual technological developments during this time in AT and language engineering.

2. Understanding known and unknown languages in *Doctor Who*

Two innovative television series—*Doctor Who* (BBC1, 1963–1989, 1996, and 2005 to the present) and *Star Trek* (NBC and Paramount Pictures, 1966–1969, 1987–2005)—were aired for the first time during the 1960s, and suggested some of the newest notions about communication with "Others." Both have been very successful, and include various franchises as the original television series, television sequels, animated series, special episodes, movies, graphic novels, literary adaptions, and more.

The two series are very different in nature. *Doctor Who* depicts a re-incarnated alien Time Lord, called "the Doctor," and his companion. In the early 1960s, while BBC producers developed the concept of the series, they aimed to present British values and history via the program. They looked for a British style "handsome young man hero [...] [and a] handsome well-dressed heroine aged about 30" (Chapman 2014: 46). In 1963, *Doctor Who* was designed as a shallow weekend program about a man lost in space and time, but swiftly shifted into a complicated SF narrative concerning known human history as well as imaginary monsters and aliens who often intend to invade Earth (Chapman 2014: 49).

A main characteristic of the Doctor is his ability to regenerate. From 1963 to 2017, for a dozen times, the Doctor was regenerated as a man, although not always as a young man. In July 2017, BBC1 announced that the next Doctor's regeneration, in December 2017 Christmas special is a woman (actress Jodie Whittaker).[1] This surprising announcement was followed by the actress' statement, in which she asks *Doctor Who*'s fans to not be "scared" by her gender. This changing gender issue is not only a matter of fans' worries or rejections, but an important cultural mirror for the changing attitudes toward a variety of feminine (and not only feminist) aspects. A female Doctor concerns lingual and communicational functioning and challenges concepts of male supremacy in language. She marks the edges of the inner gendered self. This feminine shift is very important to our discussion, as we can see later.

But from the very first episodes of *Doctor Who*, the clear need of communication with "Other"—as in the cases of a Stone Age child, Renaissance-Venetian Marco Polo, or a future alien "Dalek"—was essential to the plots. Consequently, *Doctor Who*'s first screenwriters, Anthony T. Coburn, Terry Nation, John Vincent Lucarotti, David Whitetaker, and others, had to find a permanent solution for this issue. They introduced two solutions:

1. The first concerns the Doctor only, and is based on Chomsky's theory of language universals. As a Time Lord, the Doctor naturally knows all possible natural languages from all times and from all over the universe (yet almost always everything sounds like English, a plot device that favors the viewers).
2. The second solution is technical in nature. The screenwriters "invented" a "translation circuit." This is a mechanical device for machine translation (MT) that has been assimilated into the Doctor's feminine and super intelligent bio-spaceship, the "TARDIS." It is able to translate from any language to any language, but due to the medium and in favor of the viewers' understanding, translation is made from and to British English most of the time.

The translation circuit is taken for granted in most of the episodes. It is not referred to in detail and is not a part of the rising action of the narrative so long as it functions well. This device enables the Doctor's companions to "hear" and "produce" ancient, foreign, or alien languages, much like the Doctor himself/herself. It automatically, and almost stimulatingly, deciphers either oral or written messages. In favor of the viewers, the translation is made into and from English (or German, French, Italian, and other languages in the dubbed versions). In addition, a major characteristic of the Doctor is his/her affection to contemporary and ancient English dialects. The Doctor's dialogs in the early episodes include a "very British, very BBC [dialect]" in order to both educate and entertain. In fact, about a half of his dialogs serve as explanations, or rather inter-translations, in favor of the viewers (October 2014: 8–9). But, with time, the Doctor's language changes. For instance, when the character of the Doctor is played by David Tennant, between 2005 and 2010, he speaks contemporary English, uses black English dialect, as well as American English, but fails to understand local lexis in Pagan English (Hsy 2014: 118). In general, however, the Doctor's linguistic passion, combined with the alleged ultimate power of the bio-machine translation of the TARDIS, gives him/her an advantage in communicating with others (Sandapen 2014: 81).

The screenwriters of *Doctor Who* suggested a sophisticated (yet, fictional) semi-AT, which manipulated the human brain, and could operate inside and alongside the TARDIS herself (since she is a female self-conscious bio-machine), and be inducted on a large radius around it. But, as mentioned before, the focus on translation itself appears in this series only when the Doctor and/or the translation circuit in the TARDIS do not function, since this malfunction creates the "problem" from which the story is developed. According to Hsy, the TARDIS itself/herself should be regarded simply as a "translation vehicle," and should be referred to as a translator. When the tenth Doctor (David Tennant) and his companion Donna Nobel (Catherine Tate) arrive at the Roman city of Pompeii in the episode of "The Fires of Pompeii" (2008), the bio-machine translator fails. Donna's English is translated by the TARDIS into Celtic instead of Roman, and the viewers, as well as the characters in the scene, hear Celtic. This malfunctioning affects the plot because Donna is immediately identified as a stranger (Hsy 2014: 109).

3. The final technological frontier (*Star Trek*): The evolution of a "Universal Translator" from SF to language engineering

Unlike the solitude of the anglophile Doctor, and the bio-mechanical translator, the TARDIS, or her "Translation Circuit," *Star Trek* suggests an artificial intelligent (AI) device for massive use. Yet, both suggest to the viewers an innovative technology that ciphers spoken languages. This fictional device is based on such an advanced idea that even today, about fifty years later, it cannot be created off the screen (Sternbach, Okuda, and Roddenberry, 1991: 98; Gresh and Weinberg 1999: 8; Weldes 2003: 17; Ehsani et al. 2010: 167). Spoken language is much more versatile than written language. It is much more tolerant of incorrect syntax, incorrect grammar, variety of accents and individual pronunciation. In translating spoken languages, the margins of error are enormous in comparison with the translation of a written text.

Star Trek suggests an ultimate translation device. It was originally motivated by the need to communicate during various first encounters of the "Federation" (earth-based) officers with civilized aliens. This concept was developed by screenwriter Gene Roddenberry (1921–1991), and introduced to the viewers in the beginning of each episode as a final frontier of contacting new civilizations: "[...] to boldly go where no man has gone before" ("Where No Man Has Gone Before" 1966), thus going where no man communicated before. All languages of this hypothetical final frontier are unknown to mankind; all are new. Thus, a translation device which operates without any previous knowledge is a useful tool. Chomsky and other generative linguistics founded the basis for this notion. According to Chomsky, we are all born with an inner device which is called a "language acquisition device" (Chomsky 1986: 3). This device enables us to learn languages from birth, since we are genetically programmed to acquire any language.

In general, the *Star Trek* series wishes to illustrate the daily life of multi-nations and multi-species officers in their spacecraft or in a deep space base in the future. The question of understanding other human and/or aliens' languages and cultures, is a fundamental need in the series. Accurate translation of first encounters is crucial to the crew's survival (Neumann 2001: 614). For that purpose, Roddenberry and his team created a technical multi-functional device for translating aliens' communication acts, both spoken and written, that is referred to as a "Universal Translator" (UT). In 1966, *Star Trek's* UT, was a powerful portable digital simultaneous translator, which was far beyond realistic plausibility. Although the UT was inspired by the idea of communication with "Others" through telepathy, since it was based on stimulating the human and non-human brains, the UT was clearly a device which operated in a universal mode, meaning that it was based on three assumptions:

1. Language is a structural logic communication system, and is not restricted to verbal nor visual sign systems.
2. Everything is translatable.
3. All languages operate the same, an idea that is inspired by Chomsky's "Universal Grammar." (However, after about twenty years this idea was challenged in *Star Trek* itself by questioning whether chemical communication ("Home Soil" 1988) or binary language ("11001001" 1988) can be designated as languages.

In one of the very first episodes, Captain James T. Kirk, the *Enterprise's* commander, refers implicitly to Chomsky's theory by telling his chief officers, Spock and McCoy: "There are certain universal ideas and concepts that are common to all intelligent life" ("Metamorphosis" 1967). There, Kirk explains that the "Universal Translator" functions by scanning and comparing a frequency of the speaker's brain waves patterns, recognizing concepts, and converting those concepts into familiar concepts by using a familiar pattern of grammar and syntax in the receiver's brain. This implies that all vocal speech acts are redundant while using a UT. With time, as we see during the seasons, the telepathy feature is removed or at least canceled, and ciphering the vocal input of a spoken language becomes a main function of the UT. Like in *Doctor Who*, in favor of the viewers, the translated "output" sounds as English (or German, French, Italian, etc. in dubbed versions).

During the first seasons of the *Star Trek* television series, the UT was designated as a two-way portable pipe-shaped device, and it only read a given speaker(s)' brain waves and projected the translation directly to a given listener(s)' and vice versa (Okuda, Okuda and Mirek 1999: 537). The main UT computer was launched on the chief deck, and was operated by the Communication Officer. UT's first operator, according to the filmography, rather than the reconstructed timeline, was Lieutenant Nyota Uhura. She was an Afro-American woman, and a translator who had specialized in linguistics and cryptology. Her gender, origin, and education, often seemed to have no importance to the plot, since Uhura mainly operated the UT as a technician, as we can see in "Journey to Babel" (1967):

> **First Officer Lieutenant Commander Spock** [half-Human half-Vulcan]   Sensors indicate the size of a scout ship, but the configuration is unfamiliar. Most unusual.
>
> **Captain James T. Kirk**   Does she answer a hail?
>
> **Communication Officer Lieutenant Nyota Uhura**   I've tried all frequencies and hooked the Universal Translator. No response, sir.
>
> **Captain Kirk**   Maintain translator broadcast. Check records for authorized ships.
>
> "Journey to Babel" 1967

As seasons pass, the UT gradually changes. It evolves into a learning computer program that can be installed on any Federation computer, or on any mobile device, as well as in the android Data in *Star Trek: The Next Generation* (1987–1994). The UT works on multiple combinations of communication channels, including spoken languages, written languages and/or telepathy. The result is a sophisticated software that could also be vulnerable to various malfunctions, as will be discussed hereafter.

In 2001, in the first episode of a new prequel series by the name of *Star Trek: Enterprise,* the viewers receive the benefit of a full history of the UT: It was initiated in 2151, but still failed to operate fully in the language of Klaang the Klingon ("Broken Bow, Part 1" 2001). Yet, during the time that this episode is said to have taken place, every *Star Trek*'s first season officer wore the device on missions, and it enabled him (or her, but mostly him) to communicate with every intelligent life form in the universe in a direct way, without the need of a mediator (a person) or a mediating tool (such as a mediating language).

Therefore, the UT seem to forecast a series of portable devices that exist in real life today, such as Google Translate, Skype translation, YouTube automatic subtitles, iPhone's Word Lens, Facebook "translate" button, etc. AT users, whether through Google, iPhone, or Skype, know that these devices operate best if English is either the source or the target language. Otherwise, since English is the default language in these applications, chances are that the program would use a mediating language (such as Turkish to English, followed by English to Farsi). As language engineers may suggest, a satisfactory translation will result only if the application or the digital feature is tuned to specific lingual domains (Dale 2015: 327). Translation researchers will conclude this issue by eliminating the need of a mediatory language, i.e., that all translation processes will be carried directly one from source to target. This is exactly the way in which the ideal UT works, rapidly and directly, alleged to possess ultimate potential to know every possible language without the need for a mediating language, even without a relevant personal experience, exactly as a child acquires a new language (Chomsky 1986: 55).

4. The importance of being a middleman

But despite the desire for a direct translation, a middleman may be useful in the translation process, especially when the ideal translator, the translation circuit or the UT, fails. At the end of the 1960s, the idea of a universal cipher machine that can analyze any source language and representing any target language through an automatic translation process, was a pure fantasy. It embedded another revolutionary idea, which is mentioned above: the concept of universal translatability, according to which everything can be translated; moreover: that nothing ought to be lost in translation. But as many experienced translators know, this is an impossible task. One can neither adequately nor functionally translate a text in the absence of major cultural components.

Imagine a culture that is based on concepts that are strange and unfamiliar in your world. Thus, the conceptual-intentional of thought and action, as Chomsky calls the most silent language capacity (Chomsky 2017: 201), is incapable of producing those concepts in your language. But if these concepts exist in another world, its cultural capacity of thoughts, translated into words, may be useful to you. This process is indirect and recruits a third part, a mediatory language.

In the case of the *Star Trek* episode "Home Soil" (1988), the starship officers are looking at a suspect material, which consumes some parts of the starship, in their science lab. The starship main computer acts as a bio-chemical analyzing station, and analyzes the strange material. It announces the results with a male voice. The android Lieutenant Commander Data represents the results and explains to the officers the uses of each chemical element, as components of transistor, conductor, and a lighting system. The alien material in the container shimmers in synchronization with the sounds. After finding out that, adding to these electronic circles, the analysis detects water and sodium salts as well, Lieutenant Commander Worf, a Klingon who serves as security chief officer, wonders whether the suspected material is alive. The starship main computer approves the possibility. But only the android Data and the UT can solve the mystery, as they interpret the lights and a dissonant tuned noise as something that is trying to make itself intelligent and verbal. Data operates a "conceptual-intentional thought" to understand another "conceptual-intentional action," and the UT does the same:

> **Data**   The Universal Translator is coming on line.
>
> **Computer voice**   Ugly … Ugly … Giants … Bags of mostly water.
>
> **Captain Picard**   Bags of mostly water?!
>
> **Data**   An accurate description, sir, of humans. You are after all ninety per cent water, surrounded by a flexible container.
>
> "Home Soil" 1988

The phrase "Ugly, ugly giants, bags of mostly water" is the "authentic" translation made by the UT for the alien material message, which the UT and Data reveal is made by a living collective of Nano-creatures: the Nano-alien concept for humans, a life form that they have neither cultural nor scientific knowledge of. Their description of humans is both subjective or aesthetic ("ugly") and objective or relative ("giants," "bags of water"). Only the android Data, by virtue of his logical non-human information processing protocols, is able to re-translate the UT's literal output, based on the Nano-aliens' conceptual thoughts.

But only Deana Troi, a half-human female diplomatic officer, who has the gift of telepathy, can say telepathically to the aliens: "We see and hear you now. You are beautiful to us. All life is beautiful." By saying so, she saves the starship *Enterprise* from destruction by these Nano-aliens. In addition to Data's functional translation, Troi acts as a mediator and bridges the cultural conceptual gaps in an emphatic way that no AT can produce.

5. The advantage of hybrid and technophile mediators

Although the technology of the "Universal Circuit" or the "Universal Translator" present a portable feature, with audible output, instead of a human living interpreter, humans and humanoids often serve as mediators in situations that are related to linguistic interaction, both in *Doctor Who* and *Star Trek*. Surprisingly, their meditative contribution becomes increasingly dominant in these series with time, as opposed to AT technology's huge development in recent years. As Michael Cronin suggests in his discussion of known contemporary technology, it "do[es] not so much eliminate the translator as middleman as turn potentially every middleman into a translator" (Cronin 2013: 43).

The translation circuit of the TARDIS works fine in "Chomskian" lingo-environments, converting "Universal Grammar" structures to soundless or invisible "conceptual-intentional thought or action" messages. But imagine a language which is based on tempting floral smells, such as the Vrill's in the final episode of "Survival of the Fittest" (2012), a *Doctor Who*'s radio series by BBC-R4. In that episode, each smell functions as a lexeme, and their sequel, or their unique simultaneous combination, acts as a phrase or a sentence. The smells are soundless and invisible; allegedly they suggest no semantic meaning. One needs to cipher or decode the smells' chemistry in order to gain a meaningful message. As an ultimate bio-machine, the TARDIS is not restricted to ordinary lingual structures, and she can cipher a language which is based on smells (e.g., on conceptual actions). Viewers might expect such a "floral language" to carry positive messages. But this is not necessarily the case. This language is based on chemistry and on scientific formulas and codes, and, in this episode, it is used to invoke Nazi ideology. The Vrills are hostile aliens. They are bee-like communal winged insects, which aim to demolish mankind. They collaborate with the Nazis to create a fatal nerve gas in order to eliminate Humanity. Together, they test it on human victims. Although the TARDIS is able to translate the language of smells into spoken English, the Doctor faces some difficulties in interpreting the dreadful meaning that is suggested through the TARDIS due to some paradoxical concepts. As a result, the Doctor loses precious time, and can only evacuate as many humans as possible from the vicinity of the Vrills. As he leaves, he is concerned about the lack of translation that will render the remaining humans "deaf" and vulnerable to the Vrills' sinister intentions:

Doctor Who The moment the TARDIS leaves this continuum, the gift will be revoked.

Elizabeth The what?

Doctor Who The translation! There will be no more translation. Vrill and Human will be unable to communicate. [. . .] There's no more communication between us, Stefan, us and the Vrill. We are deaf to each other.

"Survival of the Fittest, part 4" 2012

A common communication failure in *Doctor Who* is also found in "The Christmas Invasion" (2005). Rose, the Doctor's companion in this episode, is left, along with a number of other characters, with the Sycorax, a malicious race of alien warriors. In this case, the Doctor vanishes for a while, and a malfunction within the translation circuit stops the TARDIS telepathic translation. Rose tries her best to communicate with the hostile Sycorax, who wish to demolish Earth. She asks the Sycorax Leader to leave in peace. She speaks in English, but he is answering her in Sycoraxic. The fact that Rose, as the viewer, hears meaningless sounds, suggests a possible malfunction. A translation is needed immediately in order for Rose and the other characters to stay alive. Alex, a young man who works as assistant for MP Harriet Jones, carries a small tablet-like mobile device, which is used for translation. Alex, Rose, MP Jones, and the others are so preoccupied with their translation efforts that they do not notice the Doctor's arrival. He fixes the translation circuit, and the Sycoraxic turns into English again:

Alex   Hold on, that's English.

MP Harriet Jones   He's talking English!

Rose   You're talking English!

Sycorax Leader   I've never dirty my tongue with your primitive bile!

Rose   That's English, can you hear English?

MP Harriet Jones   Yes. [...]

Alex   Definitively English.

Sycorax Leader (*yelling*)   I speak only Sycoraxic!!!

"The Christmas Invasion" 2005

Of course, after "hearing" English, Rose and the others realize that the TARDIS was repaired by the Doctor, and that now she is able to translate again. Rose and Alex stop acting as mediators. But the need of a mediator, a person that is able to bridge different sets of concepts is integrated into *Doctor Who*'s fictional world.

In one of the climaxes in this series, in the episode "A Good Man goes to War" (2011), the mature woman, Prof. River Song, a time traveler, archeologist, and language specialist, reveals her true identity to her husband, the Doctor, and her biological parents, Amy Pond and Rory Williams. River Song was named Melody Pond at birth. But to the Doctor and to Amy and Rory, her parents, she says at first that her name is River Song. Young Amy Pond, the Doctor's companion in this episode, recognizes at last that her kidnapped newborn baby, Melody, appears in the present time as River Song, a mature woman, older than herself. Prof. Song acts as a mediator for Amy, interpreting for her the concepts of the Language of the Forest in which she was re-named River Song instead of Melody Pond:

River Song   It's the TARDIS translation matrix. It takes a while to kick in with the written word. You have to concentrate.

Amy Pond   I still can't read it.

River Song   It's because it's Gallifreyan and doesn't translate. But this will … It's your daughter's name in the Language of the Forest.

Amy Pond   I know my daughter's name!

River Song   Except they don't have a word for "pond" because the only water in the Forest is the River. The Doctor will find your daughter and will care for her … whatever it takes, and I know that. [The English written letters are changed from "Pond" to "River" as the mediated telepathic translation is slowly figured out by Amy] It's me. I'm your daughter.

"A Good Man Goes to War" 2011

Prof. Song's role as an interpreter introduces the issues of cultural gaps and semantic voids. Even if the viewer had already revealed her secret, here again the technical translation, even its telepathic aspect, isn't enough. A human mediator is needed in addition to the TARDIS translation matrix in order to gain a full understanding of the chiastic and unnatural metamorphosis: a baby girl that appears as a mature woman that seems to be older than her biological mother.

In *Star Trek: The Next Generation* (1987–1994), the need of a humanized mediator in addition to the "Universal Translator" becomes much clearer (Inayatullah 2003: 59). Accordingly, the character of Lieutenant Commander Deanna Troi, as starship counselor is introduced. Lieutenant Commander Troi is half-Human and half-Betazoid. Due to her Betazoid genes, she is able to sense the feelings of almost all living forms via telepathy, and explain them verbally with much empathy to the others. She serves as the *Enterprise*'s counselor, and seldom acts as an inter-alien species interpreter. She is very important to the wellbeing of the crew, and above all, her mediation is crucial for gaining a full understanding of the UT output. In a way, creating a feminine counselor/interpreter figure in *Star Trek* is an echo for many of the Doctor's companions who act as translators. However, it should not be surprising, since the majority of translators and interpreters in SF are women, and they often act as mediators between different cultures and ways of thinking (Wolf 2014: 24–25). This can also be explained by the understanding that language concerns behavior and cultural gestures (Stollznow 2014: 198) as well as psychological effects (Weldes 2003: 70) which are often women's fields of interest or occupation (Weitekamp 2013: 32).

In contrast with either a human translator or the TARDIS, the UT is by definition a genderless machine. But in *Star Trek*'s masculine technological world, to be genderless is to be exceptional, even for a machine. For example, the android Data and most of the Borgs (assimilated hostile bio-machines) are created with a masculine body (Roberts 1999: 24, 91). The UT has a distinctive male voice. Therefore, it is not truly genderless. Gender is important in context of inter-cultural translation. In the real world, for centuries, women translators were regarded as cultural interpreters (Simon 2003: 38). Bassnett points out an interesting point: many female translators of the twentieth century were also known academics, established feminists, and all were immigrants or persons who lived in a different country than their motherland, and translated to and from several other languages, additional to their first language and the language of their adopted country (Bassnett 2014: 62). Hence, we can claim that a feminine interpretation is a supplemental interpreting tool, an additional point of view that facilitates mutual understanding.

6. Women building cultural bridges in deep space

Although both *Doctor Who* and *Star Trek* introduce sophisticated translation devices, it seems that the question of the human aspect behind these super-powered machines (or bio-machines) is often neglected. Who functions as a translator when the technology fails? It is neither the anglophile Doctor, who knows historic dialects and chats in Shakespearian English, nor the technology experts of the first deck in *Star Trek*, who have a rich experience in special real-time problem solving. Instead, the translators, as has already been mentioned above, are often women with full or partial human genes system, and full or partial Earthly education. The two series narrate explorations, survival, and studying new worlds, which are stereotypically very masculine fields of interest. From the 1960s to the present, the number of episodes which refer to translation circuit's malfunction or UT's failure is rising, as the developmental work on real-time digital spoken language translation in real life becomes more and more visible. But the question remains: Why are women most often described as translators and mediators?

We already met a few of *Doctor Who*'s female mediators, who are all the

Doctor's friends, allies, and companions in his/her travels through time: two of them are the instinctive Rose, or the sophisticated Prof. Song, who is also the Doctor's wife. In various episodes, they all offer more than a pure textual interpretation, as all of them suggest a cultural insight, bridging cultural gaps and semantic voids, and point out inter-cultural differences.

In the *Star Trek: The Next Generation* episode "Dark Page" (1993), we meet the flamboyant character of Lwaxana, the mother of Deanna Troi (who is mentioned earlier). Lwaxana is on board for a special mission: she is an honored Betazoid, a daughter of a noble family, and she is a Federation ambassador. Her mission on board is to establish diplomatic relations with the Cairns, a telepathic species that has no concept of spoken language.

The Cairns have neither a spoken nor a written language, since they communicate only through telepathy. They have to use a special device in order to produce sounds for vocal communication. Through her diplomatic efforts, Lwaxana succeeds in teaching the Cairns' delegation some English, which is the official Federation language. Maques, who leads the Cairns' diplomatic mission, is on board with his adolescent daughter, Hedril, who learns to speak English very quickly. Deanna Troi, who is capable of telepathy, has a hard time trying to explain to Hedril a handful of semantic voids using only spoken English. Alas, her interpreting work fails, and her mother has to translate the cultural gap through telepathy:

Counselor Deanna Troi   This is the ship's arboretum.

Hedril   Arbor means tree.

Deanna Troi   Very good, Hedril. People like to come here to relax, enjoy themselves in a natural setting. [Hedril's father, Maques, is inspecting a rose bush and is pricked by a thorn. Deanna is citing book IV line 241 from Milton's *Paradise Lost*:] "Flowers of all hue, and without thorn the rose" . . . that's from an old Earth poem by John Milton.

Maques   Please, what is a poem?

Deanna Troi   A Poem is . . . an art form that uses words, put together in new and unexpected ways . . . sometimes in rhymes. Milton was speculating that in heaven, roses wouldn't have thorns.

Hedril   Heaven?

Deanna Troi   Oh. Oh, uh, heaven is, well, it's um . . . how can I put it?

Maques   [after Lwaxana explains telepathically] Yes, I see. Thank you. "Heaven."

Deanna Troi   Mother, you're supposed to be avoiding telepathy.

Lwaxana Troi   I'm only trying to help, dear.

"Dark Page" 1993

This dialog demonstrates Chomsky's theory of the capacity of language, which clears "the difference between what reaches the mind for semantic interpretation and what reaches the mouth and ear" (Chomsky 2017: 202). Lwaxana Troi's special mission is only a "middle stage" between telepathic and translation aid to the UT. In a later prequel series, *Star Trek: Enterprise* (2001–2005), we meet for the first time a new type of a main character: a language specialist. Hoshi Sato is a human female linguist who serves as a communication officer. Sato is one of the first officers, the first female officer, and the only living language specialist on board. In the first episode of this new series, we learn that she is a fresh recruit who has arrived to the Federation's fleet directly form a Brazilian academy, shortly after the first operative version of the UT was launched ("Broken Bow, Part 1" 2001). For the first time in the history of the original television series, its prequels and its sequels, the UT is accompanied by a living person, suggesting human perspective, comprehension, and interpretation as an element that completes the results of automatic translation. Captain Archer, who asks Sato to be a part of his first deck crew, tells her: "I need someone with your ear" (Broken Bow, Part 1 2001).

Unlike Lieutenant Nyota Uhura in the original series, Sato's characterization as a linguist (rather than a technician) is essential to the plot and to the fictive world that is presented in the innovative starship in the twenty-first century series. As a communication officer, her work is expected to supplement the work of the UT.

Sato, who used to work as a professor of linguistics in Brazil, knows more than forty languages, and continues to learn new languages in deep space. During her short vacation on planet Risa, she aims to learn the local language, which is presented as extremely complex and difficult to learn. Thus, she intentionally leaves her translator on board:

Hoshi Sato   I have been relying on the Universal Translator for too much. Before I left Earth, I learned thirty-eight languages, and now all I do is push a button and the computer does all the work.

Engineer Michael Rostov   Isn't that what it's for?

Hoshi Sato   Not this time, I left my translator on *Enterprise*.

"Two Days and Two Nights" 2002

7. Summary, or Boldly Go Where No *Man* Has Gone Before

Communication with "Other" in SF televisions series from 1960s to the present reflects the change from "Universal Grammar" to "Capacity of Language." Thinking in metaphors, conceptual intentions, acts, and potential lingual differences among species become more important than the assumptions that everything is translatable.

Both *Doctor Who* and *Star Trek* (either as television series and franchises) have changed their attitudes. At first, in the 1960s and the 1970s, they featured an innovating learning super-powered device, which is chiefly based on spoken English, as an ultimate translation tool. Since the 1980s to the present, a more modest notion is suggested and reaches its climax in empowering female translators and language specialists, such as the archeologist, Prof. River Song from the new seasons of *Doctor Who,* or the linguist, Prof. Hoshi Sato from *Star Trek: Enterprise.* As the Doctor tells his time and space travels' companion, Rose: "There's a lot of things you need to get across this universe. Warp drive ... wormhole refractors ... You know the thing you need most of all? You need a hand to hold" ("Fear Her" 2006). This metaphoric hand, a conceptual-intended action, is the human touch, the human thought, and the human bridge between species and cultures.

At the beginning of the twenty-first century, while language engineers and application developers are creating sophisticated translation tools for real-time spoken messages in a growing variety of languages, these two SF series take what might be seen as a step backward, and prefer human translation to machine translation. Female translation, or rather intuitive and empathic translation, is proved to be more accurate than "masculine" or machine translation. In the examples above, accuracy is achieved through the unspoken and invisible gift of empathy, which is imprinted in humans as the ability to acquire language. In *Doctor Who* and *Star Trek*, men often go to war, face dangers, reach the edges of the world, and females (including the TARDIS), due to either their innate talent or social conditioning, build bridges of communication to prevent wars and bring men back in peace. To use Chomsky's terms, they mediate between human conceptual-intentional thoughts and alien action.

Glossary

Automatic translation (AT) or automated translation is a software, a plug-in application or an on-demand virtual system which transfers a full text from a source language (SL) into a target language (TL). It is often based on sets of given rules of each of those languages (vocabulary, grammar, and syntax), yet some of the AT systems are also "learning systems." They are able to create new rules and new definitions by themselves. First experimental AT systems were suggested in the 1960s. Nowadays AT is a common built-in feature in most social networks and word processor programs.

Human translation (HT) is the oldest translation method, known since the dawn of history. HT is always done by a living person, or a group of persons, who know(s) both the SL and TL. In some cases, HT is accomplished by using a middle (mediating) language (ML).

Machine translation (MT) is another name for AT. It is always a non-human translation. MT can be a direct translation (SL>TL) or an indirect translation (SL>ML>TL).

Universal Translator (UT) was suggested in 1964 as a futuristic holistic communication device in the *Star Trek* television series. The fictional UT is a learning system which can either translate from audible/visual data of known languages or decipher audible/visual lingual data from unknown languages into audible/visual lingual data in English. In the twenty-first century, the fictive idea of UT begins to embroider a realistic shape as an innovative on-demand AT learning system, mostly based on ML translations. No ultimate *Star-Trek*-like UT has been successfully created to date.

Note

1   This chapter was written in August 2017.

References

"11001001," *Star Trek: The Next Generation* (1988), [Television series, season 1, episode 15] NBC, February 1.

"A Good Man Goes to War," *Doctor Who* (2011), [Television series, episode 218] BBC1, June 4.

Bassnett, S. (2014), *Translation*, London, New York: Routledge.

"Broken Bow, Part 1," *Star Trek: Enterprise* (2001), [Television series, season 1, episode 1] UPN, September 26.

Chapman, J. (2014), "Fifty years in the Tardis: the historical moments of Doctor Who," *Critical Studies in Television: The International Journal of Television Studies*, 9 (1): 43–61.

Chomsky, N. (1986), *Knowledge of Language: Its Nature, Origin and Use*, Westport, CT, London: Praeger.

Chomsky, N. (2005), "Three factors in language design," *Linguistic Inquiry*, 36 (1): 1–22.

Chomsky, N. (2006), *Language and Mind*, Cambridge: Cambridge University Press.

Chomsky, N. (2009), *Cartesian Linguistics: A Chapter in the History of Rationalist Thought*, (3rd edition), Cambridge: Cambridge University Press.

Chomsky, N. (2017), "The Language Capacity: Architecture and Evolution," *Psychonomic Bulletin and Review*, 24 (1): 200–203.

Cronin, M. (2013), *Translation in the Digital Age*, New York: Routledge.

Dale, R. (2015), "Industry Watch: The Limits of Intelligent Personal assistants," *Natural Language Engineering*, 21 (2): 325–329.

"Dark Page," *Star Trek: The Next Generation* (1993), [Television series, season 7, episode 7] NBC, November 1.

Ehsani, F., R. Frederking, M. Rayner, M. and P. Bouillon (2010), "Spoken Language Translation," in F. Chen, and Ch. Jokinen (eds.), *Speech Technology*, 167–193, New York and London: Springer.

"Fear Her (176)," *Doctor Who* (2006), [Television series] BBC1, June 24.

Gonzalez, G.A. (2017), *The Absolute and Star Trek*, London: Palgrave-Pivot.

Gresh, L.H. and R. Weinberg (1999), *Computers of Star Trek*, New York: Basic Books.

"Home Soil," *Star Trek: The Next Generation* (1988), [Television series, season 1, episode 17] NBC, February 20.

Hsy, J. (2014), "Translation Failure: The TARDIS, Cross-temporal Language Contact, and Medieval Travel Narrative," in J. Barr and C.D.G. Mustachio (eds.), *The Language of Doctor Who: From Shakespeare to Alien Tongues*, 109–124, Lanham, Boulder, New York, and London: Rowman and Littlefield.

Inayatullah, N. (2003), "Bumpy Space: Imperialism and Resistance in *Star Trek: The Next Generation*," in J. Weldes (ed.), *To Seek Out New Worlds*, 53–78, New York: Palgrave Macmillan US.

James, E. and F. Mendlesohn, (2003), *The Cambridge Companion to Science Fiction*, Cambridge: Cambridge University Press.

"Journey to Babel," *Star Trek* (1967), [Television series, season 2, episode 10], NBC, November 17.

Lasbury, M.E. (2017), *The Realization of Star Trek Technologies*, New York and London: Springer.

"Metamorphosis," *Star Trek*, (1967), [Television series, season 2, episode 9] NBC, November 10.

Milton, J. (2011 [1667]), *Paradise Lost*, New York: Random House and Modern Library.

Mossop, B. (1996), "The Image of Translation in Science Fiction and Astronomy," *The Translator*, 2 (1): 1–26.

Neumann, I.B. (2001), "'Grab a Phaser, Ambassador': Diplomacy in Star Trek," *Millennium*, 30 (3): 603–624.

October, D. (2014), "Performativity and the First Doctor," in J. Barr and C.D.G. Mustachio (eds.), *The Language of Doctor Who: From Shakespeare to Alien Tongues*, 1–20, Lanham, Boulder, New York, and London: Rowman and Littlefield.

Okuda, M., D. Okuda, and D. Mirek (1999), *The Star Trek Encyclopedia*, New York: Simon and Schuster.

Roberts, R. (1999), *Sexual Generations: "Star Trek, the Next Generation" and Gender*, Urbana and Chicago: University of Illinois Press.

Sandapen, S. (2014), "The Doctor's Wondrous Wandering Dialectic Approach to the Universe," in J. Barr and C.D.G. Mustachio (eds.), *The Language of Doctor Who: From Shakespeare to Alien Tongues*, 77–94, Lanham, Boulder, New York, and London: Rowman and Littlefield.

Simon, S. (2003), *Gender in Translation: Cultural Identities and Politics of Transmission*, London, New York: Routledge.

Star Trek IV: The Undiscovered Country (1991), [Film] Dir. Nicholas Meyer, USA: Paramount Pictures.

Sternbach, R., M. Okuda and G. Roddenberry (1991), *Star Trek: The Next Generation: Technical Manual*, New York: Simon and Schuster.

Stollznow, K. (2014), *Language Myths, Mysteries and Magic*, New York: Palgrave Macmillan UK.

"Survival of the Fittest, part 4," *Doctor Who* (2012), [Radio broadcast] BBC-R4, May 29, 18:30.

"The Christmas Invasion (167)," *Doctor Who* (2005), [Television series] BBC1, December 25.

"The Fires of Pompeii (190)," *Doctor Who* (2008), [Television series] BBC1, April 28.

"Two Days and Two Nights," *Star Trek: Enterprise*, (2002) [Television series, season 1, episode 25], UPN, May 15.

Weitekamp M.A. (2013), "More than 'Just Uhura': Understanding *Star Trek*'s Lt. Uhura, Civil Rights, and Space History," in N. Reagin (ed.), *Star Trek and History*, 22–38, New Jersey: John Wiley & Sons.

Weldes, J. (2003), "Popular culture, science fiction, and world politics," in J. Weldes (ed.), *To Seek Out New Worlds*, 1–27, New York: Palgrave Macmillan US.

"Where No Man Has Gone Before," *Star Trek*, (1966) [Television series, season 1, episode 3], NBC, September 22, 8:30.

Wolf, M. (2014), "The Creation of 'A Room of One's Own': Feminist Translators as Mediators between Cultures and Genders," in J. Santaemilia (ed.), *Gender, Sex, and Translation: The Manipulations of Identities*, 15–25, Oxon and New York: Routledge.

Wozniak, M. (2014), "Technobabble on screen: Translating science fiction film," *inTRAlinea Special Issue: Across Screens Across Boundaries*. Available online: http://www.intralinea.org/specials/article/technobabble_on_screen (accessed February 18, 2017).

2

The Translator as Protagonist

Editor's Introductory Note

The second chapter in this collection explores translation as a cultural event that transcends the boundaries between translators, performers, and creative personnel within a broad context of cultural production. By tracing the introduction of *Hamlet* in China during the second half of the twentieth century, the chapter describes this important cultural project as more than a case of Shakespearean reception: it is a meta-translation, intro-translation, and inter-translation that can hardly be credited either to a single, or even a number of translators. Whether one discusses actors, translators, or directors, the introduction of *Hamlet* in China was entrusted to an elite group of artists, scholars, and cultural leaders whose interpretation of Shakespeare's work cannot be separated from their own scholarly and literary activity.

Following Sun Daolin, who, in 1958, lent his voice to the dubbed Chinese version of Laurence Olivier's film adaptation of *Hamlet* (1948), the reader finds that the dubbing artist was also a preeminent film star, director, expert reciter, poet, author, and an important social and cultural agent in twentieth-century China. Accordingly, his contribution to the introduction of *Hamlet* in China goes far beyond reading the part of Hamlet in the film. Drawing on auteur theory in film and media studies (which, to some extent, is reminiscent of Michel Foucault's "author function"), the chapter both contextualizes translation and adaptation within a wide culture and political context, and extends the scope of authorship to consider the many participants in any cultural production.

To the Western reader, this chapter is a fascinating source of knowledge about Communist China and its cultural landscape through several radically different political eras. But this does not detract from the chapter's theoretical significance: the creation of an inclusive definition of a "translation function" that encompasses the story—not of the translated work—but of its significance to the target culture. In this case: the self-reflection of individual subjectivities and the dilemma of intellectuals in Communist China.

In Search of a Chinese *Hamlet*: Translation, Interpretation, and Personalities in Postwar Film-Cultural Exchange

Ying Xiao

1. Introduction

For the Chinese, Hamlet is identified and has been widely associated with a particular voice and name: Sun Daolin. Sun[1] interpreted, dubbed, and recreated the celebrated character with subtlety, depth, and personal charisma. When Laurence Olivier's masterpiece, *Hamlet* (1948), was imported and translated in China in 1958, it instantly became a big hit across the nation and an unparalleled apotheosis of translation into Chinese accomplished through Bian Zhilin's masterful translation, Chen Shuyi's seasoned directing, and Sun Daolin's virtuoso dubbing and performance. The three of them were prominent artists, scholars, stars, celebrities, and cultural officials in mid-late twentieth-century China. My chapter explores and traces the reception, reinterpretation, and recontextualization of *Hamlet* in China across different epochs, from its huge success in the early People's Republic of China (PRC), through the censure of the work during the Cultural Revolution, to its resurrection and even broader appeal during the post-socialist, reform era.

Central to this historiography is my attention to the critical, (pro)active, and fluid roles that translators, performers, and creative personnel have played in the process of translation and adaptation. I probe the intricate manner in which these esteemed interpreters and cultural workers have negotiated and shifted between a variety of texts, cultures, languages, and sociopolitical settings—with particular attention to Sun Daolin who has often been lauded as the "Chinese prince" whose life has been seen as sheer poetry.[2]

In doing so, I demonstrate that the search for a Chinese *Hamlet* is not only a translation, but also a meta-translation (translation-in-translation), an intro-translation (self-reflection) of the position and dilemma of intellectuals and individual subjectivities in socialist China, and an inter-translation between literature, theater, film, popular culture, and social life. Moreover, the translation and the translated provide another vibrant angle to investigate Chinese film and cultural production as well as a comparative framework for understanding China's sociopolitical changes and international relations during the second half of the twentieth century.

2. Translating foreign-language film in the early PRC

The study of Chinese film history often takes as its premise that mainland China during the postwar period had become a deplorable cultural desert in film and other artistic creativities, given the severe censorship, the relatively low output, a homogenous mode of production and distribution, and the mainland's isolation from other parts of the world, particularly in relation with its Euro-American opponents. Contrary to this common presumptive and binary view, this period saw a range of developments and innovations in film as well as in other cultural sectors. During the first three decades of the PRC, since its establishment in 1949 to the end of the Maoist era in 1978—a period that historians and scholars generally portray as a riotous time of social upheaval, political totalitarianism, and cultural backlash—about 1,109 titles, including nearly 800 fiction films, were produced in the restructured film studios in places such as Shanghai, which was long celebrated as the Hollywood of the Orient, to the newly erected film studios in the distant plateaus as far as Urumchi and Huhehot.[3]

This, on the one hand, represents a pivotal move of nationalization and popularization of film in the PRC in its early phase. Within the all-encompassing, grand project of building a new socialist regime, film has been decisively identified as the most proper instrument and effective medium to promulgate the Party's policies and state ideologies, in which every citizen was involved, from urban centers to the countryside, and from the top to the bottom of the social ladder. Thus, one of the most notable achievements in socialist China was the enormous investment and a shift of focus to film distribution, conspicuously modeled after the Soviet Union and evidenced by a rapid proliferation of film projection teams that took films to a much broader and diverse audience base, especially to the rural masses, many of whom may thus far come across this foreign-derived art for the first time. On the other hand, a further step towards cinefication and sinification of an originatively Western form has presided over the socialist cinema of the Seventeen Years (1949–1966) and played an equally important role in the large frame of Chinese social and cultural life during the Cultural Revolution (1966–1976).

Despite the fact that Hollywood films, which had for long monopolized the Chinese film market since the beginning of the twentieth century, were banished and utterly eliminated from the socialist screen with the outbreak of the Korean War, the PRC continued to show imported films and engaged in international film exchange during the Cold War era. As Tina Mai Chen delineates in her seminal study of Sino-Soviet film exchange in 1950s and 1960s China, populating the Maoist theater were primarily pictures from the socialist bloc such as the Soviet Union, Eastern Europe, Vietnam, and North Korea as well as a great deal of productions from Japan, Hong Kong, India, France, Spain, and Britain.[4] It may be striking to see that China during the revolutionary period has imported numerous foreign titles. In fact, this lump even overtook China's own output at times. For instance, following its foundation in 1949, the PRC during the first decade (1949–1959) had imported, translated, and screened 412 foreign pictures while about 401 films were supplied by the PRC itself. Between 1960 and 1965, prior to the Cultural Revolution, the ratio of imported foreign films to domestic productions was approximately 159 to 240. During the Cultural Revolution (1966–1976)—the oft-cited ten years of catastrophe (*shinian haojie*)—when the country was submerged in large-scale political campaigns and social movements, the Chinese film industry had undergone a significant downward spiral with a slender yield of 106 films in comparison to 117 foreign films that were introduced and dubbed.[5] It is no exaggeration to argue that the very exposure and extensive translation of foreign films not only manifests an evidently transnational imaginary and a distinct form of Worldism (*shijie zhuyi*), but is also a constitutive part of the sociocultural life and national identity in the early PRC.

A shift in reliance from American film stock toward that of the Soviet Union characterized the cinematic landscape of the early PRC when a nascent socialist film industry took shape and went through profound restructuring. This has led to a substantial transition and particularly a technological and formal change when it came to foreign-language film. Before I begin a close examination of the translation of *Hamlet* and the vital role that the foreign-language film plays in socialist China, I think it is of necessity to trace the convoluted discourse of film translation and place it within a larger historical-filmic context. In the 1930s, with the advent of talking pictures, Hollywood faced a critical challenge in its approach to audiences in the non-English speaking world. The assorted strategies of exhibiting sound pictures in relation to translation has always been a concern to Hollywood studios that took the largest share of the box office in Republican China during the first half of the twentieth century. Therefore, in an effort to preserve their dominance in the film market, Hollywood studios undertook some initiatives toward translation since the rise of sound pictures. In the late 1930s, the Paramount engineers developed a particular device to project subtitles onto the screen alongside the playing of the film, which would help Chinese audience to understand the film. This was soon replaced by a more common practice of adding the subtitles directly to a printed edition of the film that was specifically made for Chinese viewers ("Jile," 1938). For example, *The Lives of a Bengal Lancer* (1935) extended its screening days in Shanghai by subsequently projecting an alternate subtitled version ("Zhandi," 1936). Accordingly, when *Heidi* (1937) was released and premiered in Shanghai in 1938, the film advertisement made a special note, highlighting in their publicity promotion the added feature of Mandarin subtitles onto the copy.[6] Likewise, a group of German films were exported with ready-made Chinese subtitles ("Dapi," 1938).

At the end of 1930s, the Grand Theater (*daguangming dianyingyuan*), touted as the most prestigious and the best equipped cinema of the Far East, embarked on an experimentation with a translation system. Each seat came up with a translation device. With a cost of as little as one dime, the patronage could acquire a pair of individual earphones (*yiyifeng*) to enjoy the foreign-language film accompanied by the brief summary and interpretation of the motion picture by "Miss Yiyifeng" who had a mellifluous voice and a good command of English.[7] The 1940s saw a decline of *yiyifeng* and the beginning of film dubbing first adopted by a stack of American newsreels and propagandist documentaries through which the US aimed to forge an alliance with the Chinese Nationalist government during the Second World War and in the immediate postwar period ("Meipian," 1947). The new measure of film dubbing was further carried to commercial pictures such as *Tarzan's New York Adventure* (1942) ("Cong," 1947) and involved several Soviet films including the award-winning fantasy film, *The Stone Flower* (Каменный цветок, 1946), which was entered in the Cannes Film Festival, and which dubbed version made a notable impact on the Chinese cinematic milieu and society at large (Ma 1946).

It should be noted, however, that despite these advancements, film translation or dubbing did not gain much wide currency due to the limited resources, the costs of facilities, and the discrepancies between the goals of production companies and the demands of their target audience. Over time, however, the Chinese government took an ideological interest in film translation. This, in turn, propelled the formation and formalization of film dubbing to become a standard practice for the imported foreign films in the PRC. Many studies of

Chinese film history take the "experimental dubbing" of *Private Alexander Matrosov* (*Рядовой Александр Матросов*, 1947) by Northeastern Film Studio (the former name for Changchun Film Studio) with Soviet assistance in 1948 as a watershed that marks the beginning of film dubbing in the PRC. Epitomic of China's century-long and strenuous search for modernity and linkage to the world, film dubbing is not only a singular practice and a form of translation associated with the technological appropriation of sound, the sociopolitical background of the reproduction, and the very dialectic of self-reflection and transnational imaginary, but also a specific mode of film circulation and cultural consumption deeply anchored and imbricated with the mass popular culture and everyday life in postwar socialist China.

Parallel to the birth and evolution of the PRC, the film dubbing industry sprouted, bourgeoned, and spanned throughout varied stages of the Maoist era, followed by the reformist era of the 1980s until the late 1990s when China reopened the floodgates to Hollywood blockbusters. To a great extent, it can be argued that China's film dubbing industry evolves with and is a product of Cold War politics, nationalization, and standardization of Chinese language in particular. It provides a site in which different languages, cultures, and discourses of national identities and transnational imagination collide, converge, negotiate, and are contested and rearticulated. Yet, this significant strand of film transit and reconciliation has gone largely unnoticed in the current literature. In contrast with copious writings focusing on the Fifth Generation, the Sixth Generation, and the underground, independent film, far less attention has been devoted to the examination and conception of film translation from a critical and systemic perspective. A handful of books and essays cast valuable glimpses on the very topic.[8] As they point out, the mechanism of translation and circulation of foreign-language film is of paramount importance to PRC's nation-building project, which functioned to fill "a cultural void in Chinese society" and "contributed to building a modern Chinese identity" (Yang and Feng 2016: 206). However, these attempts still fall into a constricted Cold War reading, which predominantly concentrates on a thread of film exchange in one single national, cinematic, or historical context.

The recent years saw a growing interest in this subject matter among scholars and a cohort of young cinephiles as well as middle-aged aficionados who have witnessed and grown along with the fledgling and full-blown film dubbing industry in the PRC. Old productions were excavated and re-embraced with a markedly nostalgic sentiment. Tagged as "Dubbed Classics" (*yizhi pian jingdian*), the works, which gained wide popularity during the socialist era, were refurbished and released in the new DVD format and quite often repacked into a special collection of the so-called retrospect of the dubbed genre. Film posters and memoirs of dubbing professionals and actors were put together to advance a reassessment of dubbing and the socialist cultural landscape in general. Scholarly studies also lament the previous neglect of activity and describe their newly sparked interests in these titles as a tide of reverence for dubbed films that resurged on the mainland at the turn of the new millennium.[9] These and other explorations, albeit representing a revisionist viewpoint, are not interdisciplinary; they neither adequately scrutinize film translation from a global perspective, nor do they consider the multimedia context and the film's interplay with other forms of audiovisual cultures. My work aims to move beyond what a single-handed statistical analysis and geopolitical reading have done for this group of imported foreign products, and to reappraise and resurrect them through a semiotic, "translation" lens, placing them back in the double context of global/local, East/West, tradition/modernity, public/private space, and collective/individual memory. I use Laurence Olivier's *Hamlet* and its subsequent reception, re-articulation, and translation into Chinese as an example that demonstrates the extent to which film translation is a fluid, contingent, and polyvalent process that retains a complex relationship with the original work, the translator, popular culture, intellectual history, and sociopolitical life. All of these are most aptly embodied through Sun Daolin's work, as he has not only impersonated, dubbed, incarnated, and brought this famed Shakespearean character to life on the Chinese screen, but was also simultaneously a pre-eminent film star, director, expert reciter, poet, author, and all in all, an important social and cultural agent in twentieth-century China.

3. The voice of others/self: imagining, playing, and rendering a Chinese *Hamlet*

Richard Dyer's pioneering research remains the most influential scholarly enquiry into the studies of film stardom, which conceptual frame, I suggest, can be extended and applied to the investigation of the translator who plays an essential role in the successful distribution and promotion of the work of the others. Dyer outlines the defining features of the film star who is to be understood as a constructed image, a commodity, and an ideology. The key part of stardom is a paradox of the person in that the constructed body presents and "copes with those divisions" of the present/absent, the ordinary/extraordinary, the public/private, and the dialectic of producing/consuming. Dyer asserts that "stars are about all of that, and are one of the most significant ways we have for making sense of it all. That is why they matter to us, and why they are worth thinking about." (Dyer 2004: 2). It is along this line of thinking that I set out to delineate and re-evaluate the translation and translators of *Hamlet*, a project which presents many layers, contradictions, and identities.

3.1 Shakespearean reception in China during the Maoist era

A substantial scholarship has delved into the comparative and translation study of China's convoluted and intensive encounters with Shakespeare in a wide scope of literature, theater, cinema, and visual art throughout modern-contemporary history. In their varied navigations of Shakespeare's manifestation in Chinese culture, Ruru Li and Murray J. Levith point out that, during the 1950s, three film adaptations of Shakespeare plays were admitted to China, namely: the Soviet-made *Twelfth Night* (Двенадцатая ночь, 1955) and *Othello* (Отелло, 1955) as well as Laurence Olivier's award-winning *Hamlet*.[10] All of them were dubbed into Mandarin Chinese in the Shanghai Dubbing Studio—a first-rate film translation and production company—and were consecutively released in 1956, 1957, and 1958. Among them, Olivier's *Hamlet* has won the most attendance as well as the critical acclaim of film scholars and critics. This is first of all owing to Bian Zhilin's sterling translation of the literary work, upon which the Chinese version of the film script was primarily based.

Bian Zhilin (1910–2000) was a famous poet who published volumes of poetry since the 1930s and made a strong impact on the modern Chinese poetry movement of the twentieth century. He graduated from the English Department of Peking University, and was a devoted translator and researcher of foreign-language literature. After the founding of the PRC, Bian took the position of a professor of English at Peking University. In the 1950s and 1960s, he was employed as one of the foremost researchers at the Institute of Literature and supervised and facilitated the establishment of the Institute of Foreign Literature in the Chinese Academy of Social Sciences. During his two-decade tenure of teaching and research, he turned his focus to translation, and specifically to the translation and study of Shakespeare's plays. He also served as the vice-president of the Chinese Association for Shakespeare Studies. Bian is best known for his translation of *Hamlet*, which was completed in 1954, published and reprinted by the People's Literature Press three times between 1956 and 1958. This time frame coincides with the introduction of Shakespearean films in China as previously mentioned.

During the Maoist era, as the juggernaut of state autocracy and nation-building prevailed, it comes as no surprise that Bian's interpretation and reworking of *Hamlet* were saliently an effort to respond to socialist ideology. In an article published in 1959 in *Literary Review* (*Wenxue pinglun*)—the PRC's top journal of literary studies—Bian Zhilin provides an elaborate account of the inception and evolvement of foreign literature translation and research during the first decade of PRC (Bian, Ye, Yuan, and Chen 1959). Together with his colleagues, he posits that foreign literature translation and research thrive on a larger scale and in a better quality in New China under the auspices of the Party, especially under the "correct direction" (*zhengque de fangxiang*) of Marxist thought. Marx and Engels's remarks on Shakespeare served as the principal guidelines for Chinese Shakespearean studies. Bian cites Marx's postulation as the latter both criticized and urged Ferdinand Lassalle: "You would then have Shakespearized more; at present, there is too much Schillerism, which means making individuals into mere mouth-pieces of the spirit of the times, and this is your main fault." (Baxandall and Morawski 1974: 107). In other words, Shakespeare becomes a paragon of art that symbolizes "the spirit of the times," and he is considered a great realistic artist that "not only belongs to one time but all our times," as Bian declares in another lengthy article about Shakespeare's oeuvre (Bian 1964).

Bian further illustrates that *Hamlet* represents a most remarkable and sophisticated work that would stand at the center of the sacred pantheon of Shakespeare. First, it shows a discerning synthesis of what Engels has called "greater intellectual profundity" and "a consciously historical content" with "Shakespearean vivacity and wealth of action." (Baxandall and Morawski 1974: 145). Second, it fits into Engels's idea of realism, which "implies, besides truth of detail, the truthful reproduction of typical characters under typical circumstances." (Engels 2001: 167). Bian explains that what Engels means here is that the faithful portrayal of the characters in Shakespeare's work would serve as a fair index of the historical moment in which they were made. Moreover, *Hamlet* must be read in the new, "post-typical" context of contemporary sociocultural, linguist environment in which it was transmitted, reinterpreted, and recreated. Linking Shakespeare, the thrust of realism, and "typical characters" together, Bian defines his artistic vision and the nature of translation and literary criticism in socialist China:

In terms of the principle of reflecting reality, we should not only introduce the social background of the work, but also (more importantly) pay attention to the (internal relationship and) social content within the work. For the spirit of the time as reflected in the work, we need to invoke the important method of class analysis. We also need to consider its particular meaning in the current social landscape and not to overlook its broader meaning; while we conjure the broader meaning of the product, we shall never forget its historical traits. When we probe into the intrinsic nature of how an important work mirrors reality, we can always find certain links of how it impels sociohistorical happenings, although it might not directly reflect the main struggles or historical events of the present society.

Bian, Ye, Yuan, and Chen 1959: 75

In this light, we may contend that Sun Daolin, who assumed the voice of Hamlet in Olivier's movie, is the incarnation and "reproduction of typical characters under typical circumstances."

3.2 The construction of intellectual bodies and Sun Daolin's voice role as Hamlet

Indeed, a deliberate and uncanny craft of "typicalness"—or rather the typical paradox of stardom, to borrow Dyer's formulation—perpetuates Sun Daolin's prolific, multifaceted artistic life. Coming from an affluent family and having graduated from Peking University with a major in philosophy, Sun Daolin (1921–2007) led an eventful life both on and off screen. He is a well-known actor who came to prominence through his vivid portrayal of a timid but sincere, and, at last, politically awakened schoolteacher in *Crows and Sparrows* (*Wuya yu maque*, 1949), a masterpiece that has been canonized in film history for its timely grasp and realistic depiction of an utmost historical turning point of China on the eve of a transition to a new socialist regime. Under the authority of the PRC, Sun Daolin played a great diversity of roles in more than twenty films.[11] Sun was mostly cast as a positive character, especially known for his screen persona of a socially engaged, politically sensitive but somewhat ambivalent hero with a distinctly intellectual undertone.

Yet, it is far from sufficient to classify Sun Daolin only as a film star. In the post-Cultural-Revolutionary period, Sun started to write screen scripts and direct films himself, as in: *Thunderstorm* (*Leiyu*, 1984), *The Provisional President* (*Feichang da zhongtong*, 1986), and *Stepmother* (*Jimu*, 1992). He also played the leading protagonists in the first two pieces. On top of his stellar career of starring in more than twenty films, Sun was an extremely versatile artist who has been active and well accomplished in poetry, drama, theatrical performance, television drama, and broadcasting. In addition, he was one of the most prominent dubbing actors in the PRC, who interpreted and gave excellent voice performance in dozens of translated foreign films. Among all his other projects, his voice role in the Chinese translation of *Hamlet* is by all means the most memorable and recognized. It has been firmly anchored in the collective memory of Chinese society, and still holds a high position in twentieth-century film and cultural history. In the zeitgeist of a cultural renaissance, when a cult of Shakespeare regained great esteem, and the related productions and studies resurged and thrived in post-revolutionary China, the Shanghai subdivision of the China Phonograph Company produced two tapes of "Classical Dialogues from Shakespeare's Plays" in 1986, a program paying tribute to Shakespeare and its cohort of Chinese translators and performers who have contributed to the profound and wide influence of Shakespeare in the Chinese public. A number of renowned performers, including Sun Daolin who was invited to rehearse his iconic role of Hamlet, have participated in the recording.[12]

An instructive methodological reference that might help to situate and explore Sun Daolin in a larger frame of film translation, cultural production, and (trans)nationalism, is Christine Gledhill's conceptualization of the star's text, intertext, and context. Drawing on Dyer's theory, Gledhill goes further to suggest that the film star is

> an intertextual construct produced across a range of media and cultural practices, capable of intervening in the working of particular films, but also demanding analysis as a text in its own right. While semiotics provides methods for analyzing such "texts," sociology asks how they function in society. Thus study of stars becomes an issue in the social production and circulation of meaning, linking industry and text, films and society.
>
> Gledhill 1991: xii

In this perspective, the Chinese translation of Olivier's *Hamlet* is a vantage point from which one can shed light on the sociopolitical meanings and identity of the translators/actors. Sun Daolin becomes an important social agent in his interpretation and dubbing of Hamlet, informed at once by a fundamental parallel as well as a contradiction between manifold texts; between on-screen personality and off-screen lifestyle, individual and collective, private and public, and the self and the other.

3.3 Bian Zhilin and Sun Daolin's approaches to *Hamlet*

In the Foreword to his translation of *Hamlet*, Bian Zhilin expresses his notion of art and the artist's role with a quote of the main character:

> The purpose of playing, whose end both at the first and now, was and is, to hold as 'twere the mirror up to nature: to show virtue her feature, scorn <u>her</u> own image, and the very age and body of the time his form and pressure.
>
> 3.2.19–22
>
> 莎士比亚自己在剧本里借托哈姆雷特、关于演戏（也就是关于剧作和一般文学创作）发表议论说，它的目的是"给自然照一面镜子；给德行看一看自己的面貌，给 <u>荒唐</u> 看一看自己的姿态，给时代和社会看一看自己的形象和印记"。
>
> Bian 1980: 41

To Hamlet, as well as Shakespeare, drama essentially serves a social end to reflect its time, and must be interpreted in the sociohistorical context in which it is shaped. When realization of the vile crimes that were performed by his uncle and the danger that he must face gradually dawns on him, Hamlet does more than simply grieve the death of his father and his own adverse circumstance. He devises a plan to use a play to reflect "typical characters under typical circumstances." Hamlet then begins to carry out his plan. He meets with the performers, and proceeds to lecture them on the manner and reasons for acting. While Hamlet seems to suggest that the purpose of playing is to hold a mirror up to nature and to truthfully reproduce reality, he also emphasizes art as a metaphor and a form of social critique, which is to uncover and "scorn" the corruptions of the time.

Hamlet's standpoint on art was greatly shared by his Chinese translators and players as they continued to hold the core value of art as an imitation of life. On the other hand, the particular emphasis of the Chinese translation was that a measure of irony would facilitate "an understanding of our own time, the nature of social development, and that of our life." (Bian 1980: 41). This explains the fact that, whereas the Chinese version tries to stay as close as it can to the original meaning of the English text, Bian Zhilin also takes the liberty to interpret and add "*huangtang*" (absurdity) in place of the pronoun "her" in the expression of "scorn <u>her</u> own image" (as underlined in the preceding quote). Indeed, the manner in which *Hamlet* has registered social reality, or to be more accurate, a reality of drastic changes [*dabian*: "sea change"], suggests that a particular mode of satire can be aptly employed to tackle the truth. This quality formed the dominant perception of the play when it was first introduced in China in the 1950s, and when it was recollected and resuscitated with an even broader viewership in the post-Mao era.

Following the establishment of the PRC in 1949, the first decade of an inchoate nation was marked by a series of massive political cleansing and ideological transformation movements such as suppressing the Counter-revolutionary Movement (1950–1953), and criticizing of *The Tale of Wu Xun* (1951), Three-anti (1951), Five-anti (1952), anti-Hu Feng (1955), and anti-Rightist Movement (1957). Many of these campaigns treated intellectuals, democrats, and upper-middle-class urbanites as the main target of denunciation. In particular, during the 1957 anti-Rightist Campaign, nearly half a million Chinese intellectuals were singled out and labeled "bourgeois reactionaries." They were accused of not aligning themselves with the new socialist state, and of being preoccupied with their habitual bourgeois lifestyle and artwork that were severely reprobated as "anti-Party and anti-People poisonous weeds (*ducao*)." A great number of artists suffered, including some of the previously most trusted writers, such as Ding Ling, Ai Qing, and the prestigious film star, Zhao Dan. Bian Zhilin and Sun Daolin were no exceptions. Like their contemporaries, they hardly had any choice but to submit to an overwhelming political power and reformulate themselves in accordance with the new setting. To be sure, the effect of such self-correction on the translation and dubbing of *Hamlet* is quite notable.

In the famous scene when the once beloved prince Hamlet begins to realize and endure betrayal, mishap, and pain, he conveys his despair and divulges his chilling thought about human existence upon the cliff of a storming ocean:

> To be, or not to be—that is the question.
> Whether 'tis nobler in the mind to suffer
> The slings and arrows of <u>outrageous fortune,</u>
> Or to take arms against a sea of troubles
> And by opposing end them. To die, to sleep—
> No more—and <u>by a sleep to say we end</u>
> The heartache and the thousand <u>natural shocks</u>
> <u>That flesh is heir to, 'tis a consummation</u>
> Devoutly to be wished . . .
> There's the respect
> That makes calamity of so long life.
> For who would bear the whips and scorns of time,

The 'oppressor's wrong, <u>the proud man's contumely,</u>
The pang's despised love, the law's delay,
<u>The insolence of office</u>, and the spurns
That <u>patient merit</u> of th'unworthy takes,
Who would fardels bear,
To grunt and sweat under a weary life
But that the dread of something under death,
<u>The undiscovered country, from whose bourn</u>
No traveler returns, puzzles the will
And makes us rather bear those ills we have
Than fly to <u>others</u> that we know not of?

3.1.57–83

Bian Zhilin and Sun Daolin's interpretation of Hamlet's monologue is as follows:

活着，还是不活，这是个问题。究竟那样更高贵，去忍受那狂暴的命运 <u>无情的摧残</u> 还是挺身去反抗那无边的烦恼，把他扫一个干净。去死，去 睡，就结束了， 如果睡眠能结束 <u>我们心灵的创伤</u> ，和肉体所承受的<u>千 百种 痛苦</u> ，那真是求之不得的天大的好事......就这点顾虑使人 受着终身的折磨，谁甘心忍受那鞭打和嘲 弄，受人压迫，<u>受尽侮蔑和轻 视</u> ，忍受那失恋的痛苦，法庭的拖延，衙门的<u>横征暴敛</u> 。<u>默默无闻的劳 碌</u> 却只换来多少凌辱......谁也不甘心，呻吟流汗拖着这残生， 可是对死后又感觉到恐惧，又从来没有任何人从 <u>死亡的国土里</u> 回来，因 此动摇了，宁愿忍受着目前的苦难，而不愿投奔向另一种 <u>苦难</u> ？

Hamlet 1948

Bian and Sun's work has been hailed as the best and the most exquisite in comparison with other Chinese versions, a paragon of translation that has been written as a textbook about Translation Studies in China (Sun 2012). Their mesmeric interpretation remains largely true to the original and turns to be even more compelling and powerful with emphatic punctuation and the addition of pain, affliction, and agony to the text. As shown in the underlined part of the above quotes, the additional phrase, "our spiritual trauma," is tagged to the line, "by a sleep to say we end." "Natural shocks" is translated into "millions of ways of sufferings"; "the proud man's contumely" is reworked as "take all kinds of humiliation and contempt"; "the insolence of office" is translated as "the exploitation and cruelty of the office"; "patient merit" is translated as "silent, arduous, exhausting work"; "the undiscovered country, from whose bourn" is translated into "the kingdom of death"; and, above all, the appendage of "*kunan*" (great tribulation) is added to "fly to others." These subtle changes highlight a dominant mode of suffering and render it more explicitly in the Chinese context.

In a similar vein, the film scene reflects the excruciating pain of the individual in the face of social change. This is demonstrated through a wearisome, unusual two-minute long take, a rapid zoom onto the extreme close-up of Hamlet's afflicted face, and his dumbfounded posture. In addition, the same theme is underscored through Sun's deep, sonorous, and philosophical oration. Intercut and resonant with the thunderous, recurring torrents on the screen, a keen aural-visual symbol of turbulent change, Sun's voiceover is endowed with rich and new meanings through his unique interpretation and re-enactment. In a sense, Sun Daolin delivers the soliloquy of "to be or not to be," not only to the Chinese audience, but also in tribute to himself and many others like him who have long suffered endless trouble, castigation, captivity, betrayal, and a tumultuous life in the riotous, drastically changing sociopolitical environment of socialist China.

Thus, Hamlet has both literally and figuratively become the voice and a reflection of a struggling Chinese self, who is equally entangled in an incessant game of political struggle, persecution, and vengeance. Olivier's film begins with a sense of disbelief and disorder, and culminates in a final scene of self-validation, as the prince completes his revenge and his dead body is borne by soldiers through the extended hall, staircases, to the topmost tower with a sense of respect and justice, and to the sound of the reverberating cannon of the royal family. To echo this theme of redemption, rather than transliterating Hamlet's name as the title of the film, it was titled *Wangzi fucouji* (*The Prince's Revenge*) in Chinese, which has conspicuously replaced the foreign name with a catchy and emotionally charged stock phrase. While foregrounding "the typical characters under typical circumstances" and imparting the main theme of the film, the Chinese title also created a mystic and melodramatic touch characteristic to suspense, thriller, or action films. Moreover, this has, to a great extent, smoothed out some of the foreignness of the picture and helped reach the Chinese local audience in a generic and vernacular fashion.

In addition, there are some other factors that could explain the success of the Chinese version. At the end of Hamlet's famous soliloquy, and before the camera dissolves into the next act in which the viewers follow his decisive action, Hamlet questions his own resolve and retreats mournfully from the podium of his monologue:

Thus conscience doth make cowards of us all,
And thus the native hue of resolution
Is sicklied o'er with the pale cast of thought,
And enterprises of great pith and moment,
With this regard their currents turn away ...
And lose the name of action.

3.1.84–89

顾虑就使我们都变成了懦夫，使得那果断的本色蒙上了一层思虑的惨白的容颜。本来可以做出伟大的事业，由于思虑就化为乌有了......丧失了行动的能力。

Hamlet 1948

Through Hamlet's sardonic soliloquy and seemingly mad words, the film evinces a cutting criticism of politics, society, and the sinister underside of human nature. Instead of being a masculine, strong-willed, and chauvinist hero, as is predominantly the case in revenge narratives and action thrillers, Olivier's Hamlet is rather weak, pale, repeatedly at a loss and in a state of uncertainty. The feeble, hesitant prince may seem at odds with the interests and broader landscape of revolutionary China that, similar to Olivier's England, has undergone enormous change, destruction, and the subsequent building of a new nation in the postwar period. However, Hamlet's indecision and delay to avenge and fight against evils cannot be seen as his personal flaw, but an attestation to his moral integrity, immense intelligence, and deeply ingrained humanist concern that made the character emblematic of the Renaissance and (in relation to the film version) of postwar England. Moreover, Hamlet's thoughtful hesitation, sorrow, and immense adversities strike a deep chord of empathy with a large viewership in China. Scholars have argued that some qualities found in Hamlet would align the character with a Confucian hero—a "Confucian Hamlet" so to speak—who shares a distinct trait of *youfen* (melancholic reflection, dignity, and great anxiety about the fate of his country), as well as similar moral standards, political ideals, and a strong sense of social responsibility (Zhang 1996: 213–216).

Both forms of the Confucian hero and the Western style of the Hamlet-like hero were reprimanded as obnoxious and reactionary arts and hence banned during the Great Proletarian Cultural Revolution. But while the Chinese version of *Hamlet* and its translators met with disapproval and were subjected to harsh criticism and interrogation in the 1960s and 1970s, it returned to the spotlight, stirred up the nation, and acquired a new degree of relevance in post-Mao China. At the historical juncture of the 1980s, Hamlet and Sun Daolin's idiosyncratic performance and exclamation of "to be or not to be" were summoned up to entail a serious and thorough inspection of the political errors, traumas, and suffering that Chinese people have gone through, and the long-anticipated redemption after the chaotic decade of the Cultural Revolution. The Hamlet-like interpellation was likewise invoked to rebuild and promote the ideal of humanity, freedom, an atmosphere of liberalization, and the new directions of reform and open-door policy in the post-socialist era. As Bian Zhilin indicates, even though *Hamlet* is at large a tragedy,

> the theme of this tragedy is the conflicts between the ideal and reality. Human beings fight for the ideal. Even if they fail at time, their fight illuminates the glory of the ideal. This, therefore, strengthens and consolidates human beings' confidence in their ability to reform reality.
>
> Bian 1957: 98

4. Conclusion: The significance of the cinematic reception of *Hamlet* in postwar China

In the Chinese context, the interpretation of *Hamlet* was particularly useful because it is a rich text loaded with complex implications, contradictions, and ironies, as well as a symbol of idealized humanity across both national and spatiotemporal boundaries. More importantly, the work serves as an intertextual construct that forcefully interweaves various cultural practices, media representations, and social-artistic roles together. To put it another way: in an extended and ongoing path of searching for Hamlet, China and Chinese interpreters, actors, and intellectuals such as Bian Zhilin and Sun Daolin, seek their own identity through the articulation and engagement with the Western other. Within this process, the Western other is experienced as a nuanced projection of the Chinese, Confucian self.

We may also find such traces of Hamlet's conundrum and his signature skepticism and reflection in Sun Daolin's own writing and life. During the 1940s, when Sun Daolin was still a university student of philosophy in Beijing, a time during which the country was plagued by years of devastating war against Japanese invaders, he was extremely active in stage performance and experimented with the translation and production of many world-famous plays. Among these are Dumas's *The Lady of the Camellias*, Gogol's *The Government Inspector*, and Shakespeare's *King Lear* and *Twelfth Night*. Furthermore, he was a distinguished poet acclaimed by the school of modern Chinese poetry, and particularly celebrated as part of the movement of resistance poetry during wartime. In 1942, amidst the prolonged war, Sun bitterly wrote of himself a composition titled "Solo" (*Duwang*):

> Even if I spot a seat at the banquet
> Do I have my place tomorrow?
> They admire only the singing of the northern wind
> While I never crave only that
> Musical tunes without echoes.
> I do not intend to gladly surprise all attendants
> With any magical powers
> Like the musician at the banquet.
> Tomorrow, at the grand river, across the windows
> I will listen to your eulogies
> But the host already took away my seat
> Saying I am a passerby
> A Beggar without soul.
> By then, I should begin to doubt my abilities.
> If I have intelligence endowed by the mundane world
> How can I be satisfied with that?
> Musical tunes without echoes.[13]

Sun 1997: 294

The poem is but an utterance of Sun's deeply felt loneliness, grief, and trouble during wartime, as he exemplifies a Confucian scholar, hero, and model in modern China. Moreover, the work is simultaneously a befitting portrayal of the very Hamlet-like paradox that continues to resonate and find its universalist, humanist pertinence in postwar, revolutionary China. Over a decade after the poem was written, Sun Daolin was yet unable to find a suitable seat "at the banquet," of China's tumultuous sociopolitical changes. When he took up the role and spoke for Hamlet, he might have been thinking of himself and performing his own personal dilemma which, to a great extent, resembles and intersects with the specter of Hamlet.

Glossary

Film dubbing: A verbal translation of the foreign-language film into the audience's native language. It often involves a change of soundtrack where the original dialog is replaced by a new dialog in a different language yet synchronizing with the existing actions and lip movements of the actors on the screen.

Film translation: Adapting a film from one language to another, through various methods, for the benefit of a target audience. The practice of film translation primarily takes two forms: subtitling and film dubbing. Each method has undergone a complex trajectory of formation and evolvement throughout film history, and involves distinct audiovisual measures and ideological and aesthetic concerns. Both methods provoke important questions about translation, adaptation, cross-cultural circulation, and the global dimension of the cinema.

Hamlet **(1948):** A renowned film adaptation of Shakespeare's play, *Hamlet*, starring and directed by Lawrence Oliver in 1948. Olivier's *Hamlet* is considered one of the greatest and most critically acclaimed adaptations of the work. The film was introduced and dubbed into Chinese in 1958, and became a classic piece of adaptation in Chinese film history. It was translated to Chinese by Bian Zhilin, an eminent scholar and poet in the second half of twentieth-century China. Sun Daolin, a celebrated star, filmmaker, poet, and personality, dubbed and played the voice role of Hamlet in the Chinese version of the film.

Personality: The quality or fact of being a unique individual with distinctive traits, sociopolitical views, life experiences, and a recognized body of work with characteristic style. Drawing from auteur theory in film and media studies, the notion of personality extends the scope of authorship. Rather than regarding the director as the sole author of the work, one sees other production members such as actors, scriptwriters, cinematographers, interpreters, and other participants, as jointly playing creative roles and as important social and cultural agents in the process of film production and distribution.

Shakespeare Studies in China: A rich body of scholarship that examines the influence, reception, and translation of Shakespeare's work in the Chinese context and its interactions with a wide range of Chinese national and regional literary and cultural forms in modern and contemporary periods. To explore the intersections between Shakespeare and China, the research makes critical contributions to the global study of Shakespeare and creates dynamic dialogs across geographical, linguistic, and disciplinary boundaries.

Notes

1   Note on Chinese names and translation: In this chapter, I observe the Chinese custom of referring to the Chinese name in the order of last name followed by first

name if the full name is mentioned. When the Chinese translation is invoked for the sake of argumentation and clarification, I have adopted the simplified form of Chinese characters—which is the standard writing system of the People's Republic of China—to represent its original source and context.

2 For a related discussion, see Huang (1997: 1–8).

3 See Marion (1996) and China Film Archives and China Film Art Research Center (1981).

4 For more discussions, see Chen (2004), Chen (2009a), and Chen (2009b).

5 Up to this point, few sources and official documents can be found. In addition, a unanimous opinion has not been reached with regard to the precise number of films imported from other countries during the socialist era. My account in this essay is not intended to be an exhaustive list, but a preliminary overview. More importantly, it is meant to call for a more systematic and critical study on this topic. The data were obtained and based upon, respectively, *Zhongguo dianying fangxing fangying tongji ziliao jianbian (1949–1957)* [*A Compendium of Chinese Film Distribution and Exhibition Statistics*] (1958), Yuan (2015), and CCTV-Movie Channel's special program for the 65th anniversary of Film Dubbing in PRC [Xin zhongguo yizhipian 65 zhounian zhuanti jiemu], which, aired from December 22–31, 2014, comprises a weekly showcase of the important pieces, interviews with the renowned filmmakers, actors, and, interpreters, and a retrospective commemoration of the Chinese dubbing industry.

6 See Zhang (2006: 41–46).

7 See Hua (1939) and "Yiyifeng" (1939).

8 See Clark (1987), Chen (2004), Chen (2009a), Chen (2009b), and Yang and Feng (2016).

9 The main publications provoked by and in turn partaking in the nostalgia of dubbed foreign films include Su (2005), Su (2008), Sun (2012), Cao (2006), and Gu (2006).

10 For further discussion, see Li (2003) and Levith (2004).

11 The important roles Sun Daolin has played, which best illustrate the range of his acting abilities, include a Communist hero in *Scouting Across the Yangtze River* (*Dujiang zhencha ji*, 1954), a resourceful militia leader in *Storm on the Southern Island* (*Nanguo fengyun*, 1955), an undercover Communist telegrapher in *The Eternal Wave* (*Yongbu xiaoshi de dianbo*, 1958), a resolute revolutionary in *A Revolutionary Family* (*Geming jiating*, 1961), a weak and deeply troubled brother in *Family* (*Jia*, 1956), a reformed national capitalist in *City Without Night* (*Buyecheng*, 1958), a confused intellectual in *Early Spring in February* (*Zaochun eryue*, 1964), a patriotic scientist in *Li Siguang* (*Li Siguang*, 1979), and a legendary chess master in *An Unfinished Go Game* (*Yipang mei xiawan de qi*, 1982).

12 For further discussion, see Sun (1997: 273–275) and Zhang (1996: 197–198).

13 I wish to thank Wang Shaochang for his remarkable translation, enthusiastic support, and his keen interest in poetry and literature that has truly inspired me in this and other projects.

References

A Revolutionary Family (1961), [Film] Dir. Shui Hua, China: Beijing Film Studio.

An Unfinished Go Game (1982), [Film] Dir. Duan Jishun and Junya Sato, China and Japan: Beijing Film Studio and Tokyo Tokuma Co.

Baxandall, L. and S. Morawski (eds.) (1974), *Karl Marx/Frederick Engels on Literature and Art: A Selection of Writings*, New York: International General, 1974.

Bian, Z. (1957), "Shashibiya de beiju hamuteite [Shakespeare's Tragedy *Hamlet*]," *Wenyi yanjiu jikan [Literary Studies]*, December: 79–137.

Bian, Z. (1964), "Shashibiya xiju chuangzuo de fazhan [The Trajectory of Shakespeare's Creation of Works]," *Wenxue pinglun [Literary Review]* 4: 52–79.

Bian, Z. (1980), "Guanyu wo yi de shashibiya beiju hamuleite: wushu youxu [On My Translated Work Shakespeare's Tragedy *Hamlet*: An Old Preface with a New Note]," *Waiguo wenxue yanjiu [Foreign Literature Studies]* 1: 38–50.

Bian, Z., S. Ye, K. Yuan, and S. Chen (1959), "Shinian lai de waiguo wenxue fanyi heyanjiu gongzuo [The Translation and Research Work of Foreign Literature in the Past Ten Years]," *Wenxue pinglun [Literary Review]* 5: 41–77.

Cao, L. (2006), *Yuanqu de huixiang: liushi bu yizhipian peiyin biji [The Fading Echoes: The Dubbing Notes for Sixty Films]*, Shanghai: Shanghai cishu chubanshe.

Chen, T.M. (2004), "Internationalism and Cultural Experience: Soviet Films and Popular Chinese Understandings of the Future in the 1950s," *Cultural Critique* 58: 82–114.

Chen, T.M. (2009a), "International Film Circuits and Global Imaginaries in the People's Republic of China, 1949–57," *Journal of Chinese Cinemas* 3.2: 149–161.

Chen, T.M. (2009b), "Socialist Geographies, Internationalist Temporalities and Travelling Film Technologies: Sino-Soviet Film Exchange in the 1950s and 1960s," in O. Khoo and S. Metzger (eds.), *Futures of Chinese Cinema: Technologies and Temporalities in Chinese Screen Cultures*, 73–93, Bristol: Intellect.

China Film Archives and China Film Art Research Center (eds.) (1981), *Zhongguo yishu yingpian bianmu (1949–1979) [The Chinese Filmography (1949–1979)]*, Beijing: Wenhua yishu chubanshe.

City Without Night (1958), [Film] Dir. Tang Xiaodan, China: Shanghai Jiangnan Film Studio.

Clark, P. (1987), *Chinese Cinema: Culture and Politics Since 1949*, New York: Cambridge University Press.

"Cong senlin zhong daole dushi, weisimole xinzuo: 'taishan dao niuyue' bi guoqu de taishan pian xinyin bushao, quanbu guoyu shuoming [From Forest to Metropolis, the New Work of Weissmuller: *Tarzan's New York Adventure* Is Much More Innovative than the Previous Tarzan Films and Is Completely Translated Into Mandarin]" (1947), *Xibao* [*Drama Daily*], January 13.

Cook, P.J. (2011), *Cinematic Hamlet: The Films of Olivier, Zeffirelli, Branagh, and Almereyda*, Athens: Ohio University Press.

Crows and Sparrows (1949), [Film] Dir. Zheng Junli, China: Kunlun Film Company.

Dai, J. and B. Sun (2014), *Hamuleite de yingwu biannian* [*The Genealogy of the Films and Dramas for Hamlet*], Shanghai: Shanghai renmin chubanshe.

Dyer, R. (2004), *Heavenly Bodies: Film Stars and Society*, New York: Routledge.

"Dapi yingpian luxu yunhu, deguopian jiang shoufu shidi, jia huawenzimu, jian yuyan zhang'an [Massive Films Will Arrive in Shanghai Gradually, German Film Will Recover Its Ground, Add Chinese Subtitles, and Overcome Language Barrier]" (1938), *Diansheng zhoukan* [*Electric Sound Weekly*] 7, 16: 309.

Early Spring in February (1964), [Film] Dir. Xie Tieli, China: Beijing Film Studio.

Engels, F. (2001), "Engels to Margaret Harkness," in *Karl Marx Frederick Engels Collected Works*, Vol. 48, London: Lawrence & Wishart.

Family (1956), [Film] Dir. Chen Xihe and Ye Ming, China: Shanghai Film Studio.

Gledhill, C. (ed.), (1991), *Stardom: Industry of Desire*, New York: Routledge.

Gu, T. (2006), *Waiguo xin dianying fanyi yu yanjiu* [*Translation and Research on Foreign Films*], Beijing: Zhongguo chuanmei daxue chubanshe.

Hamlet (1948), [Film] Dir. Laurence Olivier, UK: Two Cities Films.

Heidi (1937), [Film] Dir. Allan Dwan, USA: 20th Century Fox.

Hua (1939), "Guanzhong xianting weikuai de 'yiyifeng' [Earphone to Meet the Audience's Need and Ears]," *Yazhou yingxun* [*Asian Cinema News*] 2, 47: 2.

Huang, A. (2009), *Chinese Shakespeares: Two Centuries of Cultural Exchange*, New York: Columbia University Press.

Huang, Z. (1997), "Sun daolin shi yi shou shi: dai xu [Sun Daolin Is a Piece of Poem: Foreword]," in D. Sun, *Zou jin yangguang* [*Walking into the Sunshine*], 1–8, Shanghai: Shanghai renmin chubanshe.

"Jile pailameng zhihou, migaomei jia huawen zimu [Following Paramount Pictures, MGM also Added Chinese Subtitles]" (1938), *Diansheng zhoukan* [*Electric Sound Weekly*] 7, 15: 295.

Levith, M.J. (2004), *Shakespeare in China*, New York: Continuum.

Li, R. (2003), *Shashibiya: Staging Shakespeare in China*, Hong Kong: Hong Kong University Press.

Li Siguang (1979), [Film] Dir. Ling Zifeng, China: Beijing Film Studio.

Lv, X. (2006), "1949–1976: dui shanghai yizhipian de yizhong kaocha [1949–1976: An Exploration of the Foreign Dubbed Films in Shanghai]," in Y. Yang (ed.), *Zhongguo dianying zhuanyeshi yanjiu: dianying wenhua juan* [*A Specialized Study on Chinese Film History: A Volume of Film Culture*], 530–539, Beijing: Zhongguo dianying chubanshe.

Ma, B. (1946), "xinpian zatan 'bao shi hua' [Reflections on the New Film, *The Stone Flower*]," *Shenbao* [*Shanghai Daily*], November 17.

Marion, D.J. (1996), *The Chinese Filmography: The 2444 Feature Films Produced by Studios in the People's Republic of China from 1949 through 1995*, Jefferson: McFarland & Co.

"Meipian duibai guoyuhua: guopian shou weixie, yiyifeng yicheng le feiwu [The Mandarinization of American Film: Domestic Production at Risk, Earphone Is Passé Now]" (1947), *Xi shijie* [*Theater World*] 352: 8.

Othello (1955), [Film] Dir. Sergei Yutkevich, Soviet Union: Mosfilm.

Piao, Z. (2008), *Yingshi fanyi yanjiu* [*Research on Film and Television Translation*], Harbin: Heilongjiang renmin chubanshe.

Private Alexander Matrosov (1948), [Film] Dir. Leonid Lukov, Soviet Union: Soyuzdetfilm.

Scouting Across the Yangtze River (1954), [Film] Dir. Tang Xiaodan, China: Shanghai Film Studio.

Stepmother (1992), [Film] Dir. Sun Daolin, China: Shanghai Film Studio.

Storm on the Southern Island (1955), [Film] Dir. Bai Chen, China: Shanghai Film Studio.

Su, X. (2005), *Wo de peiyin shengya* [*My Life About Film Dubbing*], Shanghai: Wenhui chubanshe.

Su, X. (ed.), (2008), *Feng hua bi xu: shangyichang de sige laotou'er* [*Feng hua bi xu: The Four Gentlemen from Shanghai Dubbing Studio*], Shanghai: Wenhui chubanshe.

Sun, D. (1997), *Zou jin yangguang* [*Walking into the Sunshine*], Shanghai: Shanghai renmin chubanshe.

Sun, J. (2012), *Xingzou zai xiaoshi zhong* [*Walking into the Disappearing*], Shanghai: Shanghai shudian chubanshe.

Sun, Y. (2010), *Shakespeare in China*, Kaifeng: Henan University Press.

Tarzan's New York Adventure (1942), [Film] Dir. Richard Thorpe, USA: Metro-Goldwyn-Mayer.

The Eternal Wave (1958), [Film] Dir. Wang Ping, China: August First Film Studio.

The Lives of a Bengal Lancer (1935), [Film] Dir. Henry Hathaway, USA: Paramount Pictures.

The Provisional President (1986), [Film] Dir. Sun Daolin, China: Shanghai Film Studio.

The Stone Flower (1946), [Film] Dir. Aleksandr Ptushko, Soviet Union: Mosfilm.

Thunderstorm (1984), [Film] Dir. Sun Daolin, China: Shanghai Film Studio.

Twelfth Night (1955), [Film] Dir. A. Abramov and Y. Frid, Soviet Union: Lenfilm Studio.

Xin zhongguo yizhipian 65 zhounian zhuanti jiemu [*The Special Program for the 65th Anniversary of Film Dubbing in PRC*] (2014), CCTV-Movie Channel, December 22–31.

Yang, F. and D. Feng (2016), "Politics of Film Translation: Cinema and Nation-Building in China (19497–1964)," in L. D'hulst, C. O'Sullivan, M. Schreiber (eds), *Politics, Policy, and Power in Translation History*, 187–210, Berlin: Frank & Timme GmbH.

Yang, H. and Z. Ma (2010), *Dangdai zhongguo yizhi* [*Contemporary Chinese Dubbing Industry*], Beijing: Zhongguo chuanmei daxue chubanshe.

"Yiyifeng zai da guangming: shang xingqi si kaishi zhuangyong, zufei meizhi guobi yijiao zheng [Earphone in the Grand Theater: To Begin Installation Since Last Thursday with a Rental Fee of Ten Cents]" (1939), *Qingchun dianying* [*Youth Cinema*] 4, 33: 2.

Yu, L. and N. Qian (2013), *Sun daolin zhuan: meng zhi dao de puti shu* [*A Biography of Sun Daolin: A Bodhi Tree in the Dreamland*], Shanghai: Shanghai renmin chubanshe.

Yuan, Q. (2015), "1949 nian hou waiguo yizhipian zai zhongguo dalu de chuanbo [The Circulation of Foreign Dubbed Films in Mainland China After 1949]," *Xiandai zhongwen xuekan* [*Journal of Modern Chinese Studies*] 5: 114–119.

"Zhandi yinghun yanchang yinqi bing huanying yinyou huawen zimu kaobei [The Lives of a Bengal Lancer Extended Its Screening Period with a Substitute of a Chinese Subtitled Copy]" (1936), Xinwenbao benbu fukan [Appendage to the Local News], February 9.

Zhang, W. (2006), "20 shiji qianqi haolaiwu yingpian de hanyi chuanbo [The Chinese Translation and Distribution of Hollywood Film in the Early 20th Century]," *Shanghai daxue xuebao* [*Journal of Shanghai University*] 13.5: 41–46.

Zhang, X. (1996), *Shakespeare in China: A Comparative Study of Two Traditions and Cultures*, London: Associated University Press.

Zhongguo dianying fangxing fangying tongji ziliao jianbian (1949–1957) [*A Compendium of Chinese Film Distribution and Exhibition Statistics*] (1958), Beijing: Zhongguo dianying faxing fangying gongsi.

3

Translators as Social (Double) Agents

Editor's Introductory Note

The third chapter in this collection follows the representation of interpreters in films that describe wars and violent conflicts. The chapter discusses three films in different languages and about very different conflicts, both real and fictional. The films also present professional as well as amateur interpreters. Common to all three portrayals of interpreters is the engaging ethical discussion that is suggested by the different films: the moral, ethical, and professional responsibilities of the interpreter when faced with violence and warfare. To what extent are these obligations contradicting each other? And what are some of the differences between a professional interpreter and an amateur interpreter who functions either as a soldier or a civilian during war?

The chapter offers a fascinating discussion of contemporary global conflict and the investigation of potential terrorists, as well as collective memories of the Sino-Japanese War and the Asia-Pacific War. Theoretically, the chapter both surveys the manner in which interpretation is represented in film, and lays the groundwork for a thought-provoking discussion about the responsibilities of interpreters in extreme situations. Does the interpreter have an obligation to maintain professional neutrality? Or rather an obligation to aid victims as much as possible? Can the interpreter truly be faulted for protecting their own skin? Or can the interpreter be held guilty of collaboration with acts of torture and oppression? These questions extend the theoretical discussion that tries to place interpreters between the roles of translators and mediators—but they also touch the reader personally: What would any of us do in situations of injustice, violence, torture, and genocide?

Mediating Violence: Three Film Portrayals of Interpreters' Dilemmas as Participants in Conflict

Kayoko Takeda

1. Introduction

Over the past decade, research about interpreters dealing with violent discourses and situations has become an emerging area in Interpreting Studies, prompted by major global events involving interpreters, such as international criminal tribunals in the Hague and Rwanda, and post-9/11 military actions in Afghanistan and Iraq. Such research examines a range of issues, including military language policies in conflict (e.g., Footitt and Kelly 2012a, 2012b), training, and working conditions of military interpreters and interpreters for humanitarian missions (e.g., Moser-Mercer 2015), and the complex issues of the identity, role, and loyalty of the interpreter in war and conflict zones (e.g., Inghilleri 2008, 2012). Ethical issues and moral struggles of interpreters working in the midst of violence, injustice, abuse, and war crimes are also addressed in scholarly work (e.g., Monacelli and Punzo 2001; Tryuk 2015), as well as in memoirs written by interpreters (e.g., Fair 2016; Saar and Novak 2005). How do interpreters behave when forced or induced to mediate violence? Historical case studies, and academic or journalistic investigations and personal accounts of contemporary events, project their role not only as enablers of violence but also as mitigating agents of aggression (see various articles in Ruiz Rosendo and Persaud (2016)). They also reveal interpreters' moral dilemmas concerning the facilitation of violence and criminal acts. And, in the case of locals hired as interpreters by the occupier, these studies discuss the apprehension of interpreters about being treated, not only as potential security risks by their employer, but also as traitors by other locals (e.g., Lan 2016; Takeda 2014a). Furthermore, consequences of their actions as interpreters can be as grave as being convicted (and executed in some cases) as war criminals (Lan 2016; Takeda 2016) and developing long-lasting post-traumatic stress disorders (PTSD) (Fair 2016; Lomax 1995/2012).

To illuminate the dilemmas interpreters face as they weigh the benefits and risks of using their linguistic power to mitigate or facilitate hostile situations, this chapter examines three film portrayals of characters who participate as interpreters in violent actions they themselves do not condone. In movies, interpreters are often characterized either as unreliable intermediaries with divided loyalties, or as indifferent props functioning to advance a narrative (e.g., Andres 2015; Cronin 2009; O'Sullivan 2011). There are, however, some exceptions: movies which feature interpreters as well-developed and highly visible individuals, who struggle to come to terms with the work they are forced to do under strenuous circumstances. The three movies selected here fall into that category. They are: *Ip Man*, a 2008 Hong Kong martial arts film in which a local Chinese interpreter works for Japanese troops during their occupation of southern China in the Second Sino-Japanese War; *The Railway Man*, a 2013 British-Australian war film in which a Japanese military interpreter facilitates the torture of a prisoner of war (POW) during the Second World War; and *The Arrival of Wang*, a 2011 Italian science fiction film in which an Italian interpreter is induced to work in her government's interrogation and torture of an extraterrestrial who speaks Chinese. The first two movies are based on historical narratives from Japan's Fifteen-Year War,[1] and the third is a fictional story with a contemporary setting. After analyzing the depictions of these interpreters' negotiation of their role in hostile discourses, this chapter discusses the interpreters' power to control information (Anderson 1976), some of the real conflicts that interpreters face in adversarial settings, and the manner in which interpreters are perceived by the parties in violent situations. Finally, the conclusion explores the significance of cinematic representations of such interpreters in raising awareness of the dilemmas that are faced by communication mediators in violent international conflict.

2. Protecting compatriots by working for the enemy (*Ip Man*, 2008)

Although not the protagonist, a local policeman-turned-interpreter in occupied China plays a significant role in the award-winning Hong Kong martial arts film, *Ip Man*. The film is based on a biographical story of a legendary martial arts grandmaster, Ip Man, who famously taught Bruce Lee. Directed by Wilson Yip, the film premiered in 2008 and was distributed worldwide. It was met with commercial and critical success, especially in the Asian market, spawning two sequels released in 2010 and 2015. Within the film, Cantonese, Mandarin, and Japanese are used. For this study, the author references the DVD versions of *Ip Man* distributed in the Japanese and US markets. The DVD acquired in the Japanese market has Japanese subtitles, and the one in the US has English subtitles. All the references to characters' utterances are based on the English subtitles, which are credited to Mandarin Laboratory (International) Limited.

2.1 A synopsis of *Ip Man*

In 1935, Ip Man lives peacefully with his wife and son in Foshan, a lively town in southern China famous for being a center of Chinese martial arts. He is a wealthy family man, admired by locals for his martial arts skills and unassuming personality. Li Chiu is a police officer who develops respect for Ip Man and calls him Master after witnessing him handling a dispute with locals and a violent challenge by a rogue stranger. In 1937, Japan invades China and soon Foshan is occupied by the Japanese military. Civilians are killed and buildings are destroyed. Ip Man's house is seized and used as the headquarters of the Japanese military. Living in a shack in dismal conditions with his family, Ip Man engages in menial labor. Meanwhile, Li becomes an interpreter for the Japanese occupiers, attending to them and relaying their orders to the locals. The commander of the Japanese troops is General Miura, a karate master, who is accompanied by the vicious Colonel Sato. Miura orders Sato to seek locals to challenge the Japanese in martial arts matches, promising a sack of rice for every win. Miura orders Ip Man to teach Chinese martial arts to the Japanese. Ip Man initially rejects the order, but, with local people being threatened, he fights and defeats Miura in the town square. As the crowd of local onlookers grows jubilant, Sato shoots Ip Man, but not fatally. Li then kills Sato.

2.2 A tactical collaborator

Li Chiu was a police officer with a commanding presence before the Japanese invaded and occupied Foshan. The film does not inform the audience how he learned Japanese and became an interpreter for the Japanese army. Historical records indicate, however, that it was common practice for the Japanese army to teach Japanese to local police officers in their occupied territories so that they could assist the Japanese in reining in the locals (Shi 2003, Yang 2014). As an interpreter, Li functions in two ways: one is as a renderer of what is said in another language, which is what interpreters are normally expected to do; and the other is as an agent of the occupiers, engaging with locals on behalf of the

Japanese. In either role, Li appears to be a reluctant participant. He also suffers physical abuse when he cannot deliver what the Japanese want. He does not explicitly explain why he risks being condemned as a *hanjian* (traitor to the Chinese) by his fellow locals. There is a scene, however, in which he brings food home to his large family, indicating that Li took this humiliating job in order to survive and support his elderly mother, crippled brother, wife, and young children, all of whom are suffering from the hunger and destitution that the Japanese military occupation has brought.

Li tries to protect locals and thwart explosive situations by deliberately mistranslating for the Japanese and giving tips to the locals in a language that his employers do not understand. For instance, there is an exchange between Ip Man and Miura after Ip Man's first match with the Japanese, which Li Chiu interprets:

General Miura [in Japanese]   Come back again.

Li Chiu [Interpreter] [in Cantonese]   He wants you to come back again.

Ip Man [in Cantonese]   I'm not here for the rice.

Li [in Japanese]   He said ... he would come back.

Miura [in Japanese]   What's your name?

Li [in Cantonese]   He wants to know your name.

Ip Man [in Cantonese]   I'm just a Chinese.

Li [in Japanese]   His name is Ip Man.

Ip Man 2008

The deliberate mistranslation is an attempt not to upset Miura as a result of Ip Man's defiant attitude. Incidentally, his use of third-person in interpretation is another indication that Li is not a trained interpreter, at least not by contemporary professional standards. Li's inclination to side with his countrymen becomes stronger after being condemned as a traitor by Ip Man:

Ip Man   Lackey!

Li   Why I am lackey [sic]? These deaths got nothing to do with me. *I'm just an interpreter. I need to scrape a living too!* [emphasis added]

Ip   Scrape a living? You watch your countrymen get beaten to death.

Li   I don't have any [sic]. You do. You have a lot of it. If you have the guts, go beat them up! Beat as many as you can! *I'm an interpreter, not a lackey. I'm a Chinese!* [emphasis added]

Ip Man 2008

Here, Li justifies his acts by saying that he is just an interpreter and assists the enemy for his own survival; however, this conversation triggers Li's conscious effort to think about what he can do as a Chinese in his position even under difficult conditions.

Ordered to find Ip Man, Li pretends not to know where he is and is viciously beaten by Sato. When Sato finds Ip Man and threatens his family, Ip Man knocks down Sato. Ip Man and his family must then escape. Li escorts and hides them in the back of his own home. Returning to the Japanese headquarters, Li is severely beaten again. With a swollen face, Li brings food back home, where the Ip family and his own are waiting.

When the Japanese troops arrive at a factory to look for Ip Man, Sato yells in Japanese: "Where is Ip Man? Get him out!" Li pretends to be translating faithfully, but shouts at the factory workers, "Don't say a word." When the factory owner gets beaten up, Li whispers to him, "Hang in there. I'll figure out something." Here, Li is clearly protecting Ip Man and the locals while trying to lessen the danger to the workers.

Ip Man arrives. Miura orders him to teach Chinese martial arts to the Japanese troops. Li deliberately misinterprets Ip Man's response:

Ip Man [in Cantonese]   I won't teach the Japanese. You wanna see me fight? I'll fight with you.

Li [in Japanese]   He said he would think about it. He wants to have a duel with General Miura.

Ip Man 2008

Once again, Li manipulates the translation so that it will not infuriate Miura.

As Li provides opening remarks on the match between Ip Man and Miura in the town square, a Cantonese-speaking local gives voice to what seems to be on everyone's mind: "That traitor will surely be killed by the Japanese." They think that Li will also fall victim to the Japanese he serves in the end. When Ip Man defeats Miura, Sato shoots Ip Man. Li attacks Sato and kills him.

Instead of condemning and executing the Chinese interpreter who collaborates with the Japanese army as a traitor (cf., Takeda 2014b), this film gives him a chance to redeem himself through courageous acts of resistance against the hated enemy. It portrays the interpreter as a reluctant participant in the occupiers' violence, who also uses his position as the only bilingual speaker of Chinese and Japanese to mitigate harm to local civilians. It suggests what interpreters might be able to do in order to help the victims of violence even under extremely difficult conditions.

3. The "face" of torture (*The Railway Man*, 2013)

A Japanese military interpreter plays a key role in *The Railway Man*, a British-Australian war movie that is based on the memoir of Eric Lomax, a former British POW. The interpreter stands at the crux of Lomax's horrific experiences as a POW and his postwar struggle with severe PTSD. Almost fifty years after the war, Lomax confronts the Japanese interpreter who had tormented him at the POW camp and eventually they reconcile. Directed by Jonathan Teplitzky, the 2013 film stars Colin Firth as Lomax, Nicole Kidman as his wife, and Hiroyuki Sanada as the interpreter. English is predominant in this movie, but there are some Japanese lines as well. The text data used for this study is based on the DVD version available in the UK market.

3.1 A synopsis of *The Railway Man*

Eric Lomax, a British Royal Corps of Signals veteran, is severely traumatized by his wartime experiences. After the fall of Singapore to the Japanese military in 1942, the Japanese imprison Eric (along with other Allied soldiers) and force him to work as an engineer on the Thailand-Burma Railway construction site in Thailand. When the Japanese find that he built a radio receiver, Lomax is taken away and severely tortured by the *Kempeitai* (the Japanese military police, akin to Nazi Germany's Gestapo). Throughout his interrogations and torture, Takashi Nagase works as an interpreter. His voice and image torment Lomax for decades. Almost fifty years after the war, Lomax finds that Nagase is still alive and decides to travel back to Thailand to confront him. Having realized a great many POWs were brutally killed by the Japanese army, Nagase has been going on pilgrimages and volunteering as a guide at war memorials in Thailand. Lomax condemns Nagase for his wartime acts of torture, but ultimately they reconcile.

3.2 Seeking forgiveness

In *The Railway Man*, the interpreter does not function as a narrative vehicle to accommodate bilingual interactions in the film. In fact, the audience hardly sees him interpreting between two parties speaking different languages. He is also not an untrustworthy manipulator of information as interpreters are often depicted in other films. The interpreter is presented throughout the film in terms of what he means to the protagonist. This is based on the actual experiences of Eric Lomax:

over the decades after the end of the war, it was the image and voice of the interpreter that still haunted and tormented Lomax. In his autobiography, which serves as an inspiration for this movie, Lomax (1995/2012) reveals that he hated the interpreter more than those who physically assaulted him because "it was his voice that grated on and that would give me no rest" (Lomax 1995/2012: 144). To him, the interpreter occupied "the centre-stage" (236) of his unspeakable ordeal and "represented all of [the torturers]" (236). Accordingly, the wartime scenes almost always show Nagase looking into Lomax's face and shouting at him. Nagase hardly ever touches Lomax—there is only one scene where Nagase appears to push him into a place where he is tortured. Despite the interpreter's subordinate status among the *Kempeitai*, Nagase has an imposing presence on the screen, which is clearly a reflection of Lomax's point of view. Nagase almost invariably looks stern and commanding. There are, however, a few scenes in which the interpreter exhibits slightly different dispositions. He looks somewhat disturbed while observing the brutal torture of Lomax. He hesitates to interpret the bad news that Lomax divulges, claiming that the Japanese army is losing ground. This hesitation results in the frustrated commanding officer's striking Nagase. Nonetheless, to Lomax, Nagase is the face of all the brutality that he suffered.

There is no indication in the film, other than the above, that Nagase feels any sympathy towards Lomax or struggles to reconcile his job of facilitating torture with his personal morality. He never tries to help Lomax or mitigate volatile situations by manipulating information as the only bilingual speaker of English and Japanese in a given setting. Nagase uses his linguistic power, not to ease the suffering of the powerless, but to save himself upon the Japanese surrender by successfully hiding the fact that he was a member of the *Kempeitai*. An Allied officer talks to the surrendered Japanese about upcoming war crimes investigations. As Nagase starts translating his remarks into Japanese, the officer realizes that Nagase is an interpreter:

Officer   *Kempeitai?*

Nagase   No, sir. Translator.

Officer   Did you work for the *Kempeitai*? Torture? Beatings?

Nagase   Only translation.

Officer   Over there.

The Railway Man 2013

Nagase is taken aside and is separated from the rest of his *Kempeitai* unit. The members of the unit do not know about his denial of affiliation with the

Kempeitai as they do not understand English. Nagase takes advantage of his bilingualism to deceive everyone in the scene.

Several decades later, Lomax finds Nagase and confronts him at a war museum in Thailand. Remembering that Nagase once said during an interrogation: "Just tell them. Or they will make you tell them," Lomax takes the opportunity to correct Nagase and bring him to take responsibility of his action by using the first person pronoun rather than the third:

Lomax   *First person singular, not third person plural. You. . . tortured me, you see, not they. You.* [emphasis added]

Nagase   They were afraid you were . . .

Lomax   No, you is second person. You need the first person. I tortured you, Lieutenant Lomax. Try it.

Nagase   I. . . I am at a loss. I want to ask . . .

Lomax   No, no, you don't ask. I ask. I ask the questions. You answer.

The Railway Man 2013

Here, their positions are reversed. It is now Lomax who interrogates Nagase across the table. He does not like the fact that Nagase distances himself from those who ordered or executed torture. Lomax forces Nagase to admit that he was the one who tortured Lomax. To Lomax, the interpreter is the most immediate presence throughout his horrifying ordeal and the interpreter's voice has a lingering effect on him. During the torture, Lomax is most cognizant of the interpreter's utterances in the language he understands. To Lomax, an agent that facilitates torture is a torturer. And he condemns Nagase for escaping war crimes charges:

Nagase   I did not expect you to be alive.

Lomax   No, of course you didn't. You thought you'd got away with it. Why are you alive? Why are we alive? No, you. Why are you alive? You were a war criminal. Why didn't they hang you?

Nagase   *Not a war criminal. Just an interpreter.* [emphasis added]

Lomax   *You were* Kempeitai, *you knew everything!* [emphasis added] Why did they let you live?

The Railway Man 2013

Echoing the defense given by most interpreters charged with war crimes (Takeda 2016), Nagase claims that he was "*just an interpreter*," merely doing his job of conveying the messages of his superiors. In his estimation he was neither the author of evil words nor the executer of evil acts.

Nagase indirectly explains the reason that he was not recognized as a war criminal. Upon the Japanese surrender, he was recruited as an interpreter by the Allied War Grave Commission. This work led him to realize how many POWs and locals were killed by the Japanese:

Nagase We identified them. We brought them here to be buried properly.

Lomax So you went up the line. You buried the men you helped to kill.

Nagase That's when I saw … so many bodies. So very many. I had not imagined so many had died.

Lomax Murdered. The word you're looking for is murdered. So many had been murdered. Go on.

Nagase Murdered. Yes. That's what I saw. So many murdered. So I will speak. I make pilgrimages. I work for … reconciliation. I will not let them forget … the tragedy of war.

Lomax The what? The tragedy of war. No, this wasn't a tragedy. This was a crime. You're not tragic. *You're a criminal. You were an intelligent, educated man and you did nothing. You're a criminal and a liar.* [emphasis added]

Nagase Mr. Lomax … Through my work here I have found some peace in my life. If I can help you …

The Railway Man 2013

As a wartime interpreter, Nagase believed in the cause of the Imperial Japanese Army and followed his superiors' orders. Realizing later that he played a part in the atrocity of Japanese aggression and the brutality towards POWs and locals in occupied regions, he atones and seeks reconciliation with the victims.

4. The risk of becoming a righteous interpreter (*The Arrival of Wang*, 2011)

One of the main characters in *The Arrival of Wang* is a young Italian woman who is a professional Chinese interpreter and translator. She receives an urgent request to work on a special assignment: to interpret in an interrogation of Mr. Wang, a Chinese-speaking extraterrestrial. The government agent's cruel interrogation and torture make the interpreter sympathetic toward Wang. Directed by brothers Antonio and Marco Manetti, this low-budget science fiction film premiered in the Venice Film Festival in 2011 and was released in several countries, including Japan. It attracted attention when *The Wall Street Journal* posted a controversial article about xenophobia and the threat of China emerging as a superpower, as represented in the movie (Napolitano 2011). Italian and Chinese are spoken throughout the film. This study is based on the DVD versions released in the UK and Japan, with English subtitles and Japanese subtitles, respectively. The film was promoted as a comic satire in Japan, which is reflected in the Japanese title (*Uchujin Wang-san to no sogu* [Encounter with extraterrestrial Mr. Wang]) and a humor-filled poster. The text data quoted here are sourced from the English subtitles, the translator of which is not acknowledged in the DVD distributed in the UK by Pecapics.

4.1 A synopsis of *The Arrival of Wang*

Gaia Aloisi is a Chinese-Italian interpreter and translator in Rome. She receives a phone call requesting her interpreting services on an urgent but lucrative assignment for a government agency. Inspector Curti arrives, and Aloisi is taken blindfolded to an undisclosed location.

There, she is told to interpret Curti's examination of a Chinese-speaking man, who turns out to be a squid-like extraterrestrial. Called Mr. Wang, the extraterrestrial claims that he came to speak Chinese because it is the language most spoken on Earth. Curti keeps asking Wang about his purpose in coming to Earth, but his response is always "cultural exchange" and "mutual understanding." Unsatisfied, Curti grows angry. His language and behavior become aggressive and violent, escalating to the torture of Wang. Aloisi is frightened and distressed. She develops sympathy for Wang, tries to reach a human rights group to rescue him, and ultimately lets him escape by unlocking Wang's shackles with a key she snatched from the guard. Wang then activates a special device that allows the spaceships from his planet to attack and destroy the city of Rome. In the end, Wang says to Aloisi: "You're such an idiot."

4.2 Advocacy exploited

The most noticeable aspect of the interpreter's behavior in *The Arrival of Wang* is her transformation into an advocate for the extraterrestrial. Inspector Curti's relentless, aggressive interrogation upsets and distresses Aloisi. Mr. Wang is always calm and polite, even under trying circumstances, and Aloisi develops sympathy for the alien. She negotiates with Curti to provide water to Wang. Here, she is clearly stepping beyond her professional boundaries, speaking as the "author" rather than the "animator".[2] Aloisi even helps Wang drink the water as he is tied to the chair and cannot use his tentacle-like hands. She also inserts her own remarks here and there in the renditions of her translation. For instance, she apologizes to Wang for Curti's abusive behavior:

> **Aloisi** Do you feel all right, Mr. Wang?
>
> **Wang** Everything's fine, don't worry.
>
> **Aloisi** Sorry about this. We're not all like this, we terrestrials. Honestly.
>
> *The Arrival of Wang* 2011

In another scene, she wants to assure Wang that she herself does not condone Curti's actions. Wang's response is considerate, which only increases Aloisi's concern for his wellbeing:

> **Aloisi** Mr. Wang, before proceeding with the translation, I'd like to tell you that I don't approve of the methods he's using.
>
> **Wang** You are only doing your job. Don't worry.
>
> *The Arrival of Wang* 2011

Later she advises Wang to solicit help from Amnesty International. In all these interactions, Aloisi takes advantage of the fact that Curti does not understand Chinese. She is delivering her own ideas to Wang without being noticed by her client. Clearly, she is violating an ethical code of impartiality that is typically observed by professional interpreters.

Aloisi's neglect of the professional boundaries set for an interpreter is also demonstrated in her dealings with Curti. She does not hold back her thoughts about the situation. Despite the fact that Curti is her end-client, she calls him by names such as "a real twisted bastard," "crazy," and "insane." Aloisi questions and criticizes his interrogation style:

> **Aloisi** Mr. Curti, you have to stop being so aggressive like this, you'll never get any answers from him.
>
> *The Arrival of Wang* 2011

Curti keeps using offensive language toward Wang. Aloisi objects and tells him that she is modulating the language and skipping some derogatory words. This is noteworthy, as some interpreters would do so without telling their client (See research on the issue of "face" in interpreting (e.g., Mason and Stewart 2001; Pöllabauer 2007)).

> **Aloisi** Slow down. And hold the sarcasm, as I'm not sure if I have to translate it.
>
> **Curti** Do what you think is right. . . .
>
> **Aloisi** Yes, but "tentacled scientist" and "octopus spies" won't be translated.
>
> *The Arrival of Wang* 2011

When the interrogation escalates to involving torture with electric shocks, Aloisi becomes hysterical:

> **Aloisi** [To Curti] You are insane, stop this torture! The human rights convention prohibits it. . . . Stop! . . . There are laws! How do you think you'll keep me from talking? . . . He keeps repeating the same thing. . . . No! I'm no longer translating! I will no longer be an accomplice to this! . . . Stop! . . . Stop! . . . You're insane! You're murdering him. If he's telling the truth, then what? We could be losing a unique chance.
>
> *The Arrival of Wang* 2011

As Curti leaves the room to attend to an urgent matter, so does Aloisi. She tries to call Amnesty International. When a guard finds her, she attacks him, takes his keys, and escapes. Aloisi comes back to the interrogation room and frees Wang. She even helps Wang climb steps as he struggles with his tentacle-like legs. Aloisi is now an activist who engages in a dangerous act to save the "victim." When Aloisi escapes to a safe room and sees that the city of Rome is attacked by spaceships, she realizes she made a terrible mistake. This disastrous ending informs the audience that the interpreter's naive humanitarianism was taken advantage of by a cunning foreign invader.

4.3 The representation of interpreters

Beyond exploring the ethical issue of an interpreter's impartiality versus advocacy, the film educates audiences on interpreting and translation as a profession. Some aspects realistically reflect the work of interpreters and translators, but there are other aspects that are not quite in line with professional norms. At the beginning of the film, Aloisi is presented as a Chinese translator in action. She is working on subtitles for a Chinese movie. There are

Chinese-themed props in the scene—an Andy Warhol art depicting Mao Zedong on the wall while the shirt Aloisi is wearing features a Chinese character meaning "treasure" or "property." She plays a video, stops it, checks a dictionary, chuckles as she realizes the meaning, and comes up with its Italian subtitle. Subtitle translators in the real world may be surprised to see that Aloisi apparently was not provided with a script of the movie, and, moreover, uses a paper dictionary (as opposed to online resources). This is presumably a reflection of the filmmakers' assumption about the manner in which a subtitle translator's work is carried out. Nonetheless, the scene suffices to show the audience that Aloisi is a working translator of the Chinese language.

When she receives the call from an agency with a mysterious assignment, she accepts it without knowing exactly what it is. Preparation being one of the most essential components in the professional practice of interpreting, Aloisi's behavior seems very unusual and risky. She is not sufficiently briefed by her end-client (Inspector Curti) about the reasons and manners in which her service is required. In the interrogation room, she is placed on one side of a long table with Wang across from her and Curti between them. This positioning is slightly odd as the interpreter is normally either placed between the parties who are conversing or seated by the party who is examined. What is really unusual, however, is that the interrogation starts in the dark. Aloisi complains that it is very hard to interpret without seeing the speaker. She also explains the difficulty of interpreting without understanding the context of the interaction. Most interpreters would agree with her professional assessment on the importance of having a clear view of the speakers, as well as with her assertion that interpreting is not the superficial conversion of words.

Aloisi also takes notes while Wang speaks, and she renders interpretation from her notes. Here, the mechanism of consecutive interpreting is reproduced realistically. However, professional interpreters would probably question the way that she takes notes and the notepad that she uses. Generally, in interpreter training, it is recommended to use a notepad with which the interpreter can turn pages up-and-down rather than left-to-right (Gillies 2005). She also seems to write down notes line by line, while interpreters are generally trained to take notes diagonally, employing symbols and space, drawing a line after one chunk of information (Gillies 2005). Another important aspect of the professional practice of interpreting is the use of the first person, which Aloisi conforms to most of the time, except when speaking on her own behalf and using the third-person to refer to Wang.

Finally, Curti's attitude towards the interpreter should be noted. He seems to perceive the interpreter as a black box into which input in one language is automatically followed by output in another language, subscribing to a classic "conduit" model. Such an attitude is illustrated by the fact that Curti does not understand the importance of providing background information and clear visibility of the speaker. He claims that the interpreter does not need to understand the context or concepts discussed. His attitude of seeing the interpreter as a machine is most effectively demonstrated by his words: "Just translate!" which are uttered numerous times throughout the film.

5. Discussion

Three cinematic representations of interpreters in violent settings have been examined individually so far. Now, I would like to discuss three topics in Interpreting Studies by drawing comparisons and parallels between the interpreters in each film: Li Chiu, the Chinese interpreter attached to the Japanese military in *Ip Man*; Takashi Nagase, the Japanese military interpreter in *The Railway Man*; and Gaia Aloisi, the freelance Italian interpreter hired for a government assignment in *The Arrival of Wang*. First, focus is placed on ethical issues that interpreters face by analyzing the responses of the three interpreters to their employers' orders to interpret abusive language that is accompanied by violence toward individuals in vulnerable positions. Next, attention is paid to the manner in which the non-interpreters (either aggressor or victim) view the role and requirements of interpreters in violent situations. Finally, the consequences of interpreting are considered in relation to the interpreters' behavior in violent crime scenes. In all of these discussions, references are made to the current practice of interpreting and interpreter training in the real world.

5.1 Interpreters' ethical behavior

Ethics is one of the central issues in the contemporary practice and research of professional interpreting. It is usually discussed in reference to codes of ethics or standards of professional conduct for interpreters established by government organizations and professional associations (e.g., Bancroft 2005; Hale 2007). These codes and standards generally entail confidentiality, accuracy, and impartiality, among other tenets. Of the three on-screen interpreters discussed above, only Aloisi would be subject to such codes. The exchanges on the phone Aloisi has with a translation and interpreting service provider suggest that she is a member of a professional community that would presumably subscribe to a code of translator and interpreter ethics. In contrast, Li Chiu is a local police officer compelled to interpret for the Japanese military occupiers for survival. He is not a trained interpreter, nor is he aware of the way in which he should behave as a professional interpreter. *The Railway Man* does not explicitly provide information concerning what circumstances led Takashi Nagase to become a *Kempeitai* interpreter. The only information the audience may glean from the dialog and Nagase's uniform and behavior is that he is a member of the *Kempeitai* who exclusively plays the role of an interpreter. He would therefore be subject to a military code, which would override any interpreter code of ethics, if one had existed at that time. At least in the cases of Li and Nagase, the code of ethics in effect is not the one of professional interpreters; rather it is a universal ethics of humanity. Even in the case of Aloisi, the situation she faces is so extreme that it goes beyond the level at which professional standards for conduct such as impartiality are applied. It can be argued that interpreters' behavior in war, conflict, or other violent contexts should not be assessed based on the codes of ethics applied to professional interpreters under normal circumstances. The survival and physical safety of interpreters themselves are in play, and tensions arise between standing by personal moral values and fulfilling the client's demands. Now, let us quickly revisit the ways in which the three interpreters address the moral dilemmas that they face:

Li, the Chinese interpreter in *Ip Man*, struggles with the fact that he works for the Japanese military simply to stay alive but is seen as an enabler of Japanese abuse toward fellow locals, making him a *hanjian*. Inspired by Ip Man's defiant and courageous actions, Li makes an effort to protect his people by taking advantage of his position as a bilingual speaker who can control the discourse as long as the Japanese do not detect that he is doing so. In other words, he acts in his capacity as an interpreter both to oblige and to undermine the enemy. Li is a tactical collaborator (cf., Davies 2004).

Aloisi, the Italian interpreter in *The Arrival of Wang*, disregards interpreter impartiality to the point of physically fighting the perceived antagonist and freeing the perceived victim. She is depicted as an idealist first and an interpreter second. Like Li, she makes use of being the only bilingual speaker in the room to hijack the discourse and engage with the "suspect" on her own without the knowledge of her end-client, Inspector Curti. In the end, her advocacy is exploited, resulting in catastrophe.

The case of Takashi Nagase is different from those of the other two characters. Since he is depicted from the viewpoint of the protagonist, Eric Lomax, the audience does not know what goes through Nagase's mind when he is involved in torture. He is portrayed as a machine-like, unwavering executer of his superior's orders. His characterization lacks the display of internal struggle seen in the cases of Li and Aloisi. Even in the memoir of the real-life Nagase, he does not clearly discuss moral dilemmas about his role in Lomax's unspeakable ordeal (Nagase 2010). He certainly recalls its severity, but, as a Japanese military officer educated in a warmongering doctrine, he does not seem to have questioned the cause of the Japanese war effort. According to the character of Nagase in the movie, as well as in Nagase's own memoir (Nagase 2010: 38–42), it was only after he found out how many Allied POWs and local civilians were killed by the Japanese that he began to feel guilty and compelled to redeem himself.

Under strenuous and dangerous conditions, personal values and strength, rather than professional codes, seem to guide the behavior of interpreters. Weighing their own safety and survival against the urge to act morally, interpreters may take advantage of their power as the only bilingual speakers in a given setting by manipulating violent discourses to help those whom they perceive as victims.

5.2 The perceived role of interpreters

Whether or not interpreters struggle to come to terms with the work that they are forced to do under extreme circumstances, they may be perceived by others as traitors, enablers of evil acts, or tools to be exploited. In the context of war, traitors against China are referred to by a special term, *hanjian*, which carries a particularly negative connotation for collaborators with outsiders (e.g., Brook 2005; Liu 2009). There are a number of war-themed Chinese movies in which interpreters are denounced as *hanjian* (Takeda 2005). In fact, the original version of *Ip Man* had the interpreter beaten to death in the end as *hanjian* by a mob of locals (Lín Jiādòng tán 2008). China's State Administration of Radio, Film, and Television ordered the scene to be cut out because of its alleged irrelevance to the overall plot (Lín Jiādòng tán 2008). The final version manages to present the interpreter as someone who overcomes the stigma of being seen as *hanjian* and redeems himself by fighting the enemy. Although a valuable asset to the Japanese military, Li Chiu in his capacity as an interpreter is treated like a slave. In particular, the sadistic officer Sato expects far more than mere interpreting from Li. Sato holds Li personally responsible for delivering his instructions to the locals, and he responds to any perceived failure with swift brutality.

In *The Arrival of Wang*, there is no particular element that casts Gaia Aloisi, the interpreter, as a traitor to her country (or planet, for that matter), despite the fact that she is assaulting a guard, stealing his keys, and releasing the suspect. For Curti (the user of her services) she is merely a mouthpiece that is expected to render the information that he needs. He learns how interpreters work (for instance, they need to be able to see the speakers, and it is difficult to interpret statements out of context). He also learns a very hard lesson in what could happen if he does not sufficiently brief the interpreter about the purpose of a given communication. Wang seems indifferent to Aloisi's empathy at the beginning. But she becomes his best opportunity to procure an ally. And he is exploiting her naive righteousness.

Takashi Nagase, the interpreter in *The Railway Man*, is a full member of the organization (the *Kempeitai*) that employs him. He appears to be committed to the mission of the *Kempeitai* and is treated in turn as one of its own. This is the reason that Eric Lomax cannot separate Nagase from the rest of the military police as someone who was only interpreting. In fact, the interpreter embodies a consistent and immediate presence for Lomax whenever anything sinister happens to him. To him, the interpreter is a highly visible agent. This perspective is enlightening when considering the fact that at least eighty-four interpreters were convicted as war criminals in trials against the Japanese after the end of the Second World War[3] (Takeda 2016). Their prosecutions were based on the statements of POWs and local residents who were victimized by the Japanese military (Takeda 2016). Since interpreters were in close contact with the victims, they were more recognizable. Lomax's experience supports this argument.

5.3 Consequences of interpreters' action and inaction

The three interpreters examined above shed light on what could happen when interpreters either act or choose not to act beyond their professional boundaries in response to violence. In the cases of Li Chiu (*Ip Man*) and Takashi Nagase (*The Railway Man*), the consequences of their action and inaction are personal.

Overcoming the stigma of being seen as *hanjian*, Li protects Ip Man, and kills his cruel employer in the end. The film does not show what happens to Li afterwards, but it suggests that he was able to redeem himself. In contrast, Nagase did not take any action against the brutality of the Japanese when it was taking place. He was part of it. After the end of the war, however, he is troubled by what he learns about Japanese atrocities and begins to go on pilgrimages to the places in which these war crimes were committed. He wants to make peace with his own past. Nagase relives it when he is confronted by his victim, Lomax. Nagase is courageous in the sense that he tries to do what he can to repent for what he and the Japanese military did, instead of pretending that he was never involved in war crimes.

Gaia Aloisi's choices in *The Arrival of Wang* result in far-reaching consequences: the destruction of Rome and perhaps the entire planet. This outcome can be viewed as a cautionary tale for either an interpreter or anyone with a naive, unsuspecting view of strangers, and it casts light on the discussion of interpreters' roles as advocates and activists. There has been a debate over the impartiality of interpreters in settings where power imbalances exist among the parties (for instance, in interpreter-mediated communication between the deaf and the hearing, a patient and a doctor, a defendant and a judge, or an asylum seeker and an examiner). Some practitioners, trainers, and academics encourage interpreters to be advocates and to protect and advance the rights of clients who are in vulnerable positions (e.g., Barsky 1996; CHIA 2002; RID 2005). Another camp argues that interpreters should never engage in anything beyond faithful renditions of what is said since interpreters are not equipped with the knowledge needed to judge the complete picture of a given communicative situation (e.g., González et al. 1991/2012). *The Arrival of Wang* provides a relevant case, however outrageously unrealistic its premise may be, that might seem to support the latter argument: In this movie, an interpreter's righteous but naive thought and behavior result in a catastrophic ending.

6. In conclusion

The present chapter has examined the depictions of interpreters in violent settings in three films: *Ip Man*, *The Railway Man*, and *The Arrival of Wang*. The first two movies are based on real stories (with varying degrees of fictionalization) and feature interpreters who worked for the Japanese military that brutalized local civilians and POWs during the Fifteen-Year War.

The third is a science fiction movie that features an interpreter who becomes sympathetic to a victim of violence. All three movies present the difficult, almost impossible, position that interpreters are placed in during war, conflict, and other violent interactions. Participating in acts against their conscience and moral compass, interpreters struggle to come to terms with the fact that they are enablers of violence. There is little room for the consideration of professional codes of ethics under such extreme conditions. Different interpreters address such difficulties in different ways at different times. Prompted by these stories, the question of "What would you do?" can lead researchers and practitioners to a meaningful discussion about interpreters who are assigned to mediate violence.

The three movies also shine some light on the practice of interpreting and users' perceptions of interpreters. *The Arrival of Wang*, in particular, informs the audience of the process of professional consecutive interpreting and what is required for interpreters to do their job to the best of their ability. It also shows a stereotypical view of interpreters from the user's perspective—that an interpreter is a conduit that can simply render words from one language into another. Non-interpreters' views of interpreters in *Ip Man* and *The Railway Man* concern more sociopolitical matters. Interpreters locally hired in conflict can be seen as traitors by their fellow countrymen, *hanjian* in the Chinese context. To the victims, they are not merely interpreters following their superior's orders; moreover, they are participants in violence and the representatives of such violence.

In sum, cinematic representations of interpreters in war and conflict can make audiences aware of interpreters' agency in either enabling or mitigating violence. They can also unveil interpreters' dilemmas as mediators in violent international conflict, the ethical and moral difficulties that such interprets might experience. Moreover, portrayals of wartime interpreters can draw attention to the way in which interpreters can be viewed by their compatriots and by victims of violence. To them, interpreters can be seen as traitors, as well as accomplices or executers of war crimes. These movies provide food for thought for practitioners, trainers, students, and researchers of interpreting.

Glossary

British Royal Corps of Signals: A combat support service of the British Army that provides telecommunications infrastructure to British forces worldwide. Because the Corps of Signals provides field support during battle, it is involved in a great deal of combat activity, and is one of the first services to be mobilized during war.

Fifteen-Year War: A historical period (1931–1945) during which Japan was involved in three military campaigns: The Manchurian Incident (or Mukden Incident; 1931); The Second Sino-Japanese War (1937–1945); and The Pacific War (1941–1945).

Ip Man: A Chinese martial artist (1893–1972). Ip was a master teacher of *Wing Chun*. He had several students who later became martial arts masters in their own right. His most famous student was Bruce Lee. Ip is the focus of a great deal of cultural attention. The movie, *Ip Man*, was followed by two sequels, and his character inspired a number of other movies and a television series.

Kempeitai: The military police of the Imperial Japanese Army from 1881 to 1945. The *Kempeitai* fulfilled four different functions under different jurisdictions: It was a part of the Imperial Japanese Army; a military police force under the direction of the Admiralty Minister; an executive (or secret) police under the direction of the Interior Minister; and a judicial (civilian) police under the direction of the Justice Minister.

Second Sino-Japanese War (1937–1945): A military conflict between the Empire of Japan and the Republic of China that involved the occupation of parts of China by Japan until the end of the Second World War.

Notes

1   The Fifteen-Year War refers to the period from the outbreak of the Manchurian Incident (or Mukden Incident) in 1931, through the Second Sino-Japanese War, to the end of the Pacific War in 1945. While *Ip Man* takes place as part of the Second Sino-Japanese War, *The Railway Man* is situated as part of the Pacific War (or Asia-Pacific War).

2   Some interpreting scholars (e.g., Wadensjö 1998) explain this type of phenomenon as the interpreter's shifting her "footing" to speak as the "author" rather than the "animator" (seeing herself as a speaker rather than an intermediary) by drawing on Erving Goffman's participation framework (Goffman 1981).

3   The number eighty-four includes only convicts who are explicitly designated as interpreters in the trial documents. There were other convicts who served as interpreters but are referred to by other designations, such as by their military rank or as "civilians."

References

Anderson, R.B.W. (1976), "Perspectives on the Role of Interpreter," in R.W. Brislin (ed.), *Translation: Application and Research*, 208–228, New York: Gardner.

Andres, D. (2015), "Fictional Interpreters," in F. Pöchhacker (ed.), *The Routledge Encyclopedia of Interpreting Studies*, 158–160, Abington & New York: Routledge.

The Arrival of Wang (2011), [Film] Dir. Antonio and Marco Manetti, Italy: Manetti Bros.

Bancroft, M. (2005), *The Interpreter's World Tour: An Environmental Scan of Standards of Practice for Interpreters*, Washington, DC: National Council on Interpreting in Health Care.

Barsky, R.F. (1996), "The Interpreter as Intercultural Agent in Convention Refugee Hearings," *The Translator*, 2 (1): 45–63.

Brook, T. (2005), *Collaboration: Japanese Agents and Local Elites in Wartime China*, Cambridge, MA: Harvard University Press.

CHIA (2002), *California Standards for Healthcare Interpreters: Ethical Principles, Protocols, and Guidance on Roles and Interventions*, Sacramento, CA: California Healthcare Interpreters Association.

Cronin, M. (2009), *Translation Goes to the Movies*, London: Routledge.

Davies, P. (2004), *Dangerous Liaisons: Collaboration and World War Two*, Harlow: Pearson Longman.

Footitt, H. and M. Kelly (eds.) (2012a), *Languages and the Military: Alliances, Occupation and Peace Building*, Basingstoke: Palgrave Macmillan.

Footitt, H. and M. Kelly (eds.) (2012b), *Languages at War: Policies and Practices of Language Contacts in Conflict*, London: Palgrave Macmillan.

Fair, E. (2016), *Consequence: A Memoir*, New York: Henry Holt and Company.

Gillies, A. (2005), *Note-taking for Consecutive Interpreting: A Short Course*, Manchester: St. Jerome Publishing.

Goffman, E. (1981), *Forms of Talk*, Philadelphia: University of Pennsylvania Press.

González, R.D., V.F. Vasquez, and H. Mikkelson (1991/2012), *Fundamentals of Court Interpretation: Theory, Policy and Practice*, 2nd edition, Durham, NC: Carolina Academic Press.

Hale, S.B. (2007), *Community Interpreting*, Basingstoke: Palgrave Macmillan.

Inghilleri, M. (2008), "The Ethical Task of the Translator in the Geo-political Arena: From Iraq to Guantánamo Bay," *Translation Studies*, 1 (2): 212–223.

Inghilleri, M. (2012), *Interpreting Justice: Ethics, Politics and Language.* London: Routledge.

Ip Man (2008), [Film] Dir. Wilson Yip, Hong Kong: Mandarin Films.

Lan, S.M. (2016), "'Crimes' of Interpreting: Taiwanese Interpreters as War Criminals of World War II," in K. Takeda and J. Baigorri-Jalón (eds.), *New Insights in the History of Interpreting*, 193–223, Amsterdam & Philadelphia: John Benjamins.

"Lín Jiādòng tán « Yè Wèn » shān xì' [Lam Ka-tung says a scene was deleted in *Ip Man*]." (2008), *SINA*. Available online: http://ent.sina.com.cn/m/c/2008-12-26/12102315186.shtml (accessed May 25, 2017).

Liu, L. H. (2009), *The Clash of Empires: The Invention of China in Modern World Making*, Cambridge, MA: Harvard University Press.

Lomax, E. (1995/2012), *The Railway Man*, New York: Norton.

Mason, I. and M. Stewart (2001), "Interactional Pragmatics, Face and the Dialogue Interpreter," in I. Mason (ed.), *Triadic Exchanges: Studies in Dialogue Interpreting*, 51–70, Manchester: St. Jerome Publishing.

Monacelli, C. and R. Punzo (2001), "Ethics in the Fuzzy Domain of Interpreting: A 'Military' Perspective," *The Translator*, 7 (2): 265–282.

Moser-Mercer, B. (2015), "Interpreting in conflict zones," in R. Jourdenais and H. Mikkelson (eds.), *Handbook of Interpreting*, 302–316, London/New York: Routledge.

Nagase, T. (2010), *Crosses and Tigers and The Double-edged Dagger: The Cowra Incident of 1944*. Sheffield: Paulownia Press.

Napolitano, D. (2011), "New Film Explores Distrust of China," *The Wall Street Journal*, (September 5). Available online: https://blogs.wsj.com/scene/2011/09/05/new-film-explores-distrust-of-china/ (accessed May 25, 2017).

O'Sullivan, C. (2011), *Translating Popular Film*, Basingstoke: Palgrave Macmillan.

Pöllabauer, S. (2007), "Interpreting in Asylum Hearings: Issues of Saving Face," in C. Wadensjö, B. Englund Dimitrova, and A. Nilsson (eds.), *Critical Link 4: Professionalization of interpreting in the community*, 39–52, Amsterdam & Philadelphia: John Benjamins.

The Railway Man (2013), [Film] Dir. Jonathan Teplitzky, UK/Australia: Liongate.

RID (2005), *NAD-RID Code of Professional Conduct*. Available online: www.rid.org/UserFiles/File/NAD_RID_ETHICS.pdf (accessed May 25, 2017).

Ruiz Rosendo, L. and Persaud, C. (eds.) (2016), *Interpreting in Conflict Zones throughout History, Special Issue of Linguistica Antverpiensia, New Series: Themes in Translation Studies*, 15.

Saar E. and V. Novak (2005), *Inside the Wire*, New York: Penguin.

Shi, G. (2003), *Shokuminchi-shihai to Nihongo* [Colonial rule and the Japanese language], Tokyo: Sangensha.

Tryuk, M. (2015), *On Ethics and Interpreters*, Frankfurt am Main: Peter Lang.

Takeda, K. (2014a), "The Visibility of Collaborators," in A. Fernández-Ocampo and M. Wolf (eds.), *Framing the Interpreter: Towards a visual perspective*, 150–159, London and New York: Routledge.

Takeda, K. (2014b), "The Interpreter as Traitor: Multilingualism in *Guizi lai le* (*Devils on the Doorstep*)," *Linguistica Antverpiensia*, 13: 93–111.

Takeda, K. (2016), "Guilt, Survival, Opportunities, and Stigma: Japanese Interpreters in the Postwar Occupation Period (1945–1952)," in K. Takeda and J. Baigorri-Jalón (eds.), *New Insights in the History of Interpreting*, 225–246, Amsterdam and Philadelphia: John Benjamins.

Takeda, M. (2005), *Guizi-tachi no shozo: Chugokujin ga egaita nihonjin* [Portrait of Guizi: Japanese depicted by Chinese], Tokyo: Chuo-koron-sha.

Wadensjö, C. (1998). *Interpreting As Interaction*, Hoboken, NJ: Pearson Education ESL.

Yang, C. (2014). "Police Interpreting Examinations in Taiwan during the Period of Japanese Rule," *Special Issue on Policing in Asia and Australia, Asian Education and Development Studies*, 3 (3): 253–266.

4

Translation and Translators in New Media

Editor's Introductory Note

Chapter 4 introduces the technologically naive reader to fansubbing, audiencing, prosumers and other terms that are used in the bustling world of social media. More importantly, the chapter presents an intriguing facet of the representation of translation: the manner in which translations and adaptations are discussed, evaluated, and responded to by the target audience. The chapter introduces us to a sophisticated reality in which readers and viewers are no longer held hostage by the translator. They are often familiar with the source text, and thanks to the powers vested in them by social media, they are more than capable of railing against omissions, distortions, and mistranslations of various kinds.

Theoretically, translation becomes the topic of conversation rather than the source text, and thus the object of representation in a secondary discussion that privileges the narrative of the translator's choices and the context of the translation process. Practically, one should not envy the adapter or translator that wakens the wrath of highly informed and engaged recipients: in 2016, state-owned Italian network Rai2 aired the pilot episode of *How To Get Away With Murder*. In this adaptation, however, a homosexual sex scene was deleted. The scandal, fueled by the anger of *Twitter* users, was overwhelming, and marked a new era in the relationship between translators and their target audience.

This chapter investigates the various ways in which *Twitter* users expressed opinions and feelings as well as affiliation/disaffiliation with the rest of the virtual community about the manipulation of localized audiovisual content. More importantly, the discussion marks a change in the representation of translation in popular culture: from an often neglected vehicle for communicating the source text, to the focus of a popular discussion about the context, the agenda and the ethics of intercultural communication.

Reactions to Audiovisual Adaptation on Social Media: The Case of *How To Get Away With Murder*

Chiara Bucaria

1. Introduction

Up until a few years ago, before Web 2.0, the practice of audiovisual translation (AVT) tended to not be questioned by its end-users, i.e., film and TV audiences. The target-language versions of the products made available either on the big or small screen were the only ones accessible to them. If mistakes, inaccuracies, or conscious manipulation were noticed, they were either ignored by the general population of non-academics or ascribed to the audiovisual translators' poor skills, or—in the case of cut scenes or edited language—to specific editorial policies on the part of broadcasters and distributors. In the last few years, however, things have radically changed due to several factors, among which are ever more demanding audiences, increased passive knowledge of English— which is the source language for most audiovisual products exported globally— and, thanks to digitization, the multiplicity of platforms and modes of consumption, including streaming and illegal downloading. Easier access to either the source-language versions of films and TV shows or to alternative target-language versions of these products—for example fansubbed versions available online—have contributed to raising viewer expectations for target versions that are as close as possible to their source-language counterparts, which, in turn, goes hand in hand with the demand for accountability and transparency from the distributors of these contents. As a consequence of these technological advances, fandoms have become more demanding when it comes to the adaptation of their favorite films and TV shows, and more vocal in speaking out against what they perceive as violations of the source-language versions.

The internet—through personal blogs, online reviews, and, especially, through social media—provides the perfect tools for fans and even casual viewers to talk about their opinions on the subject of audiovisual adaptation and to share them with likeminded people. Professionals in the field of audiovisual translation generally tend to feel undermined by forms of crowd-sourced translation such as fansubbing (Antonini and Bucaria 2015, O'Hagan 2009; 2011; 2015) or by critiques of their work by viewers who usually lack the professional experience or certifications to fully understand the rationale behind certain adaptation choices and the subtleties of the market. However, at a time in which multiple target-language versions are simultaneously available to viewers, it appears to be especially important for scholars and practitioners of AVT alike to take into consideration the manner in which audiences perceive these different modes of adaptation. In a market in which we are seeing "major transformations in consumption patterns" (Esser et al. 2016: 2) and in which the boundaries between content consumers and producers have become more blurred (see the idea of "prosumers" in Tapscott and Williams 2006), audience preferences will inevitably be a deciding factor for the AVT industry in the future (Esser et al. 2016; Chaume 2016: 72). In fact, new developments in the AVT market are already moving in the direction of a blended system that is able to incorporate more unconventional roles. Netflix' new recruiting test for subtitlers, in which candidates are asked to answer a questionnaire and take a subtitling test, but no previous professional certification is needed in order to be hired, is a clear example. Despite the sometimes justified concerns that these new trends present for more traditional AVT production and distribution models—for example in terms of more lax quality standards or stricter adaptation timeframes—perhaps the AVT industry would benefit from looking at the ways in which end-users relate to and talk about adapted audiovisual products as a way to be more flexible and receptive to the changing market. This chapter aims at taking a first step in this direction by looking at the ways in which AVT is talked about on one specific social networking website, *Twitter*, as a way to investigate the way in which certain aspects of AVT localization are perceived by their direct end-users. Specifically, this case study looks at Italian tweeters' reactions to a 2016 incident concerning the adaptation of the US TV series *How To Get Away With Murder* (*HTGAWM*) (2014–ongoing), in which a sex scene between two men was edited out of the version that was aired on Italian national TV network Rai2 (see section 2).

Twitter is a microblogging networking service founded in 2006, which allows users to post tweets of up to 280 characters (140 at the time of writing), links, videos, and images in order to interact with other users without the need for reciprocity. Public posts can be seen by all users, even those who are not followers of the original poster. Users can interact with fellow tweeters by liking or retweeting their posts, or by directly responding to them. Typically, *Twitter* posts are accompanied by hashtags, or thematic labels preceded by the symbol #, which can function as markers or keywords for the subject that users are addressing in their post. Hashtags can therefore have an informative function—in that they help index posts according to specific topics—but also a relational and interpersonal one, as users employ them to relate to other users by tapping on to ongoing conversations in the community. This way, *Twitter* hashtags create *searcheable talk*, i.e., "online conversation[s] where people render their talk more findable and hence more affiliative" (Zappavigna 2012: 95).

With its 330 million monthly active users—about 7 million of which are in Italy—and 500 million tweets sent per day (Salam Aslam 2018), it is no surprise that *Twitter's* extremely large collection of natural language is often used as a research tool in fields that range from the social sciences to epidemiology to marketing. Some of the most common kinds of analysis that can be carried out with *Twitter* metadata are sentiment analysis, or opinion mining (which is concerned with opinions and moods expressed on social media), time series analysis (an analysis of distribution of tweets over time), and network analysis (an analysis of the networks of users that interlink on social media, e.g., who retweets or likes whose posts). In the field of Media Studies, *Twitter* is often used in the sub-discipline of Audience Studies, especially from the point of view of "audiencing," i.e., "the public performance of belonging to the distributed audience for a shared media event" (Highfield et al. 2013: 315), and "second screening" (e.g., Blake 2017), i.e., the simultaneous use of multiple screens (cell phone or computer) by viewers while they are watching TV. Through second screening, viewers can express their opinions and/or feelings on what they are watching on social media—usually at the same time as they are watching it—or engage with a community of users who are watching the same shows or live events. Studies on the use of hashtags during live events include for example the Eurovision Song Contest (Highfield et al. 2013), current events programs (D'heer and Verdegem 2015, Rossi and Giglietto 2016), and coverage of natural disasters (Bruns and Burgess 2011), in which temporality appears to be a key dimension in the viewers' interaction with multiple media platforms. Moreover, while second screening might appear to be naturally less relevant as far as fiction is concerned because of shifting viewing habits and the increasing availability of on-demand and streaming services, research suggests (Wood and Baughman 2012) that broadcasters are willing to exploit the marketing opportunities of convergence and transmedia storytelling (Jenkins 2006) to engage the viewers of serial TV as well.

As mentioned above, social media can be an important meaning-making site in which viewers make their opinions and emotions heard, for example through explicit or implicit evaluation of events, issues, and experiences. This chapter intends to start investigating the ways in which *Twitter* users express such feelings as well as affiliation/disaffiliation with the rest of the virtual community on the issue of audiovisual adaptation by applying the appraisal theory devised by Martin and White (2005), which will be described in detail in section 3.

2. The localization of *How To Get Away With Murder* in Italy

The case study taken into consideration here was selected as one of the most reported-on incidents regarding adaptation/localization in Italy in recent times. I refer to adaptation in the broader sense of not only translating dialog from a source to a target language, but preparing a given foreign TV series in this case for a local (Italian) audience (localization). In fact, the incident in question concerns a scene without dialog.

On July 8, 2016, the Italian national network Rai2 started airing the much-anticipated US TV series *How To Get Away With Murder*, which was originally broadcast on ABC in the 10 p.m. slot on Thursdays. The crime/legal drama stars Academy Award winning actress Viola Davis as Annalise Keating, a law professor at a prestigious university, who, together with some of her students and employees, becomes progressively involved in a murder plot. The series was created by Peter Nowalk and produced by Shonda Rhimes, and began airing its fifth season on September 27, 2018. A successful series overall, the pilot episode garnered over 14 million viewers in the US in September 2014.

By July 2016, the series had already been broadcasted in Italy by subscription-based channel FOXItalia for about a year and a half under the title *Le regole del delitto perfetto* (The rules for a perfect murder). When the state-owned network Rai2 aired the pilot episode at around 9 p.m. on the evening of Friday, July 8, it became apparent to fans of the series who had already seen the episode elsewhere that a sex scene between one of the main characters, Connor (Jack Falahee) and his love interest Oliver (Conrad Ricamora), had been cut out. The incident caused an overwhelming reaction among *Twitter* users, who started accusing Rai of homophobia and bigotry. Fans even brought the incident to the attention of actor Jack Falahee (@RestingPlatypus), creator Peter Nowalk (@petenowalk), and producer Shonda Rhimes (@shondarhimes), who, in turn, tweeted to condemn the censoring of their show and of beloved screen couple "Coliver." They also asked their fans to let them know if *HTGAWM* had been censored in other countries. As a consequence of the international attention and involvement of the series' actor, creator, and producer, the story went viral and was covered by both the national and international press, e.g., *Variety* (Vivarelli 2016), *The Huffington Post* (Wong 2016), *The Hollywood Reporter* (Anderson 2016), *Entertainment Weekly* (Beard 2016), and various online publications and blogs. The following day Rai2 top executive Ilaria Dallatana issued a statement about the incident:

> Non c'è stata nessuna censura, semplicemente un eccesso di pudore dovuto alla sensibilità individuale di chi si occupa di confezionare l'edizione delle serie per il prime time. Capisco l'irritazione, ma mi preme far notare che dopo anni e anni di serie esclusivamente poliziesche, Rai Due ha cominciato a proporre titoli di diverso contenuto, quali Le regole del delitto perfetto e Jane the Virgin, che tratta di maternità surrogata. Anche queste polemiche ci aiutano a prendere le giuste misure per il futuro. Come dimostrano anche le scelte fatte per i nuovi palinsesti, Rai2 sarà sempre più sensibile alla complessità del mondo contemporaneo.

> There was no censorship, only an excessive amount of modesty due to the individual sensitivity of the person who edits the series for primetime. I understand people's irritation, but I'd like to point out that after years and years of exclusively airing crime series, RaiDue has started to offer different contents as well, for example *How To Get Away With Murder* and *Jane the Virgin*, which is about surrogate pregnancy. These controversies help us identify the way to go for the future. As shown also by our new programming choices, Rai2 will be more and more attentive to the complexity of contemporary society.

> Franco 2016

The statement, which was not generally perceived as an apology but as a defensive justification for what had happened, caused even more controversy and infuriated fans even more because of a perceived refusal to be held accountable for the mistake and the backhanded attempt to attach the blame to a single individual rather than network policies. In general, the attempt is clear in the statement to distance Rai2 from the accusations of bigotry leveled online by specifically referencing the network's recent progressive programming choices. The statement was generally perceived as "too little, too late"; a clumsy attempt at patching things up after being publicly shamed in the national and international press. Of course, *Twitter* users were also quick to note that *Jane the Virgin* is not about surrogate pregnancy, a gaffe that did not help Rai2's case. After the statement was issued, Rai2 announced in a tweet that the first two episodes of *HTGAWM* would be aired in an unedited version the following day (Sunday, July 10). Rai's press office even tweeted the new schedule directly to the attention of Shonda Rhimes, specifically in response to her tweet in which she writes: "censorship of any love is inexcusable, #HTGAWM #loveislove":

@Raiofficialnews	True @shondarhimes. An integral version of the episode is scheduled to air tomorrow at 9pm on @Rai2. #LoveIsLove #htgawm

In the flurry of *Twitter* activity around this incident in early July 2016, one main new hashtag rose to prominence with Italian users who were commenting on *HTGAWM*: #RaiOmofoba (or #raiomofoba), i.e., "homophobic Rai".[1] Users first began to use #RaiOmofoba in the immediate aftermath of the edited episode broadcast, with the first occurrence appearing on July 8. After its very first occurrence, the use of this hashtag seemed to become a conscious effort to start a movement to expose Rai2's censorship, as shown in the tweets below:

@User	@RaiTv @RaiDue semplicemente OMOFOBI. #HTGAWM #Raiomofoba
	@RaiTv @RaiDue simply HOMOPHOBES. #HTGAWM #RaiOmofoba
@User	Propongo di far partire l'hashtag #RaiOmofoba, per denunciare lo scempio che @RaiDue ha fatto con #HTGAWM. Bisogna sconfiggere l'ignoranza!
	I propose to start the hashtag #RaiOmofoba, to denounce how @RaiDue butchered #HTGAWM. Ignorance needs to be defeated!

If the intention was to bring attention to the incident, Italian *Twitter* users definitely succeeded, as the hashtag topped the list of trending topics in Italy on July 9. After Rai aired the unedited episode, however, the hashtag did not stop its course. *Twitter* users—including actor Jack Falahee—tweeted exalting messages praising the positive result that fans were able to obtain through a concerted community effort against censorship.

Unfortunately, users had a chance to resurrect #RaiOmofoba in relation to a different incident that occurred less than a month after the *HTGAWM* one, on August 1, 2016. One of Rai's networks, Rai4, aired the film *Mine vaganti* (Ferzan Ozpetek 2010), which tells the story of two brothers from the southern Italian region of Puglia who come out as gay to their conservative parents. Despite the fact that the comedy shows only a kiss between two men and does not contain homosexual sex scenes, Rai4 prefaced the film with a warning about its content being suitable only for adult viewers. *Twitter* users were quick to level their harsh criticism towards Rai, with obvious references to the recent *HTGAWM* incident. In this case as well, Rai issued an apology, explaining that the warning was a "banale errore" (simple mistake) and a "svista" (oversight), which, albeit more sincere-sounding than the previous one, highlighted even more the comparison with the awkward apology issued by Rai2's director a few weeks prior.

3. *Twitter* as insight into users' attitude and engagement

As mentioned above, microblogging can provide invaluable insight into the users' interpersonal meaning expressed through evaluative language. The appraisal theory devised by Martin and White (2005) is a useful tool in attempting to categorize Italian *Twitter* users' reactions to the *HTGAWM* incident as an expression of interpersonal meaning. Following a concise description of this framework, a qualitative analysis of the collected tweets will be carried out with the help of Michele Zappavigna's (2012) application of the appraisal system to microblogging.

Couched in systemic functional linguistics (SFL) and in John Rupert Firth's (1957) and Michael Halliday's (e.g., 2004) work, appraisal theory purports that evaluation is a domain of interpersonal meaning, which uses language to express attitudes and stances about people and events. While the other metafunctions of language identified by SFL—ideational and textual—have to do respectively with construing experience and information flow (Martin and White 2005), interpersonal meaning is concerned with "negotiating social relations: how people are interacting, including the feelings they try to share" (Martin and White 2005: 7). In this context, appraisal is intended as a set of discourse semantic resources used to express interpersonal meaning. The appraisal system is composed of the three subsystems of ATTITUDE, ENGAGEMENT, and GRADUATION. Attitude is concerned with mapping feelings; engagement is concerned with adopting a stance in relation to other texts; and graduation is concerned with the gradability of meaning. In turn, the network branches out into more delicate (or finer) subsystems, and the different areas of meaning can be expressed through different linguistic resources. These aspects will be dealt with in more detail in the following sections, with particular reference to the attitude and engagement systems, whereas, for reasons of space, the graduation system will be referenced only when relevant.

The tweets containing the hashtag #RaiOmofoba, which was posted over 8,200 times, were retrieved by means of *Twitter*'s advance search feature, which apart from keywords and other parameters, allows the researcher to select a timeframe for the search. The selected window was July 8–11, 2016, which allowed us to cover the first few days (Friday to Monday) in which the hashtag #RaiOmofoba developed, between the moment that the edited episode was broadcast and the day after the unedited episode was aired. An initial qualitative analysis was carried out with the NVivo software to generate a word frequency list.

3.1 Attitude

ATTITUDE involves choices from resources of AFFECT (expressing emotion), JUDGMENT (assessing behavior), and APPRECIATION (estimating value). The same tweets often contain a mixture of these three subsystems, as they may describe a feeling, and offer judgment and/or appreciation at the same time, sometimes about different aspects of the incident.

3.1.1 Affect

AFFECT is "concerned with registering positive or negative feelings: do we feel happy or sad, confident or anxious, interested or bored?" (Martin and White 2005: 42). When it comes to how *Twitter* users expressed affect in the aftermath of the *HTGAWM* incident, the most common reactions expressed sadness, surprise, indignation, disgust, shame, disbelief/incredulousness, disappointment, frustration, and derision of Rai's decision. Both positive and negative emotions can be found in the tweets, with a preponderance of the latter.

An example of feelings on the sadness/happiness continuum can be found in the tweets below. The first user draws a parallel between the *HTGAWM* incident and the 2008 censoring of the film *Brokeback Mountain* (Ang Lee, 2006), also aired by Rai2. The second user expresses happiness about the fact that the *Twitter* community was able to create hype around the incident, which in turn caused Rai2 to air the unedited episode.

@User   Nel 2008 Brokeback Mountain, nel 2016 HTGAWM . . . **che tristezza** vedere come in Italia certe cose non cambino mai @ RaiDue #RaiOmofoba #HTGAWM

In 2008 Brokeback Mountain, in 2016 HTGAWM ... **how sad** to see that in Italy some things never change @RaiDue #RaiOmofoba #HTGAWM

@User   Sono **MOLTO felice** che i fan e non di #htgawm siano riusciti a far uscire la notizia e a mobilitare la Rai. Basta censure. #RaiOmofoba

I'm **VERY happy** that #htgawm fans and non-fans have managed to get the news out and to get Rai to act. Stop censoring. #RaiOmofoba

Other tweets contain mixed emotions, such as the following, in which the user says s/he is satisfied with the decision to air the unedited episodes, but saddened by Rai2's statement in which they blame an "excess of modesty":

@User   **Felice** della scelta di ritrasmettere i primi ep. integrali di #HTGAWM domani, **triste** per la giustificazione "eccesso di pudore"! #RaiOmofoba

Happy about the decision to re-air the first unedited episodes of #HTGAWM, **sad** about the justification of "excess of modesty"! #RaiOmofoba

In the tweets above, the feelings of sadness/happiness are expressed through the use of specific lexical items, such as the noun *tristezza* (sadness) and the adjectives *felice* (happy)—in one case intensified by the adverb *molto* (very)—and *triste* (sad).

Other users express decisively negative emotions. One reoccurring feeling is disappointment—both in general terms and more specifically directed at either Rai or at the whole country—with the noun *delusione* (disappointment) being the most recurrent:

@User   **Che delusione** #raiomofoba

What a disappointment #raiomofoba

@User   #RaiOmofoba non è neanche più una sorpresa, solo l'ennesima **delusione** che questo paese ci dà

#RaiOmofoba is not even a surprise anymore, just the umpteenth **disappointment** that this country has given us

A form of disappointment can also to be found in a number of tweets expressing the users' disenchantment about Rai's treatment of this particular TV series in light of the broadcaster's track record of pre-emptively editing films and TV shows before airing. In other words, viewers felt that they should not be surprised by this kind of behavior because Rai has always acted this way. In the following tweet, the user directly references Rai2's censoring of *Brokeback Mountain* a few years prior by attaching a GIF of a hug between the film's two protagonists.

> @User Che poi da una rete televisiva che ha censurato questo film che cosa vi aspettavate? #raiomofoba
>
> What did you expect from a TV channel that censored this film? #raiomofoba

While in the previous case the affect is inscribed in the tweets, expressed explicitly through specific lexical items, in this tweet the disappointment is implicit, or invoked, according to Martin and White's terminology (Martin and White 2005). As Zappavigna notes, it is often the case that attitude on *Twitter* is expressed through the use of hashtags instead of explicit lexis (Zappavigna 2012: 62), which is here realized by the use of #raiomofoba coupled with the rhetorical question "what did you expect?"

The most common negative reactions in the affect sphere, however, were comprised in a range going from frustration to outright indignation and disgust. Some of the most typical tweets contain the nouns *schifo* (informal for "disgust") and *vergogna* (shame) or their adjective and verb variations, respectively *schifato/a* ("disgusted") and *mi vergogno* ("I'm ashamed"). Feelings of embarrassment (adj. *imbarazzato/a*) and indignation (n. *indignazione*) often co-occur as well.

> @User **Mi vergogno** di essere italiana in sti casi dove attori dall'altra parte del mondo sgridano le nostre reti televisive. **Schifo**. #RaiOmofoba
>
> **I'm ashamed** to be Italian in these cases where actors on the other side of the world tell off our TV channels. **Disgust/Gross**. #RaiOmofoba

> @User Sono **disgustata, imbarazzata** e ancora una volta **mi vergogno** di vivere in un paese così.
>
> #RaiOmofoba
>
> I'm **disgusted, embarrassed** and once again **I'm ashamed** to live in a country like this.
>
> #RaiOmofoba

Feelings of shame are typically related not only to the inherent injustice and disrespect of Rai2's censoring choice but also to the negative attention that the incident drew to Italy on an international scale, both from the actors, creator, and producers involved in *HTGAWM* and from the press. In fact, a number of users included in their tweets links to various articles and reports on the incident published both in the Italian and international press (see below).

The tweet below is an example of graduation of the affect resources by means of an intensifier (the adjective *grande*). In Martin and White's taxonomy this is an instance of upscaling, which "frequently acts to construe the speaker/writer as maximally committed to the value position being advanced and hence as strongly aligning the reader into that value position" (Martin and White 2005: 152):

@User   Provo **grande vergogna** in questo momento è [sic] condivido
               l'**indignazione** generale su *Twitter* #RaiOmofoba #HTGAWM

               I feel **great shame** right now and I share the general **indignation**
               on Twitter #RaiOmofoba #HTGAWM

3.1.2 Judgment

Having so far discussed the resources used in the #RaiOmofoba tweets to express emotions (affect), we now move on to consider how *Twitter* users express JUDGMENT, i.e., the area of meaning that is concerned with ethics. Just like the other resources relating to attitude in the appraisal model, judgment can also be either positive or negative. However, since *Twitter* is often used to complain about daily life (Zappavigna 2012), it is not surprising to see a prevalence of instances of criticism towards other people, current events, etc. In this case, a considerable number of tweets expressed negative judgment of Rai with regard to the broadcaster's ethics ("propriety" in Martin and White's system) or lack thereof. Typically, the most common resources used to express explicit criticism are once again along the lines of *vergogna* (shame) and *schifo* (disgust). However, although they are the same nouns and verb variations used to express affect, this time judgment targets Rai directly in the sense of "shame on you" or "you should be ashamed of yourselves." The adjectives *vergognoso* (shameful) and *scandaloso* (scandalous) are also frequent occurrences.

@User   È **scandaloso** che, in un momento storico così importante per
               l'Italia, la #Rai censuri una scena omosessuale. **Vergognoso**.
               #RaiOmofoba

It's **scandalous** that at such an important historical moment for Italy #Rai censors a homosexual scene. **Shameful**. #RaiOmofoba

@User **Vergognatevi** per quello che avete fatto e per come parlate! "Eccesso di pudore"?!??! Questa è discriminazione e omofobia #RaiOmofoba

Shame on you for what you've done and for the way you talk! "Excess of modesty"?!??! This is discrimination and homophobia #RaiOmofoba

@User **che vergogna** la rai . . . già non la guardavo mai, adesso **mi fa schifo**! Siamo nel 2016 non nel tardo medioevo! #RaiOmofoba

shame on Rai . . . I already wasn't watching it, now **it disgusts me**! It's 2016, not the late Middle Ages! #RaiOmofoba

The tweets expressing judgment in the form of shame and disgust typically expose Rai's disconnect with the times and its retrograde and homophobic mentality—which is more suitable for the Middle Ages than 2016—particularly at a time when the Italian Parliament had just passed a bill on same-sex unions. The criticism appears particularly burning because of Rai2's self-proclaimed image as a young network and the new direction towards innovative and modern programming that had just been announced by Rai executives only a few weeks prior to the incident. Along the same lines, *Twitter* users highlighted the broadcaster's hypocrisy in relation to the fact that only a few months prior to the incident, during the widely popular singing competition Festival di Sanremo—which, as usual, was broadcasted live on Rai—many singers sported rainbow-colored ribbons in support of same-sex unions. This was seen in retrospect as an instrumental use of the issue by Rai, which on that occasion seemingly sided with members of the LGBTQ community but effectively failed them when it came to representing them on screen.

Other tweets target Rai's hypocrisy in censoring same-sex kisses while at the same time allowing other kinds of sexually charged content to be aired without censorship, such as graphic heterosexual sex scenes and scantily dressed showgirls and dancers, which users saw as demeaning to women's dignity. Specifically, many users referenced a 2012 incident, in which Argentine showgirl Belén Rodríguez had walked on stage during the above-mentioned Festival di Sanremo wearing a very revealing dress that left part of her crotch—and with it her strategically placed butterfly-shaped tattoo—exposed.[2] Many on *Twitter* highlighted the paradox of showing such a revealing look on national television while censoring a kiss between two men.

Apart from the explicit lexical resources described above, one of the most common responses to the whole incident was to express invoked negative judgment via sarcasm and irony. The use of satire and humor in general is of course not a new strategy as a response to current events or as social commentary—see for example political cartoons in magazines and newspapers, and stand-up comedy in comedy clubs and on television. However, computer-mediated communication (CMC) in general and social media in particular have increased the number of opportunities for users to share content online and to offer personal (often sarcastic) commentary on any number of social and political issues, and current events. A recent example is the great quantity of memes and image macros (Shifman 2013, Chiaro 2017) that have been and continue to be created since the beginning of the 2016 US presidential election, and which are widely circulated through social media. In the case of Trump opponents, the idea is of course to use social media to expose the ridiculous; to express dissent and resistance to dominant discourses (Sørensen 2016) through punching up (Krefting 2014), i.e., selecting as the target of comedy powerful social and political structures rather than the underdog and the disempowered.

As far as the reasons for using humor are concerned, in her study of the language of microblogging, Zappavigna notes that, similarly to face to face communication, humor can be used on social media to invoke solidarity and to diffuse tension, often through the use of emoticons or initialisms such as "LOL" or "Laugh Out Loud." However, with particular reference to microblogging and other social networking services, Zappavigna also introduces the idea of "ambient humor," which "invokes a putative community of users who may have no direct virtual contact but share in the expression of certain values, often aesthetic values" (Zappavigna 2012: 152). In other words, *Twitter* users tend to employ humor in order to relate to other users who are not necessarily their followers but who share similar sensibilities or attitudes towards specific events or issues. However, as Zappavigna notes, the sarcastic meaning and ambient humor might be difficult to analyze, both because of the 140-character restriction by which contextual references to understand the humor are not always provided (Zappavigna 2012: 152), and because simple quantitative analysis (for example a word frequency list) does not provide clear interpretation without the additional use of qualitative analysis (Zappavigna 2012: 58). In other words, sarcasm is more often than not invoked rather than explicit, since there are no clear linguistic markers of this meaning except for the hashtags and the other users' background knowledge of the incident. The following tweet is a case in point:

@User Quel momento in cui ti accorgi che neanche il vangelo va bene per la rai. #raiomofoba #censurai #eccessodipudore

That moment when you realize that not even the gospel is ok for rai. #raiomofoba #censurai #eccessodipudore

The tweet includes a detail of Giotto's "Kiss of Judas" fresco, which depicts the moment from the New Testament in which Judas, one of Jesus' disciples, kisses Jesus in order to signal to the Romans that that is the man they should arrest. The fresco portrays Judas in the act of approaching Jesus' face in order to carry out his betrayal. In other words, the fresco portrays a kiss between two men (the very thing that Rai had censored). Therefore, this user defiantly imagines that the broadcaster's disapproval of this kind of behavior extends to the Gospel as well. This tweet is only one example of the humorous use of *Twitter's* feature that, similarly to other social networking services, allows users to share external links, images, and videos. *Twitter* users commenting on the *HTGAWM* incident took full advantage of this feature by sharing screen grabs and GIFs mostly from the TV series in question (for example, Viola Davis' character in *HTGAWM* rolling her eyes) as well as from more local, seemingly unrelated material, such as the TV show *Uomini e donne*, which could be described roughly as an Italian version of *The Bachelor/Bachelorette* reality shows, only with a live studio audience. The association with *Uomini e Donne* in this case was made popular by the announcement that, in its next season, the show would feature a gay bachelor.

A further target for sarcasm is Rai's obligatory TV license fee (*canone*), which many Italians already see as unfair given the poor quality of the programming on national television. Numerous *Twitter* users saw the incident as an incongruity and as further evidence for the lack of respect for paying subscribers. *Twitter* users felt that by virtue of paying a subscription fee, subscribers should be at least entitled to watching the full version of the show.

@User Cara @RaiDue volevo dirti che farò dei **tagli al canone**..così, per eccesso di pudore #Coliver #htgawm #RaiOmofoba #loveislove

Dear @RaiDue I just wanted to let you know that I'll be doing **some cuts to my license fee**..just so, because of an excess of modesty #Coliver #htgawm #RaiOmofoba #loveislove

Similarly to the previous tweets containing sarcasm, the humorous content is not conveyed by the linguistic elements per se but by their interaction with the additional elements attached to the tweet, in this case the direct mention of #htgawm and #RaiOmofoba, which anchor the tweet within a specific theme.

More humor is derived by imagined scenarios in which Rai airs notoriously controversial TV series—such as *Game of Thrones*, *Orange is the New Black* and *Shameless*—but is unable to broadcast most of the content because of its raciness:

> @User   Immaginate se #Rai2 trasmettesse #gamesofthrones [sic].
>   Riuscirebbe a mandare in onda tutte le 6 stagioni in 2 ore.
>   #HTGAWM
>
>   Imagine if #gamesofthrones [sic] was on #Rai2. They would
>   manage to air all 6 seasons in 2 hours. #HTGAWM

More fodder for sarcasm and ridicule was provided by further developments in the *HTGAWM* incident. One development occurred when a *Twitter* user claimed that s/he agreed with Rai's choice to censor the gay sex scene because "il rischio che il telespettatore diventi gay guardandolo è concreto" [there's a concrete risk that viewers might become gay by watching it]. Whether the tweet was an instance of trolling (i.e., a deliberate attempt to cause disruption and enraged reactions) or not, humorous responses brought this statement to its extreme consequences. For example:

> @User   quindi sono detenuta di Litchfield che ha 11 cloni, una laurea in
>   medicina e una famiglia nel south side #RaiOmofoba
>
>   so I'm an inmate at Litchfield who has 11 clones, a degree in
>   medicine and a family on the south side #RaiOmofoba
>
> @User   Quindi se guardo "Uomini e donne" rischio di diventare una
>   semianalfabeta? #RaiOmofoba
>
>   so if I watch "Uomini e donne" I run the risk of becoming
>   semi-illiterate? #RaiOmofoba

Both tweets employ hyperbole with the clear intent of ridiculing the original user's faulty reasoning. The author of the first tweet implies that, by following the same reasoning, she has watched so much television that she is now an inmate at Lichfield Penitentiary (the primary setting of *Orange is the New Black*) who has eleven clones (similarly to the protagonist in *Orphan Black*) and a medical degree (presumably from being exposed to *Grey's Anatomy* and/or other medical dramas), and lives on the South Side of Chicago just like the working-class protagonists of *Shameless*. The second tweet includes a reference to the reality show *Uomini e donne*, which has a reputation for featuring rather low-brow, crass contestants. In both cases, the sarcasm is only obvious to other users who share background knowledge of the mentioned shows, which in turn speaks to these users' desire to partake in the ambient humor of the community discussing the *HTGAWM* incident.

Another development that spurred further sarcastic tweets is Rai4's (aforementioned) decision to preface the broadcast of Ferzan Ozpetek's film *Mine vaganti* with a "bollino rosso" (red mark), indicating that the film was only suitable for an adult audience. Even after Rai4's apology on the following day—in which the mistake was attributed to an oversight—*Twitter* users rebooted the hashtags #RaiOmofoba and #eccessodipudore as a direct reference to the *HTGAWM* case that occurred less than a month earlier.

@User	@RaiQuattro @Raiofficialnews Certo che come #MineVaganti siete proprio perfetti. Sarà un altro eccesso di pudore come #HTGAWM. #RaiOmofoba
	@RaiQuattro @Raiofficialnews You are certainly perfect as "loose cannons." It must have been another case of excess of modesty like with #HTGAWM. #RaiOmofoba
@User	Ma l'hanno capito che siamo nel 2016? La scusa sarà che chi ha messo il bollino era daltonico . . . vergogna #RaiOmofoba
	Have they understood that we're in 2016? Their excuse is going to be that the person who put the red mark was color-blind . . . shame on you #RaiOmofoba

The first tweet contains a rather sophisticated example of verbal humor playing on the meaning of the film title (similar to "loose cannons" or "time bombs") and an explicit comparison with the censoring intervention on *HTGAWM*. The second tweet, once again using a hyperbole, offers an example of a ridiculous excuse that, based on its track record, Rai is likely to put forward to apologize for another case of content "manipulation." It is notable that, even though these last two tweets were not written as a direct reaction to the *HTGAWM* incident, viewers seem to show remarkable awareness of the patterns at play within certain kinds of broadcasting policies even as far as autochthonous products are concerned, as well as an increased intolerance towards censoring choices made for them a priori by broadcasters.

3.1.3 Appreciation

Lastly, the third subsystem included in the attitude system is APPRECIATION, i.e., the area of meaning concerning the aesthetic value of a text. This discourse semantic resource is used to express attitudes about objects, states, and processes. An example can be "our 'reactions' to things (do they catch our attention; do they please us?), their 'composition' (balance and complexity) and their 'value' (how innovative, authentic, timely, etc.)" (Martin and White 2005: 56). In the context of social media, appreciation is implicit when users repost another user's tweet (retweet) or post a link to an external resource, such as a newspaper article. In this case, Zappavigna (2012) talks of meta-evaluation because, even in the absence of commentary, the act itself of referencing means that users consider the referent noteworthy.

The most notable example of appreciation in the sense of negative aesthetic evaluation found among the tweets containing #RaiOmofoba was the reference to Italy's and/or Rai's *figuraccia* or *figura di merda*. With an Italian phrase almost as untranslatable as its opposite, *bella figura*, many users expressed their displeasure in seeing that Rai's decision to censor the homosexual sex scene had garnered the attention of the international press and of the *HTGAWM* creative team, thus making Italy and Italians look bad in the eyes of the world. In fact, many tweets include modifiers to the nouns *figuraccia* or *figura di merda*, such as *mondiale, planetaria* (worldwide), *globale* (global), and *transoceanica* (transatlantic) to define the scope of this public relations disaster.

> @User   Una **figuraccia** di **proporzioni planetarie**, persino peggiore dei Bunga di Mr B. #RaiOmofoba
>
> A **gaffe** of planetary proportions, even worse than Mr B's Bunga. #RaiOmofoba
>
> @User   Anche EW parla della **figura di merda** della RAI . . . #RaiOmofoba
>
> Even EW talks about RAI's **shitty gaffe** . . . #RaiOmofoba

In order to put this *figuraccia* into perspective, the first user above unfavorably compares it to the impact of Silvio Berlusconi's infamous Bunga Bunga parties. The second user reposts a link to an *Entertainment Weekly* article referencing the fact that Rai's "shitty gaffe" (an admittedly inadequate translation) was picked up by a major US show business publication.

As a conclusion to this section on attitude, it is also worth noting that the use of swear words in the tweets taken into consideration was not limited to the case mentioned above. Although Martin and White (2005) do not cover swearing in depth, perhaps it could be cataloged as a way to heighten and reinforce attitude through linguistic means, almost as a form of upscaled graduation (see above) used to convey a more intense reaction to the issue at hand in terms of emotions, judgment, and appreciation. For example:

@User   **Cazzo** io a quest'ora dovrei essere un mostro con tutte ste serie che guardo #RaiOmofoba

With all the series I watch I should be a **fucking** monster by now #RaiOmofoba

@User   "Eccesso di pudore", io nelle tue parole leggo un eccesso di **stronzate** #RaiOmofoba

"Excess of modesty", in your words I read an excess of **bullshit** #RaiOmofoba

In the first example above, the user is responding to the previously mentioned tweet concerning the concrete possibility that viewers might become gay as a consequence of watching homosexual sex scenes. By using the Italian swearword *cazzo*, the tweeter reinforces his/her reaction, possibly adding a more colloquial, humorous tone to the observation. The second tweet, on the other hand, is built on the antithesis between the expression used by Rai2's executive in her apology, "eccesso di pudore," and the perceived "eccesso di stronzate" that that apology seemingly masks. Once again, the choice to use a swear word possibly indicates a more plain-spoken approach aimed at ridiculing Dallatana's poorly phrased excuse.

3.2 Engagement

Within the appraisal system, ENGAGEMENT is the area of meaning concerned with adopting a stance and positioning oneself in relation to other texts. It has clear connections with Bakhtin's notions of intertextuality and heteroglossia (Bakhtin 1981), since it is concerned with the dialogic relationship that speakers/ writers establish with what has been said/written before. This system of resources appears to be extremely relevant in a discussion of social media because it takes into consideration the relationships that users of these networking services enter into with respect to a community of other users. Specifically, users can employ this system to either build solidarity or distance themselves from previous social media posts or, in other words, to either align or disalign themselves with specific issues or opinions.

Some of the most common resources to express engagement on *Twitter* are retweets, direct responses to other users' tweets, hashtags, and direct mention of another user's handle in the text of the tweet. All of these strategies indicate the users' wish to enter into a conversation either with a single user (or their point of view) or with a community of users, which Zappavigna, given the lack of reciprocity that characterizes *Twitter*, refers to as "ambient audience" (Zappavigna 2012: 64). In other words, users can either engage directly with a fellow tweeter—typically by responding to their tweet or tagging their handle in a new tweet preceded by the symbol @—or engage more indirectly with the community at large by tagging their posts with the hashtag(s) relevant to a specific discourse.

In the case of the *HTGAWM* debacle, one of the most common early reactions to the realization that Rai2 had aired an edited version of the first episode was effectively to "troll" @RaiDue. The practice of trolling, defined by the *Cambridge English Dictionary* as leaving "an insulting message on the internet in order to annoy someone," was in this case carried out by deliberately tagging @RaiDue in posts containing images, GIFs, and short videos showing homosexual couples engaged in kissing or more explicit sexual behavior, all the way to pornographic images. The idea was of course to tease the powers that be with content that would almost certainly be disturbing or offending to them while at the same time clearly making their dissent heard and seen. Furthermore, while the primary purpose of this kind of trolling might not necessarily have been to create humor, a sense of elation can no doubt be perceived in this kind of posts, which challenges bigots while creating camaraderie with the vast majority of the community using #RaiOmofoba.

In terms of alignment/disalignment, a qualitative analysis of the tweets tagged #RaiOmofoba shows that the overwhelming majority of users disaligned with Rai2's censoring intervention, which also clearly transpired from the description of attitude resources in the previous section. However, a minority of users chose to align with Rai, for example by condemning the exaggerated reaction and use of the hashtag #RaiOmofoba—especially after the broadcaster's apology—or simply by expressing their disgust in seeing two men kissing on television (see examples below). These users choose to disalign with the general trend on

Twitter, but at the same time engage with the community by joining the conversation through the hashtag #RaiOmofoba.

@User	Adesso anche dopo le scuse dovete continuare ad indignarvi? Avete stufato, hanno sbagliato, e state esagerando #RaiOmofoba
	Do you have to keep being outraged even after the apology? I've had enough, they made a mistake, and you're exaggerating #RaiOmofoba
@User	Mi dispiace questo vittimismo del mondo gay che grida sui social #RaiOmofoba ritengo sia solo una moda del momento #RaiNonOmofoba @RaiDue
	I'm sorry to see that the gay world has such a persecution complex and shouts #RaiOmofoba on social media—I think it's just a fad #RaiNonOmofoba @RaiDue
@User	Io sono etero e prentendo che in tv passi roba che no [sic] mi faccia rimettere il pranzo di natale. Grazie #Rai #RaiOmofoba
	I'm heterosexual and I want TV to air stuff that doesn't make me throw up my Christmas meal. Thank you #Rai #RaiOmofoba

As in the case of the user who acknowledges a direct cause and effect connection between one's sexuality and watching homosexual sex scenes, the three Rai supporters above were either ridiculed or openly insulted by other users for their bigotry.

As already mentioned, however, the majority of tweets marked with the hashtag #RaiOmofoba tend to express their disaffiliation with Rai and, as a consequence, their alignment with the rest of the *Twitter* community using #RaiOmofoba. This overwhelming stance against what was perceived as bigoted and retrograde ideology on the part of Rai should, however, not be surprising if we consider the demographics of *Twitter* users, who on average tend to be younger and more educated than users of other social networking services such as Facebook (Agostini 2013).

A clear example of engagement that Martin and White attribute to the subcategory of distance (Martin and White 2005: 113–114) is the fact that a considerable number of tweeters directly engaged with members of the *HTGAWM* creative team who had spoken out against censorship by either responding to their tweets or directly tagging them in their own posts in English:

@User	To @shondarhimes I am Italian and I am very sorry for the #CensuredScene in #HTGAWM ! #LoveAlwaysWin #RaiOmofoba
@User	@petenowalk I'm Italian and I'm so sorry for the stupid people with no brain We're not all like them! #loveislove #RaiOmofoba

Despite their sometimes-limited English skills, the authors of the tweets above express a clear intention to apologize on behalf of Italy as a whole; to detach themselves from the idea that all Italians are homophobes; and therefore to disaffiliate themselves from certain negative qualities—such as bigotry and closed-mindedness—that Rai2 had seemingly displayed through their censoring choice.

An example of distancing is evident in a tweet by one of the major actors in the Italian mediascape and direct competitor of Rai, FOX Italia, which had been broadcasting *HTGAWM* before Rai:

@UffstampaFOX	Su @foxtvit in passato, oggi e in futuro, serie tv in versione integrale. Senza censure, sempre. #Sky. #HTGAWM #leregoledeldelittoperfetto
	On @foxtvit in the past, today and in the future, unedited TV series. Without censorship, always. #Sky. #HTGAWM #leregoledeldelittoperfetto

By capitalizing on the incident, FOX chooses to reinforce its position as a provider of uncensored content (as opposed to Rai) by promising its subscribers to keep up their commitment to always offer them unedited series. Despite the fact that FOX did not use the hashtag #RaiOmofoba, they successfully put themselves in direct opposition to Rai and polarized engagement even further. The tweet spurred hilarity among *Twitter* users—on whom the not-so-subtle dig at Rai was not lost—and the same message was included in the *HTGAWM* season 3 promo aired on FOX in December 2016.

As Zappavigna notes (Zappavigna 2012: 61), *Twitter* is often criticized for providing a platform for inane, mundane comments often concerning everyday life and its little annoyances. Social media in general, even when they are meant to be used for activism, are often seen as ineffective as they tend to provide an echo chamber for users that already think alike, without ever opening up a real conversation about a given issue. However, the *HTGAWM* incident could be considered as a case in which the engagement of Italian and international *Twitter* communities actually brought some tangible results. When Rai issued an apology and rescheduled the unedited episodes for Sunday July 10, this was seen as a victory against homophobia by the *Twitter* community as a whole, as *HTGAWM* actor Jack Falahee and creator Peter Nowalk triumphantly announced in the immediate aftermath:

@petenowalk   Good news, thanks to all the fans for making this happen. #HTGAWM #LoveIsLoveIsLove

@RestingPlatypus   WE ended censorship in this case. YOU ALL inspire me. Thank you for your voices! #loveislove

Whether or not this was a case of successful activism carried out through social media, the fact is clear that the *Twitter* community confirmed its function of "watchdog" as far as social and political issues are concerned. While this sentiment was evident in a number of posts, one user summarized it successfully by addressing @RaiDue directly:

@User   Spero di non dover più twittare #RaiOmofoba ma attenta a quello che fai @RaiDue che *Twitter* ti tiene d'occhio

            I hope I won't have to tweet #RaiOmofoba anymore but be careful what you do @RaiDue 'cause Twitter is watching you

4. Conclusion

This chapter investigates the reaction of the *Twitter* community to the airing of an episode of the US TV series *How To Get Away With Murder*, in which Italian network Rai2 had decided to delete a homosexual sex scene. By using the appraisal framework devised by Martin and White (2005), the evaluative language used in tweets including the hashtag #RaiOmofoba was qualitatively analyzed according to the resources of the attitude and engagement systems. As far as attitude was concerned, users expressed overwhelmingly negative emotions, mainly linked to feelings of disappointment, shame, and disgust. They expressed mostly negative judgment towards Rai2's choice to censor the episode as exposing the network's seemingly disconnect with the times and hypocrisy. They also expressed negative appreciation of the impact that such an incident might have on Italy's reputation worldwide. Engagement was mainly expressed through disalignment with the values represented by Rai2 in this scenario—i.e., bigoted mentality and disconnect with the times—and alignment with the rest of the virtual community that stood up for shared values in support not only of the LGBTQ community, but also of Rai's subscribers' right to watch unedited content. Humor, especially in the form of sarcasm, was also often used to put across negative judgment and to engage with the community.

A few more observations seem to be in order by way of conclusion. One significant aspect of this incident has to do with certain dynamics in the AVT distribution in Italy and specifically the idea of accountability. If we concede that Rai did not intentionally censor the scene—in other words, even if it was indeed an innocent mistake—the fact remains that if a single person was responsible for such an impactful choice this exposes a flaw in the system itself. If one accepts that there is no consistency in the process and that a single editor may decide to excise a scene that s/he personally perceives to be offensive or controversial, this reveals an anything-goes approach in which nobody can ultimately be considered accountable. However, I would argue that whether or not Rai intended to make a stance by censoring the homosexual sex scene is not the main point in our discussion. How the incident was handled, though, might be more important. The fact that Rai did not offer an apology per se but at best a somewhat piqued justification for the incident demonstrates a lack of accountability towards their viewers/subscribers, a refusal to take responsibility, if not for an intended censorship, then at least for a flawed execution of the adaptation process for the series.

A second point that is worth making pertains to the increased agency of consumers of audiovisual content and their resistance to official forms of AVT that no longer respond to their needs. The overwhelming *Twitter* reaction to what was perceived as an act of censorship is an unequivocal message—not only to Rai but to all broadcasters—that in the digital/social media age there is no room for "mistakes"; that fans are much more demanding and unforgiving; and much less willing to abide by practices that were perhaps ignored or accepted by the less technologically savvy previous generations that had no access to source-language versions and had a reduced knowledge of English. It appears that the small but demographically significant segment of the Italian population that uses *Twitter* is ready to keep the AVT industry on its toes. As Frederic Chaume notes, "the days of decisions taken by just a few agents, used to dictating what audiences like and dislike, are progressively coming to an end" (Chaume 2016: 72).

Glossary

Audiencing: The public display (usually on social media) of belonging to the audience for a given media event.

Fansubbing: Subtitling created by non-professional subtitlers, usually made available on dedicated online platforms where users can download subtitle files independent of the video content it relates to.

Microblogging: Short messages posted for an online audience, typically on platforms such as *Twitter* and *Instagram*, which might contain text, video, images, audio, or hyperlinks.

Prosumers: People who both consume and produce (producer + consumer) a given product or content, usually referring to the active role that some members of the audience take on with respect to media content.

Notes

1 Other recurring hashtags were #CensuRai—playing on the words *censura* (censorship) and *Rai*—and #eccessodipudore (excess of modesty).
2 Incidentally, "la farfallina," or little butterfly, as it started to be referred to at the time in Italian, is a childish euphemism for the female genitalia.

References

Agostini, F. (2013), "Twitter in Italia: pochi account e l'età media è la più alta del mondo [Twitter in Italy: few accounts and the average age is the highest in the world]," *Money.it*, November 29. Available online: https://www.money.it/twitter-in-italia-2013 (accessed February 18, 2018).

Anderson, A. (2016), "Italian broadcaster Rai apologizes for cutting 'How to Get Away With Murder' gay sex scene," *The Hollywood Reporter*, July 10. Available online: http://www.hollywoodreporter.com/news/italian-broadcaster-rai-apologizes-cutting-909631 (accessed February 18, 2018).

Antonini, R. and C. Bucaria (eds) (2015), *Non-Professional Interpreting and Translation in the Media*, Frankfurt: Peter Lang.

Aslam, S. (2018), "Twitter by the Numbers: Stats, Demographics & Fun Facts," *OmnicoreAgency*. Available online: https://www.omnicoreagency.com/twitter-statistics (accessed February 18, 2018).

Bakhtin, M.M. (1981), *The Dialogic Imagination. Four Essays*, Austin: University of Texas Press.

Beard, L. (2016), "How to Get Away With Murder: Shonda Rhimes responds to Italian TV's censorship of gay sex scene," *Entertainment Weekly*, July 11. Available online: http://ew.com/article/2016/07/11/shonda-rhimes-censorship-gay-sex-scene-how-get-away- murder (accessed February 18, 2018).

Blake, James (2017), *Television and the Second Screen: Interactive TV in the Age of Social Participation*. London and New York: Routledge.

Bruns, A. and Jean E. Burgess (2011), "The Use of *Twitter* Hashtags in the Formation of ad hoc Publics," in *Proceedings of the 6th European Consortium for Political Research* (ECPR) General conference 2011, University of Iceland, Reykjavik. Available online: https://eprints.qut.edu.au/46515/1/The_Use_of_Twitter_Hashtags_in_the_Formatio n_of_Ad_Hoc_Publics_%28final%29.pdf (accessed April 6, 2018).

Chaume, F. (2016), "Audiovisual Translation Trends: Growing Diversity, Choice, and Enhanced Localization," in A. Esser, Á.B. Merino, and I.R. Smith (eds.), *Media Across Borders: Localizing TV, Film and Video Games*, 68–84, London: Routledge.

Chiaro, D. (2017), *The Language of Jokes in the Digital Age: Viral Humour*, London: Routledge.

D'heer, E. and P. Verdegem, (2015), "What Social Media Data Mean for Audience Studies; A Multidimensional Investigation of *Twitter* Use During a Current Affairs TV Programme," *Information, Communication & Society*, 18 (2): 221–234.

Esser, Á.B. (2016), "Defining 'the Local' in Localization or 'Adapting for Whom?'" in A. Esser, Á.B. Merino, and I.R. Smith (eds.), *Media Across Borders: Localizing TV, Film and Video Games*, 19–35, London: Routledge.

Esser, Á.B. Merino, and I.R. Smith (eds.) (2016), *Media Across Borders: Localizing TV, Film and Video Games*, London: Routledge.

Esser, Á.B. Merino, and I.R. Smith (2016), "Introduction," in A. Esser, Á.B. Merino, and I.R. Smith (eds.), *Media Across Borders: Localizing TV, Film and Video Games*, 1–18, London: Routledge.

Firth, J.R. (1957), *Papers in Linguistics 1934–1951*, London: Oxford University Press.

Franco, R. (2016), "Bacio gay: Rai2 lo censura. Polemica social, la replica: «Eccesso di pudore» [Gay kiss: Rai2 censorship. Social controversy, the reply: 'Excess of modesty']." *Corriere della Sera*, July 9. Available online: http://www.corriere.it/spettacoli/16_luglio_09/bacio- gay-rai2-censura-a8277610-45b8-11e6-be0f-475f9043ad28.shtml?refresh_ce-cp (accessed April 6, 2018).

Halliday, M.A.K. (2004), *An Introduction to Functional Grammar*, 3rd edition, London: Arnold.

Highfield, T., S. Harrington, and A. Bruns (2013), "*Twitter* as a Technology for Audiencing and Fandom: The #Eurovision phenomenon," *Information, Communication & Society*, 16 (3): 315–339.

Jenkins, H. (2006), *Convergence Culture: Where Old and New Media Collide*, New York: New York University Press.

Krefting, R. (2014), *All Joking Aside. American Humor and Its Discontents*, Baltimore: Johns Hopkins University Press.

Martin, J.R. and P.R.R.R. White (2005), *The Language of Evaluation: Appraisal in English*, Basingstoke: Palgrave Macmillan.

O'Hagan, M. (2009), "Evolution of User-generated Translation: Fansubs, Translation Hacking and Crowdsourcing," *Journal of Internationalisation and Localisation*, 1: 94–121.

O'Hagan, M. (2011), "Community translation: Translation as a Social Activity and Its Possible Consequences in the Advent of Web 2.0 and Beyond," *Linguistica Antverpiensia*, 10: 13–23.

O'Hagan, M. (2015), "Reflections on Professional Translation in the Age of Translation Crowdsourcing," in R. Antonini, R. and C. Bucaria (eds.), *Non-Professional Interpreting and Translation in the Media*, 115–131, Frankfurt: Peter Lang.

Rossi, L. and F. Giglietto (2016), "*Twitter* Use During TV: A Full-Season Analysis of #serviziopubblico Hashtag," *Journal of Broadcasting & Electronic Media*, 60 (2): 331–346.

Shifman, L. (2013), *Memes in Digital Culture*, Boston: MIT Press.

Sørensen, M. (2016), *Humour in Political Activism: Creative Nonviolent Resistance*, Basingstoke, UK: Palgrave Macmillan.

Tapscott, D. and A.D. Williams, (2006), *Wikinomics: How Mass Collaboration Changes Everything*, New York: Portfolio.

Vivarelli, N. (2016), "Italian Broadcaster Rai Censors Gay Sex Scene in "HTGAWM," Shonda Rhimes & Cast Respond," *Variety*, July 11. Available online: http://variety.com/2016/tv/global/censored-gay-sex-scene-htgawm-htgawm-prompts-italys- rai-to-face-homophobia-complaints-1201811676 (accessed February 18, 2018).

Wong, C.M. (2016), "How To Get Away With Murder Crew Won't Stand For Anti-Gay Edit," *The Huffington Post*, July 12. Available online: http://www.huffingtonpost.com/entry/how-to- get-away-with-murder-gay-italy_us_57851929e4b07c356cfe90d6 (accessed February 18, 2018).

Wood, M.M. and L. Baughman, (2012), "Glee Fandom and *Twitter*: Something New, or More of the Same Old Thing?" *Communication Studies*, 63 (3): 328–344.

Zappavigna, M. (2012), *Discourse of Twitter and Social Media: How We Use Language to Create Affiliation on the Web*, London and New York: Bloomsbury.

Translation and/as Global Communication

Editor's Introductory Note

Chapter 5 provides a refreshing venue for discussion as it suggests that translation can be used for comic effect. Of course, the comic effect is most readily found in mistranslation, mock-translation, and ineffective translation between characters that are brought together by the lack of a common language. The effect is intensified further when miscommunication occurs between lovers who speak in different languages. Therefore, the chapter examines films in which cross-language, cross-cultural and star-crossed couples fall in love despite a language barrier.

The humor is lost, however, when the representation of translation (or, rather, of mistranslation) is based on the assumption of ignorance and a lack of sophistication, or serves to ridicule and to underscore certain cultural stereotypes. The chapter contextualizes the seemingly romantic juxtaposition in which lovers abandon their native languages for the benefit of universal human traits and an international language of love. Several films are examined, taken from different historical periods, and representing various models of "postcarding," and "translanguaging." In doing so, the chapter provides an ethical discussion of the translational equivalent of "trouble in paradise": macaronic Italian, mixing romance languages, linguistic inauthenticity, and linguistic fetishisms which, much like many of the romantic infatuation by which they are contextualized, lead to complicated and unequal relationships.

Cross-Languaging Romance on Screen

Delia Chiaro

1. Introduction

The beginning of the third millennium appears to have seen an exponential rise in the number of films and fictional products for television involving characters from diverse linguistic backgrounds with the result that the content of such products is more than likely to occur in more than one language. As discussed at length by Giuseppe De Bonis (2014, 2015), this phenomenon is not new as the occurrence of more languages in one movie has been customary since the birth of the talkies. Alongside English-speaking protagonists, westerns in the 1950s and 1960s typically depicted Native Americans talking in what would now be considered politically incorrect "Hollywood injun English" (Meek 2006: 9), while Japanese and German language were persistently present in Second World War movies. Today, the constant and massive flux of migrants crossing continents, coupled with technology that has speeded up communication, has brought people together from far and wide despite language barriers. Multilingual cities are a rule rather than an exception, and it should come as no surprise that fictional audiovisual media reflects the post-multilingual reality of today's society through the rise of the same multilingualism on screen.

As I argue elsewhere, multilingual filmic products, i.e., those containing dialogs in which speakers converse in two or more different languages, can be roughly divided into two broad categories, depending on whether the aim of the narrative is to create a sense of conflict or confusion (Chiaro 2015, 26). In order to be credible, films portraying conflict, such as those set against a backdrop of war or international espionage, will usually require at least two languages. In the spy thriller, *Atomic Blonde* (2017), Lorraine Broughton (played by Charlize Theron) is an undercover MI6 agent in Berlin just before the fall of the Wall. While she investigates the murder of a fellow agent and tries to recover a missing list of double agents, she has to use several languages. Now, if critics may justly accuse the film of being extremely far-fetched in terms of plot and action, linguistically it is perfectly credible. In fact, as well as English, dialogs occur in German, Russian, French, and Swedish. In *Atomic Blonde* and other films like it, the presence of languages other than English add to the tension felt by the monolingual English-speaking audience at whom it is principally aimed.

In comedy, utilizing the same tension and conflict that is created in non-comic films, the use of more than one language can create misunderstandings that lead to confusion and, ultimately, to the audience's laughter and exhilaration. The notion of romance between two people who do not share the same language has attracted the imagination of film directors for decades (Chiaro 2009, 221–223). Romantic comedies concerning couples who do not speak the same language, conventionally promote a series of cross-linguistic misunderstandings and cross-cultural faux pas that are eventually resolved when the pair form a relationship that leads to a happy conclusion. Bilingual, cross-cultural romance can occur in other serious dramatic products as well.

This chapter sets out to examine the manners in which directors and actors imagine cross-language romance. The concept of translanguaging or: "... the deployment of a speaker's full linguistic repertoire without regard for watchful adherence to the socially and politically defined boundaries of named (and usually national and state) languages" (Otheguy et al. 2015), is a handy tool to describe dialog in which two speakers do not share a common language yet need to make themselves understood. In order to do so, they must resort to their entire gamut of linguistic knowledge that will include perceptions of the language of their interlocutor or the employment of a third language they happen to know in the hope that it is similar to the language required. When the languages of star-crossed and linguistically challenged lovers clash, attempts at translanguaging may well become something that can further highlight tension, or else, become a humorous device. After all, how do these fictional couples negotiate their linguistic imbalance without causing mix-ups? Or could it be that the process of falling in love is something that transcends language?

Working from a small number of carefully chosen movies involving English-speaking protagonists in a love relationship with a speaker of another language, I shall examine the extent to which the crossing of two languages on screen between lovers can become a comic device. I will be focusing on comedy, rather than drama, because it would appear that the intersection of two languages against a romantic backdrop can generate, not only thought-provoking comic characteristics, but evidence for the importance of humor in romantic relationships—and relationships in general.

2. The sound of silence

Susan Ervin-Tripp's study of American-Japanese couples with no pivot language, reported that they tended to speak to one another in "the language of the eyes" (Ervin-Tripp 1968: 202). Similarly, romance on screen seems to follow this trend. When bilingual, cross-cultural couples fall in love on screen, there is a tendency, in the initial moments of their romance, for them to base their communication on long, drawn out gazes. Yet, in *Pocahontas* (1995), a full-length cartoon loosely based on the romance between an English soldier, John Smith, and the daughter of an Algonquin chief, Grandmother Willow urges the couple to communicate with an organ other than the eyes, advising them to: "Listen with your heart; you will understand . . ." Never mind the ears and the heart, the *topos* of "the language of the eyes" is present in many films involving cross-language couples where we find that the expression "love at first sight" seems to ring especially true.

It is literally love at first sight for Italian Chiara (played by Giulia Steigerwalt) and Polish builder Pawel (played by Szajda Pawel) who meet while harvesting olives in *Under the Tuscan Sun* (2003). And if not at first sight, it is certainly with their eyes that Lieutenant Dunbar (played by Kevin Costner) and a Lakota speaker named Stands-With-A-Fist (played by Mary McDonnell) fall in love in *Dances with Wolves* (1990). The interplay of eyes is also responsible for Nathan Algren (played by Tom Cruise) and Japanese Taka (played by Koyuki) falling in love in *The Last Samurai* (2013). It is even more strikingly love at first sight for Stanley Ford (played by Jack Lemmon) when scantily-clad Virna Lisi pops out of a huge cake at a stag party which he is drunkenly attending in *How to Murder your Wife* (1965). Their romance blossoms when, for more than a minute, the camera zooms back and forth between Lisi's beautiful huge green eyes and Stanley's hypnotized gaze. The camera also significantly focuses on Lisi's lips and her tongue as, when the couple wakes up the following morning to find they are married, we soon learn that the new Mrs. Ford does not speak a word of English. This same scene portraying the chemistry of eyes and lips is mirrored in the final scene of the movie. Stanley's butler, Charles (played by Terry Thomas), finds a middle-aged woman in his room. Exactly as in the earlier "cake" scene, the eyes of the couple meet and the camera goes backwards and forwards focusing first, at length, on the their eyes, and then on the woman's lips. The woman, who has by now bewitched Charles, utters: "*Buona sera. Sono la mamma della Signora Ford*" [Good evening. I am Mrs. Ford's mother]. Once more, it is literally a case of love at first sight between two people who do not share the same language.

For roughly half the film, Mrs. Ford speaks no English and interacts with her husband, not only with her eyes, but with her whole body. In a number of scenes in which Stanley tries to communicate his distress at finding himself suddenly married, his wife will suddenly cover him with kisses and throw herself onto the nearest sofa or bed, taking him with her without any verbal exchanges occurring. Each time she does this, the same slow, sexy music accompanies the scene that soon fades out into oblivion as the couple embrace and kiss. We are in the 1960s, so the scene will typically cut before the couple goes any further. As repetition "may be the single most important mechanism in comedy" (Charney 1978: 82), each time they hear the music and see Mrs. Ford embrace her husband, the audience knows what is coming and is triggered to either smile or laugh at the irony of the situation.

The subplot of *Les poupées russes* (2005) involves the romance between William (played by Kevin Bishop), an English stagehand at the Royal Albert Hall, and Natacha, a Russian ballerina (played by Evguenya Obraztsova). During rehearsals for *Swan Lake*, the stage is buzzing with dancers and theater staff so both Russian and English can be heard in the background. Natacha is working with her teacher and both converse in Russian. William watches from his workstation above the stage, and soon his eyes focus on Natacha who is now alone practicing her steps before he switches off the lights. Natacha calls up to William, in Russian (accompanied by subtitles), asking him to turn the stage lights back on so that she can practice longer. William replies "I . . . I don't . . . I don't speak Russian. Sorry." Totally bewitched by Natacha, William stares at her as she climbs up the ladder to reach him:

William   Be careful.

Natacha [in Russian]   Hi. I was talking about the lights. I have to work a little bit longer. Just a bit.

William   I don't understand. Sorry.

Natacha [in Russian]   I need . . . the light. To work. Like that. Like the sun. On the stage.

William   Sunset? Light? OK, OK. So you want the lights on.

Natacha [in Russian]   Yes

William [Turns the lights back on]   OK. Sure, sure. Sorry.

Natacha [in Russian]   Thank you very much. I'll just be a little while. My name is Natacha.

William   I'm Wi . . . William.

Natacha [in Russian]   William. Thank you, William. Bye.

Les poupées russes 2005

From this moment onwards, William's relationship with Natacha is based on his gaze in her direction as well as a number of long, lingering glances between them both. He explains to his friend, Xavier (played by Romain Duris) that:

The very first time I saw her I knew at that point, cross my heart hope to die . . . my life'd never be the same again [. . .] well, we saw each other every day before and after each performance. And I would watch the show every single night, and the only person I could see was her . . .

Les poupées russes 2005

Viewers see a flashback of Natacha performing on stage, alternated with close ups of Kevin's enthralled facial expression. Significantly, William uses the verbs "to see" and "to watch" four times in describing his romance to Xavier. In addition, each time Natacha exits the stage, William would be there and they would exchange a prolonged "Hello William"/"Hello Natacha" in which Kevin's eyes reveal that he is besotted with her. They make awkward attempts at conversing, Natacha asking in Russian if he likes how she dances, but William does not understand so their conversation involves copious gesticulation, nodding, smiling, and, of course, eye contact. Finally, when the company leaves London, Natacha gives Kevin her address on a piece of paper, but when he unfolds it, he sees that it is in Cyrillic. Xavier (and the viewers) is curious to know what happens next:

Xavier   So, so you saw her again? You went to St. Petersburg?

William   Yeah . . . but it took me a year to get there.

Xavier   Why?

William   Well, because I had to learn Russian for a year first!

Les poupées russes 2005

The fact that Kevin decides to learn Russian before embarking on a serious liaison with Natacha raises a laugh because he embodies the uncouth uneducated English *chav*, but also adds credibility to the narrative. Although eye contact and gazes continue to dominate their relationship, William has taken the trouble to familiarize himself with Russian.

3. Me Tarzan, you Jane?

In *How to Murder your Wife*, the morning after his wedding, Stanley is concerned to find that he is no longer the previously staunch bachelor he had been until the day before. In fact, Stanley wakes up to find himself in bed with the new Mrs. Ford who is in a state of undress. As soon as his wife wakes up, Stanley delivers a long tirade as to how they had mistakenly ended up married and how they would immediately get divorced:

> You're awake. Well, that's fine. [...] Before anything else happens, we have to have a little talk. [...] First of all, I would like to apologize for last night. Quite obviously, a mistake has been made. On my part! It's nothing that can't be rectified. It can be rectified if we keep our heads [...] Last night at old Tobey's bachelor dinner, you ... came out of a cake. That's natural. Young ladies often come out of cakes at bachelor dinners. [...] I asked you to marry me ... while I was intoxicated, [...] And, apparently, you accepted. [...] Before I knew what hit me, there's Judge Blackstone, two guys holding him up ... "Now pronouncing you man and wife." Anyway, that's where things stand, my dear, at the moment. As I say, it's nothing that can't be rectified [...] And you'll get a handsome settlement. I happen to be very well off. Six weeks in Las Vegas. Ooh, boy. All there is too it.
>
> *How to Murder your Wife* 1965

While Stanley speaks, his new wife listens attentively, with a puzzled expression on her face. However, her look of perplexity soon vanishes as she begins to nod, smile, laugh and finally to clap with joy. Mrs. Ford tries to interrupt her husband but she is unable to get a word in edgeways and it is only towards the end of Stanley's rant, that she takes his hands in hers, caresses his face and covers it with kisses, after which, in rapid-fire Italian she declares:

> *Oh marito mio, disgraziatamente io non ho capito una parola di quello che hai detto, però quando parli, parli con questo fare così, così meraviglioso, così splendido che il mio cuore si riempie di felicità. Pensare che un uomo come te mi ha scelto tra tante donne per essere sua moglie, beh, questo è troppo, i miei occhi si riempiono di lacrime ... oh vieni qui marito mio, abbracciami come hai fatto la notte passata* [kissing his face] *stringimi forte, forte, forte ...*
>
> Oh my dear husband, unfortunately I haven't understood a single word of what you have said but when you speak, you sound marvelous, so splendid that you fill my heart with joy. To think that a man like you has chosen me out of so many other women is too much. My eyes fill with tears ... come here husband of

mine, embrace me like you did last night [kissing his face], squeeze me tight ...
How to Murder your Wife 1965

Like newlywed Stanley, a monolingual English-speaking audience is unlikely to understand a word of what his wife has just said although it will be clear that she is more than happy to be married to him, seeing as she cannot keep her hands off him. Unless audiences are familiar with Virna Lisi and know that she was Italian, her behavior, and mystified facial expressions during Stanley's tirade will not be so funny. Like Stanley, the audience will be simply flummoxed by her Italian outburst. To someone unfamiliar with Italian it will simply sound like a fast stream of words that they do not understand, which in itself may seem comic. Furthermore, there is a tradition of laughing at the stereotypically fast-talking Italian who is wildly gesticulating. However, humor also arises from Stanley's bewildered expression as he, too, does not understand a word. "My God, you're Italian!" he says in astonishment, followed by: "*Vous ne parlez ...* You don't sp ... No speaka da English?" The concept of all Romance languages being the same is a Hollywood trope. Stanley first uses French, although he understands that she is Italian and his first attempt at French soon turns into macaronic Italian: "No speaka da English?" to which his wife answers, "No": He then asks, "Italian?" and she triumphantly replies "Yes!"

The use of this type of macaronic Italian is a common comic device when an English speaker interacts with an Italian speaker. Like the late nineteenth-century poems of Thomas Augustine Daly, Stanley is emulating the stereotypical Italian pronunciation of English. The first verse of Daly's poem "Mia Carlotta" reads:

> Giuseppe, da barber, he gotta da cash,
> He gotta da clo'es an' da bigga moustache,
> He gotta da seely young girls for da "mash,"
> But notta–
> You bat my life, notta—Carlotta.
> I gotta!

Daly 1936: 6

In Daly's poem, several features of Italian pronunciation seep through into Giuseppe's English. Daly exaggerates Italians' inability to pronounce the interdental fricative. Instead of saying "the," Italians may say "da." Italian speakers might also have a tendency to add the schwa sound at the end of words ("gotta," "notta," etc.). Daly also highlights many Italians' difficulty in pronouncing short vowels ("seely") and uses these characteristics to make fun of the way that Italians speak. Stanley uses this kind of English to speak to his Italian wife, and although, unlike Daly, his intention is not to make fun of Italians, the same comic effect is partly created by the Italian pidgin English he uses to make himself understood. As in the immortal line, "Me Tarzan, you Jane," Stanley tells his wife: "You get am dressed ... me go talk butler." Nevertheless, when Mrs. Ford stretches her arms out and says: "*vieni qui*" ("come here") he just smiles and mutters: "What does that mean?" This somewhat patronizing way of speaking to his Italian wife continues throughout the movie in utterances such as: "you, me, we, go talk-am lawyer." He also patronizes her by raising his voice in an exaggeratedly slow fashion, although fast or slow will make no difference if she speaks no English! Although not all Italians speak English with such a poor and comic accent, this disdainful way of portraying their speech is still a common way of depicting Italian identity in a variety of text-types including advertisements (Chiaro 2004, 322–324). Given that the film is from the 1960s, presumably this type of ethnic ridicule was still acceptable. And yet, today, while it would be unheard of to mock the speech of a person of color, on screen, it would appear that it is still permissible to ridicule Italians by means of this kind of pseudo Italian.

The scornful "No speaka da English?" would nowadays be regarded as offensive. According to Joel Sherzer, this "mock language" is a common form of verbal play based on code-switching: ". . . usually one that is characteristic of groups low on the political-economic and social hierarchy of a community—[which] is inserted into the discourse of the dominant language of the same society, in a purposely parodic form" (Sherzer 2002: 93–94). Sherzer provides the examples of "*hasta la vista baby*" and "*no problema*," both used pejoratively by non-Spanish speaking Americans. A similar mockery takes place as people consistently speak to Mrs. Ford in this uncomplimentary way. When Stanley's attorney, Harold (played by Eddie Mayehoff) introduces her to his wife, he says "Oh, Mrs. Ford, this MY wife. But she speak *mucho good* Italian, go Berlitz, take lessons. Learn Italian. $300 worth. $300 is many, many lira." The attorney uses a Spanish term and then simplified Italian, to which his wife quite rightly responds: "Yeah, shut up, Harold. You sound like a feeble-minded Indian," and then turns to Mrs. Ford and, in perfectly good Italian, says, "*Congratulazioni, mia cara*"—"Congratulations my Dear." Edna, the attorney's wife (played by Clare Trevor), speaks fluent Italian and is able both to converse with, and act as interpreter for Mrs. Ford. In these scenes, the film displays some self-aware irony that is perhaps critical of linguistic stereotypes. While the two men are reduced to an elementary speech-style in an attempt to speak Italian, interestingly, the two women are linguistically talented.

Edna speaks enough basic Italian to communicate with Mrs. Ford, who, while not speaking a word of English, does understand the word "divorce" being bandied around the attorney's office. Her reaction is in perfectly understandable broken English: "Divorce? Divorce? Ah, no, no. Italia, no divorce, no." In the end, although the men are treating their wives with a touch of linguistic arrogance, it would appear that the laugh is on them rather than on the two women.

Moreover, Mrs. Ford learns English by watching television in bed with the volume turned up so loud that Stanley has difficulty sleeping. As he tosses and turns, Mrs. Ford says: "Work, work, pressure, pressure, the tension mounts and before you know it, it strikes." Stanley is surprised by her sudden fluency in English but she has an explanation: "Oh, they talk always about this on television." She goes on to quote the jingle of an advertisement for painkillers: "Oh, oh, darling, I have a three-way formula … How they say? Faster, faster, faster. Oh, relief." The double entendre is then played out as camera fades out on the embracing couple and the rest is left to the audience's imagination.

4. All romance languages sound the same

In Hollywood movies, it sometimes appears that languages other than English are unimportant, and it is a commonplace that Romance languages are seen as mutually intelligible. As we have seen, while aware of the fact that she is Italian, Stanley uses French terms when speaking to his wife on more than one occasion, such as when he asks her to wait "cinq minutes." And Harold uses the Spanish adverb when he tells Mrs. Ford that his wife's Italian is "mucho good." Both Stanley and Harold speak to her in a form of simplified Italian, almost as though she were lacking in intelligence: "$300 is many, many lira." Similarly, in *Grumpier Old Men* (1995), in his pursuit of Italian speaking Mama Ragetti (played by Ann Morgan Guilbert), Grandpa Gustafson (played by Burgess Meredith) addresses her with the Spanish term, "*Señorita.*" It is a cliché that Spanish and Italian are reciprocally understandable, and some Romance languages certainly seem to be considered one and the same in dominant Anglocentric culture.

One of the four plots in Richard Curtis' blockbuster *Love Actually* (2003) is aptly titled "Love in a Second Language" and concerns the unrequited passion between English writer Jamie (played by Colin Firth) and his Portuguese housekeeper, Aurelia (played by Lucia Moniz). They fall in love but have difficulty in communicating their feelings owing to their lack of proficiency in each other's language, so their relationship stumbles along mainly through gesture, facial expressions, and a good dose of Jamie's awkward mixture of Spanish and Italian in his attempts at speaking Portuguese. Jamie uses a concoction of (what he considers to be) Romance-sounding languages in his attempt to communicate with Aurelia. But, above all, he inserts the name of a famous Portuguese European football (soccer) player, Eusebio, into the conversation. The presence of the name Eusebio is nonsensical, but it typifies a way of connecting with someone of another culture by displaying a knowledge of one of its sociocultural elements. However, while on one level it is amusing that Jamie muddies a number of languages, at the same time, by thinking they are all the same, the individuality of each is rejected. English is the dominant language in the film and all other (Romance) languages are considered equivalent. It therefore appears that it is unimportant which one he uses. It is also interesting to note that Jamie makes an effort to study Portuguese. Certainly compared to twentieth-century films, in more recent productions such as this one, we can notice an attempt to obtain a higher level of linguistic authenticity.

The idea that languages other than English are all the same can be extended to the notion that all speakers of other languages are the same. In *Les poupées russes*, when Kevin takes Xavier and his sister Wendy (played by Kelly Reilly) to a performance of Swan Lake in St. Petersburg, only Kevin is able to distinguish Natacha from the rest of the *corps de danse*. All dressed identically in white tutus and fascinators, only Kevin's "look of love" is able to tell Natacha apart from the other swans.

Wendy [watching Natacha dance]   Now which one . . .?

William   That one there, look.

Wendy   The one on the end?

William   No. Look. Right . . . Second from the left.

Xavier   The blonde one?

Wendy   But they're all blonde!

William   That one! See, look. Second from the left. That one.

Wendy   They all look the same.

Les poupées russes 2005

The idea that the "others" all look the same crops up in other multilingual films as well. In *Another Time, Another Place* (1983), a dramatic film about a group of Italian prisoners of war billeted in Scotland, the Italian prisoners are indistinguishable to the women of the Scottish community. When a local woman is raped, an Italian is wrongly accused because, after all, "they all look the same."

5. Dirty talk?

In *Les poupées russes*, the "dominant language" (Heiss: 2004) is French, yet there are long stretches of dialog in English and Russian, or only in English, for which subtitles are provided for a monolingual French audience. However, what is of interest here are not the translational solutions provided by the subtitles. What is of interest is how the couples adopt translanguaging to push their liaison further. Translanguaging involves the use of a speaker's entire linguistic repertoire that goes beyond the defined restrictions of named languages. Neither speaker uses the correct language of their partner, but often just a rough approximation. Through translanguaging, speakers draw on their entire range of language options and eschew the "legitimate" target language as the only mode of communication. In order for the couple to understand each other, almost anything goes.

Romance on screen is rarely limited to innocent gazing and kissing. Eventually the issue of sex will emerge and, in both drama and comedy, communicating sexual needs in another language may be troublesome. *Another Time, Another Place* (1983) takes place in the Scottish Highlands during the Second World War. Janie (played by Phyllis Logan), a young woman in a lackluster marriage with an older man becomes vulnerable to the charms of Italian prisoner of war Luigi (played by Giovanni Mauriello). Luigi's agenda in relation to Janie is not completely honorable. Although he is "a fast-talking, essentially harmless scamp" (Canby 1984), Luigi's hidden agenda is to seduce her. When Luigi is alone with her, he shows her a photograph of his mother and asks: "You like my mother?" to which Janie replies that she does, opening the way for Luigi to ask: "You like me?" When Janie says that she does like him, Luigi then asks: "Is possible we make jiggy jiggy?" The verb "to like" can have scores of meanings including that of sexual attraction. And although "jiggy jiggy" is not a common term, there is no question as to its meaning. By using this onomatopoeic term to refer to sexual intercourse, Luigi is not trying to be amusing; he is simply using his knowledge of languages—he speaks in both Standard Italian and Neapolitan (plus his idiosyncratic version of English)—to convey the meaning he wants. Presumably, the term is an attempt to ask for sex both figuratively and euphemistically at the same time, and Janie understands exactly what he wants. Luigi, does not stop at this first attempt at seducing Janie, and he soon replaces the term "jiggy jiggy" with a far more distant allusion:

> **Luigi**   *Bella*! E' possibile? *Ja! Solo 'na vota*, is possible *per favore*?—Is possible? Come on! Just once . . . please.

Janie   No possible! Never possible! Understand?

Another Time, Another Place 1983

Luigi does not openly mention sex at all. In his second request, Luigi codeswitches between Italian (*per favore*—"please") and Neapolitan (*Ja! Solo 'na vota*—"come on, just once") together with a translanguaged calque: "Is possible" (i.e., with an absent subject, "it," as Italian does not require one in the expression: *E' possibile?*). Luigi does not directly ask for sex. It is his eyes and desperate stance that convey his request. And whether ironically, or to make herself understood, Janie responds in broken English, thereby closely echoing Luigi's grammatical inaccuracy. With her firm and angry "No possible! Never possible! Understand?" Janie too is translanguaging. In fact, Luigi nods in agreement and repeats "Understand. Understand," followed by "*Scusate Signò . . . nun 'o faccio cchiù*" [Neapolitan for "Sorry Madam, I shan't do it again"] in an almost frightened tone, and then closes in English with "Sorry. Understand. I go. OK. OK."

Luigi, however, does finally succeed in seducing Janie. Depressed because of the bleak weather and the fact that he receives no letters from home, he vents his grief on Janie: "*Niente lettera* [no letter] one month . . . two month . . . in Naples the war is finished . . . *io aggia biosgna 'e te si no nun campo* [Neapolitan: "I need you or else I do not live"]. Janie consoles him. And as he weeps, Luigi obtains what he wanted all along—sex. Still not satisfied, Luigi soon returns for more. "Is possible one more time?" asks Luigi. Janie consents and in the aftermath of the couples' second sexual encounter, insecure Janie uses the Italian words "*sempre* [always]" and "*ragazze*" [girls]" in an attempt to be understood while the now sexually satisfied Luigi tells her what she wants to hear, namely that he loves her, in his broken English. Janie knows he is not being completely truthful and that, in a sense, they are saying what is expected of them. Furthermore, it is clear to the audience that they are both aware of the fact that they are unlikely to meet again.

Janie   Will you always love me? *Sempre* Luigi? [Always Luigi?]

Luigi   *Certo, sempre, certo.* [Of course, always, of course.]

Janie   Napoli you get other girls, *ragazze.*

Luigi   No I love you.

Janie   I'll not see you again.

Luigi   One day you come in Naples, soon.

Another Time, Another Place 1983

Comedy contains instances of sexual innuendo that some might consider verging on the vulgar. *Grumpier Old Men* (1995) is a romantic comedy in which elderly Grandpa Gustafson attempts to seduce equally elderly Italian Mama Ragetti when he spots her in a supermarket clutching a cucumber:[1]

Grandpa Gustafson   You need a hand with that [cucumber]? My name's Gustafson.

Mama Ragetti   *Il mio nome Francesca Ragetti* [My name is Francesca Ragetti.]

Grandpa Gustafson   Woo hoo hoo Italian girl. What do you say we go back to my place? I'll show you my cannelloni.

Grumpier Old Men 1995

Grandpa Gustafson comes straight to the point by alluding to his virility neatly indicated by the term "cannelloni," a classic Italian food item. In a clip displaying different rejected cuts of the supermarket scene,[2] Meredith attempts to seduce Italian Mama Ragetti by suggesting he shows her his "... spicy pepi ... peperoni"; "... man-sized manicotti" and "beefy boloney." In these rejected dialogs, there is also an attempt at alliteration that was abandoned in the final cut. Before falling on the euphemistic choice of "cannelloni" for the final cut, the old man uses other Italian food terms. Mama Ragetti is clutching a large cucumber, so sexual allusion is already visible. And despite the fact that Gustafson uses the plural form of each food item, innuendo is clearly heightened. As in the earlier example in which the namesake of soccer player Eusebio is inserted into the conversation, there is something derogatory about reducing a culture to stereotypical traits whether they are Italian food or a Portuguese athlete.

In a later seduction scene, Grandpa Gustafson uses a classic wordplay technique in which he invents a name of place that sounds as if it is in another language. As he is talking about Hawaii, he invents the name of an island that sounds Polynesian but simultaneously carries an erotic connotation in English. In other words, he exemplifies what Delabastita labels translation based monolingual target-language wordplay (Delabastita 2005: 162–173):

Grandpa Gustafson   I have been to Hawaii.

Mama Ragetti   Oh yeah? Which island?

Grandpa Gustafson   Come-on-I-wanna-lay-ya.

Mama Ragetti   I find you disgusting.

Grandpa Gustafson   Well, just as long as you find me.

Grumpier Old Men 1995

Again, if we examine the previously mentioned unused takes, before arriving at the island of "I-wanna-lay-ya," actor Burgess Meredith improvises with "I-kinda-like-a-pok-ya," "You-like-a-licky-dicky" and "I'm-a-kinda-kinky." All the examples are compatible with the speech of the improper character Meredith portrays and carry an erotic connotation.

Food words also occur in a very famous comic sex scene in *A Fish Called Wanda* (1988). Wanda (played by Jamie Lee Curtis), can only become sexually aroused if her partner speaks to her in a foreign language. Otto, (played by Kevin Kline) invents nonsensical Italian in order to make love to her:

Otto   *E molto pericoloso signorina, molto perico . . . Carissima.*

Wanda   Oh speak it! Speak it!

Otto   *Un ossobuco milanese con piselli. Melanzane parmigiana con spinaci. Dov'è la farmacia?*

Wanda   Yes, yes, yes! No, no, no!

Otto   *Sì sì si! Ecco l'uomo . . . oooh le due cupole grandi della cattedrale di Milano . . . Benito Mussolini! Dov'è il Vaticano? Oh, ecco Roma . . . Volare . . . Oh oh . . . Cantare . . . oh . . .*

A Fish Called Wanda 1988

He invents examples from tourist phrasebooks that range from ordering food to asking directions and ending with the first bar of the popular Italian song, *Volare*. Similarly to the speech of Grandpa Gustafson in *Grumpier Old Men*, Otto exemplifies Sherzer's argument about the appropriation of foreign words in English, as both of them throw in randomly stereotypical elements of the target culture in order to sound (in their case) Italian. It is highly likely that the audience is aware that Otto's dialog is completely ludicrous. Similarly, in a scene from *Les poupées russes*, William arrives in Paris and immediately engages in the same kind of linguistic behavior:

William   Hello Paris! I'm a Parisian! Gimme some escargot and red wine! [sees some girls walking by and speaks to them in French] *Parlez vous francais?*

Girl   *Oui.*

William   *Voulez-vous coucher avec moi?* Always wanted to say that to a French girl!

Les poupées russes 2005

Once again, food is involved as William reduces French cuisine to snails and red wine. He then propositions a girl in the street with the riff of a 1970s disco song because he "always wanted to say that to a French girl." People's limited knowledge of a foreign language is invariably composed of the vocabulary of food. William thinks that he is being funny and presumably, some audiences will appreciate this style of humor. Although we are in the realm of humorous discourse where often anything goes, there is a serious observation to be made about the highhanded way in which "other" languages are being used. Another seduction scene from *A Fish Called Wanda* involves Archie (played by John Cleese) who is something of a polyglot:

Wanda   Archie? Do you speak Italian?

Archie   I am Italian! *Sono italiano in spirito. Ma ho sposato una donna che preferisce lavorare in giardino a fare l'amore appassionato. Uno sbaglio grande* [I am Italian in spirit. But I have married a woman who prefers gardening to making passionate love. A big mistake]! But it's such an ugly language. How about . . . Russian?

A Fish Called Wanda, 1983

Archie then goes on to speak in Russian. But what he actually does is to recite a poem titled "Molitva" by Mikhail Lermontov. The character, and apparently the actor as well ("A Fish Called Wanda (1988)," n.d.), had no idea what the words actually meant. What Archie is saying is meaningless in the given situation, and it is likely that the audience is aware of this. However, because it is a comic scene concerning a woman who can only be aroused in a foreign language, this linguistic gibberish becomes not only acceptable, but designed to be hilarious. Wanda displays a "language fetish" in the Freudian sense.

More seriously, according to Cronin, a similar "cavalier approach" to linguistic inauthenticity underscores the limits of intercultural communication. The dominance of English means that other languages lose their distinctive identities and merge into an undistinguishable and interchangeable other. What matters most is that they are "not English" (Cronin 2009: 77—8). As with Jamie, whose initial words to Aurelia contain a mixture of Spanish and Italian as a stand in for Portuguese, it matters little to Wanda which language her lover speaks: provided it is foreign, it makes no difference to her at all.

6. Postcarding

The 1960s and 1970s witnessed numerous US romcoms set in Italy, such as: *Roman Holiday* (1953); *It Started in Naples* (1960); *Buonasera Mrs. Campbell* (1968) and *Avanti!* (1972). In these movies, well-known US actors would typically be set off against beautiful young female Italian stars. In *It Started in Naples*, Clark Gable plays against a young Sofia Loren; and Telly Savallas plays against Gina Lollobrigida in *Buonasera Mrs. Campbell*. Actors such as Loren and Lollobrigida had an excellent command of English so there was no need for translanguaging. They simply exaggerated their accents for the purpose of the film. However, these films contained many instances of "postcarding" (Wahl 2005). Postcarding involves sprinkling a movie here and there with words in the language of the place where it is set. These are words that most people will know, like *"grazie," "ja,"* or *"bonsoir." Buonasera Mrs. Campbell,* as the title suggests, reverses postcarding. The film is set in Italy, but Carla Campbell (played by Gina Lollobrigida) names herself after the well-known American soup label. Similarly, *It Started in Naples* contains a famous scene in which Loren sings and dances to the well-known Neapolitan boogie-woogie *"Tu vuo' fá l' Americano* [You wanna be American]" (1956). The same song was later to be performed by Rosario Fiorello in *The Talented Mr. Ripley* (1999). The song is a satire of post-war southern Italy that was still a rural and traditional society, but in which people emulated American customs. What the song does is to reduce "Americanness" to drinking whiskey and soda, smoking Camel cigarettes, playing baseball, etc. This appropriation of American culture made Italians of the time seem trendier and *"a la moda"*:

> Tu vuo' fá l' americano, mericano, 'mericano Siente a me chi t''o ffa fá?
>
> Tu vuoi vivere alla moda, ma se bevi Whisky and Soda , po' te siente 'e disturbá
>
> Tu abballe 'o Rock and Roll, tu giochi a Base Ball Ma 'e solde p''e Ccamel, chi te li dá?
>
> La borsetta di mammá!?
>
> Tu vuo' fá l'americano, 'mericano, 'mericano ma si''nato in Italy!
>
> Siente a me: Nun ce sta niente 'a fá Okay, Napolitan!
>
> Tu vuo' fá l' american! Tu vuo' fá l' american!
>
> *"Tu vuo' fá l' americano"* 1956

You want to be americano, 'mericano, 'mericano

You were born in Italy

Used to living a la moda, But if you drink Whisky and Soda

All you do is sing off key,

You dance the rock 'n roll, you play at baseball those cigarettes you smoke
leave mama broke they should only make you choke
You want be americano, 'mericano, 'mericano you were born in Italy!
Don't you know it's not New York city, Okay Napulitan,
You want to be American,
American, American.

English version sung by Sofia Loren in It Started in Naples, 1960

Reducing US life to values that are right on the tip of Edward Hall's famous iceberg model of culture (Hall 1976) might be amusing at first. However, the song does display a number of what seem to be casually chosen features to portray a culture. Just as the complexity of Italian culture can be reduced to food in an attempt to identify Italian-ness outside the Italian community, this song reduces the USA to cigarettes and rock and roll. But, for an American audience, mention or occurrence of food such as spaghetti and pizza that typify Italian culture in scores of movies is always good for a laugh. Stanley would like to murder his wife for many reasons, amongst which is her insistence on feeding him too much: "Stanley, darling. *Rigatoni, pollo, vino rosso* ... Lunch. *Mangia tutto*." Not only does Mrs. Ford make her husband gain weight on her diet of lasagne and sizzling Italian sausages, but she also transforms his ex-bachelor pad into an Italian delicatessen by hanging salami and cheeses from the ceiling. It makes sense that some audiences might actually believe that it is the norm to find salami and provolone hanging from the ceilings of Italian homes, although nothing could be further from the truth.

In order to promote *The Millionairess* (1960), in which Peter Sellers plays the part of Ahmed el Kabir, an Indian doctor, and Sofia Loren plays an arrogant heiress, the two actors recorded a comedy duet titled: "Goodness Gracious Me." Nowadays it would be unthinkable for a non-Asian to play the part of an Indian doctor in the film, let alone for him to put on a derisive pseudo-Indian accent. At the time, however, both film and record were a huge success and led to a second recording by the duo, this time contrasting Italian Sofia with cockney Sellers. The lyrics of the song play on the Italian obsession with food—already present in films such as *How to Murder your Wife*—with *Bangers and Mash*:

Sellers sings:

I met 'er down in Napoli and didn't she look great
And so I brought 'er back to Blighty just to show me mates

And though we're married 'appily, I'll tell ya furthermore
I 'aven't 'ad a decent meal since Nineteen-Forty-Four.[3]

The Millionairess 1960

The reason for Sellers' angst in the song lies in the fact that Loren nags him to "Eat your minestrone, Joe!" and "Eat your macaroni, Joe!" when what he really wants is "a bash at the bangers and mash me muvver [mother] used to make." Significantly, at a certain point, the couple switches roles. Loren begins to ask for bangers and mash in a cockney accent and Sellers for *tagliatelle* and vermicelli in an Italian accent. While Loren's attempt at cockney is acceptable (she simply drops her aitches and changes her vowel sounds), Sellers' Italian accent is macaronic and rather disparaging.

7. Different cultures, different values

We have considered so far a number of films in which Italians are depicted as stereotypical others, reduced to fast-talking pasta-eaters. In *It Started in Naples* (1960), before Mike Hamilton (played by Clark Gable) falls in love with Lucia (played by Sofia Loren), his idea of Capri is that of a "terrible place [...] No washing machine. No ice cubes. No peanut butter. The end of the world." This way of thinking is very much in line with a vision of Italy as a pre-industrial society compared to up-to-the-minute USA. There may be no reference to pasta in this stereotype, but people living on Capri in 1960 were experiencing the threshold of an economic boom, and most of them certainly owned, or were about to own, both a washing machine and a refrigerator.

The Latin Lover is another Italian stereotype. Marcello (played by Raul Bova) flatters American Francesca (*Under the Tuscan Sun*) by telling her that she has "beautiful eyes" and that he wishes he "could swim inside them." This makes Francesca laugh because " ... that's exactly what American women think Italian men say." Francesca then goes on to explain that she "was married for a long time, and since then there hasn't, there hasn't been anybody. Would you like to help me change that?" When Marcello asks her to confirm that she is asking him to sleep with her he laughs and says: "That's exactly the kind of thing Italian men think American women say."

In *La Ragazza con la Pistola* [*Girl with a Pistol*] (1968), Assunta Patané, a stereotypically hot-blooded Sicilian (played by Monica Vitti), is surprised that her English boyfriend John (played by Anthony Booth) prefers watching rugby on television to making love. John is absorbed by a rugby match on television and Assunta tells him that she is puzzled by the fact that they are alone at home and all he does is watch sports. Feeling encouraged by her remark, John makes a pass at her, but not only does Assunta resist his advances, but she physically and violently keeps him away:

Assunta *Ma tu che uomo sei?*

John *No comprendo* (continues watching television) Come on . . . come on . . .

Assunta What man are you?

John What?

Assunta You look television two hours. *Due ore.*

John I am watching sport er . . . rugby. I *gioco*, play rugby. *Sabato io gioco. Voglio vedere* shhh,

Assunta *Ma come, tu uomo, io donna, nessuno in casa e tu* look television?

John Oh, you're a little love!

John is confused and says: "I don't understand, *non capisco sei tu che mi hai provocato* [I don't get it, you provoked me]." Assunta replies in broken, simplified Italian: "*Vero uomo ci deve provare ma vera donna si deve difendere* [Real man has to try, but real woman has to defend herself]." Rejected, John goes into another room and slams the door, locking it behind him. "*Ma come? Tu ti chiudi a chiave* [What? You lock yourself in?] " asks Assunta. This scene plays into the old southern Italian stereotype that true masculinity encompasses an ability to seduce women, while a true woman is expected to defend and retain her virginity until she is married. The joke in this scene, of course, is that Assunta really wants to be seduced, but her boyfriend is unwilling to put in the effort.

Being able to ignore what their wives say was seen as a benefit for husbands in the movies of the 1950s and 1960s. Several sexist gags in films of that era played on the commonplace perception that women talk too much. When Stanley Ford (*How to Murder your Wife*) goes to his lawyer to begin divorce proceedings, his attorney is quite surprised that he is complaining that his wife cannot speak English.

Attorney My God, you're right. She is Italian. You mean that she doesn't speak A-N-Y E-N-G-L-I-S-H?

Stanley Not one word.

Attorney Not a word? You lucky devil!

How to Murder your Wife, 1965

The implication of this "joke" is that wives (women) talk far too much, that the inability of a wife to speak English is a definite advantage for a man, and that Stanley should consider himself lucky. Apart from talking too much, wives in jokes to this day spend too much of their husband's money (Chiaro 2018, 80–83). *How to Murder your Wife* takes the concept of wives' overspending a step further by rendering it bilingual: when Stanley's attorney, Harold, meets Mrs. Ford, he tells her how much he pays for his wife's Italian lessons.

8. Conclusions

This chapter provides an overview of the role of humor in romantic fiction on screen. In over a century of cinema, countless films have been made involving bilingual-cross-cultural couples. Having taken into consideration a handful of films that are mainly in English, I am well aware that I have only scratched the surface of the subject at hand. In fact, English is almost always the dominant language in my sample, and not only because the movie itself was produced in Hollywood or the UK. English is the dominant language because of its social and global importance, and the couples in my examples all reflect a relationship in which the English partner is in some way dominant—even in the Italian and French movies I have examined.

In these films, the concept of "verbal foreignness" adopted for humorous means clearly emerges together with some kind of "cross-talk" as a source of humor. The occurrence of humor combined with romance on screen frequently reveals underlying feelings and attitudes. These feelings may be of superiority, as when the speaker mocks the other. Or they may be kindhearted. Although the subject matter of romantic comedy itself may be lightweight, in the sense that drama inherently possesses more cultural capital than comedy, tracing conflict and confusion engendered in cross-linguistic and cross-cultural communication in relationships in general might prove illuminating in a wider context.

Undoubtedly, many of the films discussed in this chapter highlight linguistic fetishism. Languages other than English are adopted for symbolic purposes rather than for purely instrumental reasons. It often appears that the "other" language gives added value to the film as a whole, and in most of the cases examined, the value that it adds triggers laughter. One thing that comes across is how easily the native speaker of English can, either deliberately or in good faith, ridicule the speech of the foreign "other." In a world where political correctness in speech is paramount, it is surprising that in the name of comedy, linguistic diversity can become the butt of humor. Yet at the basis of much good humor, we find bad taste. It may well be that these films provide a safe place, a haven, in which to joke freely and where no offense will be taken by the person who is the butt of the humor. Finally, as more multilingual audiovisual texts are produced and circulated, their content opens up new and surprising avenues for future research.

Glossary

Mock Language: Code-switching that involves the insertion of terms in a minor language, often with a pejorative attitude.

Mutual Intelligibility: The ability of speakers of different but related languages to understand each other effortlessly without actually knowing each other's language.

Postcarding: Inserting words (usually commonly known) in the language of the narrative's location.

Translanguaging: Switching between languages while mixing them within a single linguistic system.

Translation Based Monolingual Target-Language Wordplay: An utterance in one language that creates a pun or a humorous effect in the target language.

Notes

1 See "The Supermarket Scene" (2013) for an accessible online version.

2 See "Grumpier Old Men Outtakes" (2014) for a number of unused takes of the Supermarket scene.

3 See "PETER SELLERS & SOPHIA LOREN" (2009) for an accessible online version.

References

A Fish Called Wanda (1988), [Film] Dir. Charles Chrichton, UK: MGM.

"A Fish Called Wanda (1988)," (n.d.), *Internet Movie Database*. Available online: http://www.imdb.com/title/tt0095159/?ref_=tttr_tr_tt (accessed September 3, 2017).

Another Time, Another Place (1983), [Film] Dir. Michael Radford, UK: Channel 4 Films.

Atomic Blonde (2017), [Film] Dir. David Leitch, USA/UK/Germany.

Avanti! (1972), [Film] Dir. Billy Wilder, USA: United Artists.

Buonasera Mrs. Campbell (1968), [Film] Dir. Melvyn Frank, USA: United Artists.

Canby, V. (1984), "Another Time, A British Import, Opens," *New York Times*, July 11. Available online: http://www.nytimes.com/movie/review?res=9B05E1D9143AF932 A25754C0A9629 48260&mcubz=1 (accessed September 10, 2017).

Charney, M. (1978), *Comedy High and Low: An Introduction to the Experience of Comedy*, New York: Oxford University Press.

Chiaro, D. (2004), "Comparison of Print and Web Advertising of Italian Agro-Food Products," *The Translator*, 10 (2), 313–329.

Chiaro, D. (2009), "Cultural Divide or Unifying Factor? Humorous Talk in the Interaction of Bilingual, Cross-cultural Couples," in N.R. Norrick and D. Chiaro (eds.), *Humor in Interaction*, 221–232, Amsterdam: John Benjamins.

Chiaro, D. (2015), "Mimesis, reality and fictitious intermediation," in R. Antonini and C. Bucaria (eds.), *Non-professional Interpreting and Translation in the Media*, 23–42. Frankfurt: Peter Lang.

Chiaro, D. (2018), *The Language of Jokes in the Digital Age*, London: Routledge.

Cronin, M. (2009), *Translation Goes to the Movies*, London: Routledge.

Daly, T.A. 1936, *Selected Poems of T. A. Daly*, San Diego (CA): Harcourt Brace.

Dances with Wolves (1990), [Film] Dir. Kevin Costner, USA: Orion Pictures.

De Bonis, G. (2014), "Dubbing Multilingual Films Between Neutralization and Preservation of Lingua-cultural Identities: A Critical Review of the Current Strategies in Italian Dubbing," in M. Pavesi, M. Formentelli, and E. Ghia (eds.), *The Languages of Dubbing*, 243–266, Frankfurt am Main: Peter Lang.

De Bonis, G. (2015), "Tradurre il multilinguismo al cinema: Lingue, Identità culturale e loro rappresentazione sullo schermo [Translating Multilingualism at the Movies: The Representation of Language and Cultural Identity on Screen]," PhD thesis, University of Bologna.

Delabastita, D. (2005), "Cross-language Comedy in Shakespeare," *HUMOR International Journal of Humor Research*, 18(2): 161–184.

Ervin-Tripp, S. (1968), "An Analysis of the Interaction of Language, Topic and Listener," in J. Fishman (ed.), *Readings in the Sociology of Language*, 192–211, The Hague: Mouton.

Grumpier Old Men (1995), [Film] Dir. Howard Deutch, USA: Warner Bros.

"Grumpier Old Men Outtakes" (2014), [video clip] Posted by Lane P, *YouTube*, June 14. Available online: https://www.youtube.com/watch?v=gvt_ql10G-A (accessed September 11, 2017).

Hall, E.T. (1976), *Beyond Culture*, New York: Anchor Books.

Heiss, C. (2004), "Dubbing Multilingual Films: A New Challenge?" *META*, 49(1): 208–220.

How to Murder your Wife (1965), [Film] Dir. Richard Quine, USA: United Artists.

It Started in Naples (1960), [Film] Dir. Melville Shavelson, USA: Paramount Pictures.

La Ragazza con la Pistola [*Girl with a Pistol*] (1968), [Film], Dir. Mario Monicelli, Italy: Documento Film.

Les poupées russes (2005), [Film] Dir. Cédric Klapisch, France: Studio Canal.

Love Actually (2003) [Film] Dir. Richard Curtis, UK: Working Title Films.

Meek, B.A. (2006), "And the Injun Goes 'How!' Representations of American Indian English in White Public Space," *Language in Society*, 35(1): 93–128.

Otheguy, R., O. García, and W. Reid, (2015), "Clarifying Translanguaging and Deconstructing Named Languages: A Perspective from Linguistics," *Applied Linguistics Review*, 6(3): 281–307.

"PETER SELLERS & SOPHIA LOREN—'Bangers And Mash'—45rpm 1961" (2009), [Video Clip] Posted by VinylFun, *YouTube*, February 21. Available online: https://www.youtube.com/watch?v=aGFpVN2xwXU (accessed September 11, 2017).

Pocahontas (1995), [Film] Dir. Mike Gabriel and Eric Goldberg, USA: Walt Disney Pictures.

Roman Holiday (1953), [Film] Dir. William Wyler, USA: Paramount Pictures.

Sherzer, J. (2002), *Speech, Play and Verbal Art,* Austin: University of Texas Press.

The Talented Mr. Ripley (1999), [Film] Dir. Anthony Minghella, USA: Paramount Pictures and Miramax.

The Last Samurai (2013), [Film] Dir. Edward Zwick, USA: Warner Bros.

The Millionairess (1960), [Film] Dir. Anthony Asquith, UK: 20th Century Fox.

"The Supermarket Scene" (2013), [video clip] Posted by YoureAJagOff, *You Tube*, November 9. Available online: https://www.youtube.com/watch?v=xNU3B4BqbPU (accessed September 21, 2017).

"*Tu vuo' fá l' Americano* [You wanna be American]" (1956), [Song lyrics] Composers: Nicola "Nisa" Salerno and Renato Carosone, Italy: Pathé.

Under the Tuscan Sun (2003), [Film] Dir. Audrey Wells, USA/Italy: Touchstone Pictures.

Wahl, C. (2005), "Discovering a Genre: The Polyglot Film," *Cinemascope*, 1. Available online: http://www.cinemascope.it (accessed July 31, 2012).

"They have eyes, but they [could see better]"

Editor's Introductory Note

Chapter 6 addresses an innovative and theoretically exciting field of study: Media Access Services. Captioning, audio descriptions, podcasts, and audio guides have been the subject of a growing area of research within Audiovisual Translation Studies. New creative technological opportunities, a growing demand, and accessibility requirements have made this a pertinent issue, first for the hard of hearing and the visually impaired, but later for a growing audience that recognizes the benefits of such services. One moves quickly from the moral imperative of aiding the disabled to the benefits for the sighted and the hearing, which are described in this chapter. Such benefits include cognitive benefits, linguistic benefits, aesthetic benefits, and social benefits. In other words: sighted people can understand better, learn more, enjoy more, and share texts with visually impaired colleagues, friends, and family members. In addition, studies suggest that sighted people have a better understanding of academic materials when they study with the aid of audio descriptions.

This chapter introduces the reader to the complex world of Media Access Services, and many of the ways in which audio descriptions already effect all of us through audio guides, podcasts, audio books, and other materials. It also lays the theoretical grounds to viewing audio descriptions as annotated translations that become important texts in their own right, sometime with equal or greater significance than the artifacts, texts, and objects that they describe. Some theoretical questions might follow: Does the object still supersede its description? Which is more important: The text or its mediation? The artifact or the description? The original or the translation? The chapter describes the benefits of audio description for sighted people within the paradigm of a universal design—an inclusive approach to environmental planning that strives to cater to the needs and expectations of as many users as possible. In this manner, the discussion does not only extend the definition of translation to commentary, and perhaps an original secondary text, but highlights the important realization that all of us are blind and hard of hearing to some extent, and that all of us need as much help as we can receive to understand the world around us.

Audio Description for All? Enhancing the Experience of Sighted Viewers through Visual Media Access Services

Iwona Mazur

1. Introduction

Audio description (AD) has been created with visually impaired persons (VIPs) in mind. It gives them access to the visual semiotic codes that would otherwise remain inaccessible to them. However, AD can also benefit and be enjoyed by sighted persons. As noted by Lou Giansante (n.d.), a writer and producer of museum audio tours meant for both sighted and visually impaired visitors, "[s]ighted people have come to expect descriptions of what their eyes can see easily," as such tours "can focus attention, making for a richer experience." In addition to being a guiding tool, AD can potentially have a number of other cognitive, linguistic, experiential (aesthetic), and social benefits, enriching the experience of persons with no visual impairment. The benefits will be discussed in the chapter below, preceded by a brief definition of AD and its primary recipients, and followed by the Universal Design paradigm applied to AD.

2. Audio description and its primary recipients

Audio description, sometimes referred to as video description or described video (Piety 2004: 453), is a type of transfer involving verbal representation of visual content of a film, a TV show, a theater play, an opera performance, a museum exhibition, a sports event, or possibly any other event that includes visuals, such as a rodeo or a funeral (Snyder 2007). Depending on the object of description, what is usually described are the spatio-temporal setting, characters, actions (in a film, a theater play or an opera performance), works of art such as paintings, sculptures, installations at an exhibition, or the performance of players or athletes at a sports event. AD can be live (theater, opera, sports event) or recorded (film, TV, museum), static (museum) or dynamic (film, theater, opera, sports event). In the case of dynamic AD, it has the form of an additional narration track that is inserted between dialogs and/or other meaningful sounds.

Using Roman Jakobson's (1966) tripartite division of translation (interpretation of the verbal sign), AD is considered an example of intersemiotic translation, though in the reversed form, i.e., describing images with words (Díaz Cintas 2005: 4). Though this definition is now commonly accepted, it is somewhat imprecise, as AD can also be isosemiotic—it can include the description of sounds that are difficult to decipher, but are essential to understand film narrative. So rather than treating it as *inter*semiotic, it seems more appropriate to classify it as *multi*semiotic.[1]

Since AD compensates for the visual code, its primary addressees are persons with visual impairments. This group includes people with both complete and partial loss of sight, such as loss of peripheral vision due to glaucoma; loss of central vision related to macular degeneration; or cloudy vision caused by cataracts. According to the World Health Organization (WHO) statistics, there are 253 million people with visual impairment around the world, including 36 million blind people and 217 million people with moderate and severe sight impairment, 81 percent of whom are fifty years of age or older. Only a small percentage of VIPs are born blind; most acquire the impairment through accident or illness, with the main medical causes being: uncorrected refractive errors (57 percent), un-operated cataracts (25 percent), age-related macular degeneration (4 percent), glaucoma (2 percent), and diabetic retinopathy (1 percent) (WHO 2017). These figures suggest that the vast majority of visually impaired people have partial vision or have lost their sight later in life, which means that they have some residual vision or have access to visual memory.[2] Furthermore, it is estimated that of those registered or registrable as blind in the UK, only 18 percent have no usable sight at all, which indicates that the remaining 82 percent can see something, though to varying degrees, depending on the nature of their impairment (ITC 2000: 6). This has some major implications for audio description: while it is commonly believed that AD is created first and foremost with completely blind people in mind (especially ones who have no visual memory), it should be created to primarily benefit those who do have some sight (or access to visual memory). Such AD could then be possibly more beneficial or acceptable to fully sighted persons, as discussed below.

3. Secondary recipients of audio description

Although, as noted above, AD is primarily targeted at the visually impaired as a way of allowing them access to the visual media by replacing the visual semiotic code, the group of potential recipients of AD is broader and includes persons without visual impairments (e.g., ADP 2009: 3; Remael et al. 2014: 17). In fact, results of a study carried out across the UK indicate that sighted persons are "potentially the largest audience to benefit from audio description" (ITC 2000: 7).

The group of potential sighted AD beneficiaries is broad and includes children with learning difficulties and attention deficits, the elderly whose cognitive abilities deteriorate with age, as well as viewers who simply find it hard or confusing to follow a fast-paced action movie or to keep track of a detailed story line. For example, in the already mentioned UK study, a group of sixty-two elderly admitted that audio description contributed to a better understanding and enjoyment of a police drama they watched as part of the study (ITC 2000: 7). But also people with no apparent cognitive challenges can enjoy or benefit from AD, such as foreign language learners who receive an additional linguistic input to the already present dialog exchanges in a film; average "sighted folks who see but who may not observe" (ADP 2009: 8); or simply those who watch or listen to television in the background. A study in which 1,000 sighted viewers were interviewed concerning their television viewing habits revealed that 39 percent of them watch television as background to other tasks that they may be doing at the time (such as cooking, knitting, ironing, etc.) in which case AD is very useful for them as they follow the show. Some of them reported that they tend to record their favorite programs with AD to listen to them later on in the car or on a train (ITC 2000: 7).

Unsurprisingly, most AD research to date focuses on the ways in which audio description can benefit VIPs as the primary recipients of AD (e.g., Frazier and Coutinho-Johnson 1995; Peli et al. 1996; Schmeidler and Kirchner 2001). However, AD scholars begin to recognize the potential of audio description also for persons with no sight impairment. For example, Elisa Perego (2016) conducted a study involving 125 sighted individuals between 18 and 28 years of age, divided into three groups: one watching a 10-minute film excerpt without AD (standard group), one with AD (AD group), and one with AD, but in a blindfolded condition (blindfolded group). The participants were then asked comprehension and appreciation questions. The primary aim of the study was to test the cognitive and evaluative effects of AD on sighted persons.

Louise Fryer and Jonathan Freeman (2012 and 2013) conducted a study in which they presented a video clip in three conditions: without AD, with standard AD (drafted in accordance with the Ofcom AD guidelines), and with cinematic AD (including filmic terms such as "a wide shot" or "cut to a close shot") to three groups of respondents: those with no usable vision, with some usable vision, and fully sighted. The studies' objectives were to learn the preferences of the participants as to AD style and to measure the degree of the sense of presence (including, for example, immersion in the film narrative) using the Independent Television Commission's Sense of Presence Inventory (ITC-SOPI).

Other studies concentrate on the manner in which audio description can be used as an additional or alternative tool to the traditional teaching methods in mainstream schools for sighted children. A group of Polish researchers (Krejtz I. et al. 2012, Krejtz K. et al. 2012) conducted an eye-tracking experiment with a view to ascertaining whether AD could support multimedia content used in educational settings (in this case a biology class). The participants were forty-four elementary school children with no visual impairment, divided into two groups: one group watched two clips from the educational film, *Once upon a Time ... Life*, with audio description (the experimental group), and the other without (the control group). All of the participants' gazes were recorded using an eye-tracker. The viewing session was followed by scene recognition tests and interviews. The research hypothesis was that the experimental group would better understand the educational content of the film (as their attention would be guided to its more essential and informative parts) and would retain more specialized vocabulary.

Another group of studies is one that explores the feasibility of using AD in a foreign language classroom. For example, in the Audio Description as a Didactic Tool to Improve (Meta)linguistic Competence in Foreign Language Teaching and Learning (ARDELE) project, 113 Dutch native speakers learning Spanish as a foreign language, aged between 20 and 22, were given audio description tasks to complete both in class and at home. They were later asked to reflect on the learning process. The aim of the project was to assess whether AD can be an effective tool for improving language skills (especially writing), increasing idiomaticity, motivating learners, and enhancing their metalinguistic competence (Ibáñez Moreno and Vermeulen 2013 and 2018). Agnieszka Walczak (2016), on the other hand, conducted a study on the use of AD as a didactic tool for foreign language acquisition (with English being the language concerned) involving thirty-six sighted and partially-sighted learners (aged 7–10 years) with Polish as their mother tongue. The tested materials were selected episodes of an animated educational series for teaching children English as a foreign language. The subjects were divided into two groups: one watching the clips with AD and the other without. They were then asked questions about the film's content and acquired vocabulary, the hypothesis being that the children (both sighted and partially sighted) watching the film with AD will outperform the other group on both counts.

Finally, as some AD guidelines suggest, and as has been indicated above, a significant target audience of AD are persons with cognitive challenges, such as children with learning difficulties or attention deficit hyperactivity disorder (ADHD). As it turns out, another potential group of AD beneficiaries may include persons with social and communicative issues. In a novel study conducted by Kim Starr (2017), autistic children, who exhibit "theory of mind" and emotion recognition deficits, were presented with three types of AD. The first was a standard visually-descriptive AD, which replaces the missing visual information for VIPs. The other two were bespoke ADs meant to explain the emotional states experienced by film protagonists: an emoto-descriptive AD that identifies and labels the emotions, and an emoto-interpretive AD that also contextualizes the emotions through a reasoning of cause-and-effect. The study involved a group of boys of 9–14 years of age, diagnosed on the autism spectrum, with average or above-average IQs and good reading and writing skills. They were shown ten film or TV extracts, each depicting one emotion that is described using the above methods. The viewing sessions were followed by an emotion recognition test and an interview in order to determine which AD type is most effective when it comes to deciphering the emotions felt by the protagonists.

Selected results of the above-mentioned studies will be referred to when discussing possible benefits of AD below.

3.1 Potential benefits of audio description for its secondary recipients

There are a number of benefits sighted viewers can possibly draw from AD, which could be roughly categorized into cognitive, linguistic, experiential (aesthetic), and social. Examples of such benefits falling under each of the categories are discussed below.

3.1.1 Cognitive benefits

It is assumed that when blind viewers watch a film with AD they have a better understanding of the plot, as the visual details they miss are verbalized for them in a manner that makes a coherent whole, and they can make the necessary links between the sounds, dialogs, and described visual content. A number of studies confirm that, in comprehension tests, those exposed to audio described materials perform better than subjects watching or listening to a program without AD (e.g., Frazier and Coutinho-Johnson 1995; Peli et al. 1996; Schmeidler and Kirchner 2001).

The question is whether viewers with no visual impairment can also draw similar benefits, as the AD supports what is conveyed via the visual code. The opinion that they draw such benefit is in line with the Dual Coding Theory, according to which people can store new information both through a verbal code and through a visual code. The two modalities reinforce each other and facilitate comprehension and information retrieval (Paivio 1986). In the case of AD, what is fed through the visual channel in the form of images (be they dynamic or static) is reinforced verbally in the form of the verbal commentary. Perego's findings (Perego 2016) seem to confirm the positive cognitive effects of AD, as stipulated by the Dual Coding Theory, for AD. In her study, the persons who watched the film clip with AD outperformed the other two groups when it comes to recognizing visual details expressed verbally (e.g., naming the color of a ribbon which is both visible on screen and described in the AD). Moreover, the AD group claimed that the AD was very helpful in understanding the whole of the film excerpt. Similar results were obtained by Krzysztof Krejtz et al. (2012), who found that in a scene recognition task, following a viewing session of an educational film for children, the group who had seen the episode with AD made decisions based on recognition (they fixated their gazes longer on scenes they had already seen), rather than elimination (i.e., fixating the gaze on unfamiliar scenes), as was the case for the control group who had not listened to AD. This suggests that AD helps store information in the memory and confirms the hypothesis that memory retrieval is strengthened when information is fed via multiple channels, in this case both visual and auditory.

Moreover, in the study reported by Izabela Krejtz et al. (2012), it was confirmed that AD helps the children focus their visual attention on the salient elements in the film. For example, in the experimental group, the children looked longer at a virus mentioned in the AD (the episode in question concerned blood), whereas the control group fixated their gaze on it less often. Furthermore, the AD suggested an order for looking at the individual elements of the scene, and the result was that children concentrated on such elements for a longer period. This, in turn, helped them better understand the educational message of the film and better memorize specialist vocabulary.[3] This is in line with the findings of Walczak (2016), who notes that the positive impact of AD could be observed when it comes to plot comprehension and recall of story elements. The AD group in her study could recount the story much more effectively, giving more details, including those concerning the appearance of characters.

In the case of autistic children, it seems that AD can serve as a form of narration, explaining elements that children on the spectrum struggle with, i.e., reading the emotions of others and interpreting their intentions ("mind reading"). In this case, AD could be conceived of as a tool that helps them learn "through the intellect" (as these children tend not to learn by observation). Starr's preliminary findings (Starr 2017) suggest that autistic children can benefit from bespoke AD variants that make use of dianoic ("between minds") strategies. The participants in Starr's study found both the emoto-descriptive strategy that identifies and labels the emotions ("Addie's extremely angry") and the emoto-interpretive one ("Addie's very angry with Moses because he's taken her money") helpful in understanding the protagonists' emotions and states of mind, with a slight preference for the former method. This shows that adopting a functionalist, skopos-based approach to audio description broadens the scope of potential beneficiaries of AD to include persons with communicative and social challenges.

Based on the premise that AD can be a tool that guides the visual attention of sighted viewers, as discussed above, and that audio describers should have increased visual literacy that allows for informing "even the sighted but casual observer" (ADP 2009: 4), AD may aid the sighted viewer in noticing significant details that may otherwise escape their attention. For example, in one of the first scenes of a film titled *Chopin. Pragnienie miłości* [*Chopin. A Desire for Love*] (2002), a young Frédéric Chopin receives a note after a private concert from a woman in the audience. The note says: "I adore you."[4] This small detail marked the beginning of a passionate love affair between the young pianist and the French writer, George Sand. The note is hardly visible on the screen and is likely to be missed during a casual viewing of the film. However, it was noticed by the Polish audio describer and included in the AD. In this way, the viewers, including the sighted ones, were clued early on to the affair that developed throughout the film, and learned an actual fact about the affair of the two lovers.

Since audio description is a type of translation, the audio describer—same as the translator—is also an intercultural communicator, especially when they describe a work set in a cultural context different than the one the AD's target recipients live in or are familiar with.[5] And much like translators, they may encounter cultural bumps[6] (Leppihalme 1994) or "translation crisis points" (Pedersen 2011: 42) that are related to extra-linguistic cultural references, which are also known as culture-bound terms, culturemes, cultural terms, or culture-specific items. Such items may range from geographical locations, to food, to everyday objects.[7] In the case of audio description, culture-specific items are included in the visual layer of an audiovisual text, and should somehow be rendered in the verbal commentary, much like in the case of translation. Translators have a range of strategies or procedures at their disposal to tackle such crisis points, and so do audio describers who resort to strategies such as explicitation, naming, generalization, specification, or retention (Szarkowska and Jankowska 2015).[8] For example, in the movie *The Wedding Planner* (2001), the main character, Maria, strides the streets of San Francisco, in which the film is set. In the background one can see the city's landmark buildings, such as the Transamerica Pyramid. To sighted persons, especially non-Americans, this cultural reference may not be known, so if the building was named in the AD, the viewers could learn something new about San Francisco's landscape and American culture in general. Along similar lines, Agnieszka Szarkowska and Anna Jankowska (2015) give the example of the famous commercial skyscraper in London, 30, St. Mary Axe (formerly known as the Swiss Re Building). In the Polish AD of Woody Allen's *Matchpoint* (2005), in which the building appears, the building is described using its informal nickname "the Gherkin" (Szarkowska and Jankowska 2015: 251–252).[9] Although the primary aim of the strategy was to familiarize the visually impaired viewers with the famous building, one can imagine that mentioning the name of the building could benefit the sighted audience in that they could learn the name of this prestigious location in London. Other examples mentioned by Szarkowska and Jankowska (2015) include: Tate Modern, the Moulin Rouge, and the London Eye. Such choices can be referred to as a retention strategy that introduces both visually impaired and sighted viewers to various ethnographic references and cultural terms. The Polish AD of *Midnight in Paris* (2011) familiarizes viewers with the famous French game, *boules* ("men play boules"), and the Polish AD of *Memoirs of a Geisha* (2005) introduces them to *okiya*, the Japanese name for the geisha house (Szarkowska and Jankowska 2015: 255).[10]

Finally, cognitive benefits can be drawn by sighted viewers from audiointroductions (AIs), which normally precede theater plays or opera performances, but can also be successfully used for films (Fryer and Romero Fresco 2014). In addition to some general information about a given production, this piece of running prose usually includes information on its style, music, camerawork in the case of film, the set and costumes in the case of live performances, etc. Although some of the information (such as the description of characters) may be superfluous for viewers without visual impairment, it is easy to imagine that they can learn more about a production they are about to see, as in the following example:

> Inglourious Basterds—the words misspelled I.n.g.l.o.u.r.i.o.u.s. B.a.s.t.e.r.d.s.—is set during World War II. But while the locations are realistic and characters such as Goebbels, Hitler and Winston Churchill resemble their real-life selves, one of the lead actors, Christoph Waltz, has described the film as "a piece of art. Not a history lesson." It's brutal but darkly funny, and Tarantino includes plenty of anachronisms. The music includes Morricone's Spaghetti Western-style themes lifted from other movies, and the flourish of an electric guitar accompanies a character's name as it flashes up on-screen, in bold, cartoon-style lettering. [...] In contrast to Tarantino's other films, like *Pulp Fiction* and *Kill Bill*, much of this movie is shot in unobtrusive, classic Hollywood style, and as close as he could get to glorious technicolour. This makes the moments where the camerawork deliberately draws attention to itself all the more remarkable. A doomed character walks forward in slow motion, crisply picked out as the background blurs. Or the camera closes in and lingers on a glass of milk, or a bowl of cream, bringing it to our attention.
>
> Fryer and Romero Fresco 2014: 14–15

Having listened to such an AI prior to watching the film, the sighted viewer can pay particular attention to the filmic language, something they may have ignored otherwise. They also receive extra information about the film's publicity (Waltz's quote) or about some of the ways in which it compares to the style of the director's other movies.

3.1.2 Linguistic benefits

Since AD is an additional narration track containing information expressed verbally, it can be assumed that it contributes to language development of its listeners. A number of studies have confirmed that AD can help boost visually impaired children's literacy and language acquisition. For example, AD accompanying educational films has been found to be a useful tool in environmental and biology classes (Walczak and Szarkowska 2012), as well as during lessons in history, biology, and physics (Walczak and Rubaj 2014), especially as regards acquisition of specialized vocabulary, use of synonym, similes, and metaphors. Palomo López (2008) has also found that watching programs with AD promotes vocabulary development and improves the pronunciation of blind children.

According to Perego, AD "seems a powerful tool that can be duly exploited in aiding literacy development, language acquisition and language learning" (Perego 2016: 440). It can be beneficial for both sighted persons and VIPs, mainly thanks to the dual coding mechanism discussed in section 3.1.1. Perego's statement has been corroborated by Krejtz I. et al. (2012), who found that in interviews following viewings of an educational film with AD,[11] the children in the experimental group were far more likely to spontaneously use the newly acquired vocabulary than their counterparts from the control group, and were better able to explain its meaning (an example being the highly specialized term, "mitosis"). In Walczak's (2016) study, the main focus of which was foreign language learning through AD,[12] the experimental videos were dubbed and audio described in Polish (the pupils' mother tongue), while the English vocabulary items to be learned in each episode were left in the original. In addition, the episodes were preceded by AIs in Polish focusing on character description. In a post-viewing exercise conducted in the children's mother tongue, those who had seen the episodes with AD described the characters using more vivid language, including words, phrases and similes taken out directly from the AD (e.g., "eyebrows like two earthworms"; "body like two boxes"). In fact, it turns out that the AD group used 40 percent more vocabulary items than the non-AD group. These results clearly point to linguistic benefits for young learners, when it comes to developing mother tongue competence.

As already mentioned above, another area of AD application is foreign language learning. Although in Walczak's (2016) study there were no statistically significant differences between the AD and non-AD groups when it came to new English vocabulary acquisition, the AD group did perform better. This insignificant difference could possibly be contributed to the fact that there was only one vocabulary item to be learned from each episode, rendering this a fairly simple task, either with or without AD. More studies involving more complex tasks are thus needed in this area. One such study, with college students as participants, is the ARDELE project,[13] in which it was found that AD-based tasks were highly motivating for Dutch-speaking students learning Spanish, as the output that they produced had a potentially significant functional and social value (it was created with the blind viewer in mind). Also, the AD exercises fostered the development of the writing skills and communicative and interpersonal competence of the students, as well as of their idiomaticity and phraseology in the foreign language. Moreover, the learners had to reflect on their learning process. As a result, their metalinguistic and metacognitive competences also increased (Ibáñez Moreno and Vermeulen 2013 and 2018).

Based on the above-mentioned findings, it could be assumed that an average-sighted person watching an AD film or program, whether in their native tongue or in a foreign language that they are learning, could draw linguistic benefits similar to those obtained by participants of the studies. It is highly probable that whenever an AD contains new information or an unfamiliar word, which is properly used in context and accompanied by the relevant image, a sighted person is likely to become familiar with them. A good example of a genre in which such terms abound are period films, which often depict items no longer used in everyday life. For instance, in *Marie Antoinette* (2006), a film which recounts the life of the Austrian-born French queen, the audio description often includes terms referring to the reality of the eighteenth-century France and court, such as clothing items, furniture, or different types of courtiers. For example, in one of the initial scenes, the newly arrived Marie Antoinette is touring her chambers in the Palace of Versailles:

> Inside the palace, in a magnificent circular chamber, lit by a huge crystal chandelier, with tall windows hung with blue drapes, with chairs upholstered in blue brocade, footmen in blue livery carry flower arrangements, and then a blue and gold wig box.
>
> *Marie Antoinette* (AD) 2006

Later, at breakfast, the queen sits with her newly married husband at a long, food-laden table, surrounded by her courtiers who "curtsy" all the time:

> The Dauphine, wearing a delicate white-blue dress and a ruffle around her slender neck, drinks water.
>
> *Marie Antoinette* (AD) 2006

From the above audio descriptions, had they not known the terms before, the viewer can learn the name of the trimming on a dress, customarily donned by upper-class ladies in eighteenth-century Europe ("ruffle"); the exquisite fabric type used in the palace ("brocade"); what uniforms worn by servants are called ("livery"); or, finally, the anachronistic verb "curtsy," which also appears in the AD numerous times.

Another group of films that have the potential of "teaching" new vocabulary to those watching them with AD are films set in a cultural context significantly different from the one of the viewers.[14] In such films, the audio description often names the foreign concepts, which otherwise would most likely remain unknown for the target viewer. For example, in the Iranian film, *A Separation* (2011), a drama telling the story of a Teheran-based couple on the verge of splitting up, the Polish audio describer choses to familiarize the viewer with the names of garments associated with the Muslim culture:

> Razieh takes off a cape covering her body, a jlbab. Her hair and neck are covered with a chimar.
>
> *A Separation* (AD) 2011

More examples can be found in the Polish audio description of the Saudi Arabian film, *Wadjda*[15] (2012), which Polish audio description includes terms such as: "abaya," "niqab," and "burqa." Moreover, the terms are explained using the specification strategy,[16] as in the following example:

> The man is wearing a white tunic down to his ankles, his head is covered with a *ghutra*, which is a white and red-checkered *arafat* head scarf. On the *ghutra* there is an *igal*—two black cord rings.
>
> Walczak and Figiel 2013

Admittedly, such explanations are likely to be found more useful by the visually impaired audience that does not have access to the visual layer of the film. But one can imagine that such a brief definition can also be helpful for viewers with full vision in the comprehension and retention of the vocabulary item in question. It should be noted that although the above benefits have been classified as linguistic, as they foster vocabulary acquisition, they might as well be considered cognitive, as the viewers learn about the reality of a foreign culture.[17]

3.1.3 Experiential (aesthetic) benefits

In addition to the cognitive and linguistic benefits discussed above, there are benefits that could be classified as experiential or aesthetic, meaning that a person's experience when watching a film with AD or visiting an audio described museum exhibition is simply more enjoyable and helps them better appreciate the aesthetic dimension of a given work or event. After a cinema screening of *Afonia i pszczoły* [*Afonia and the Bees*] (2009), a 100-minute long film with only five minutes' worth of dialogs, a sighted person (who had watched the film without AD) said that she neither enjoyed nor understood the film, while her visually impaired companion (having seen it with AD) exclaimed that she loved the film (Künstler September 27, 2017). Had the sighted person chosen to put on the headset in the cinema and turn AD on, perhaps her reception of the film would have been more positive. And although this is purely anecdotal evidence, it does point to the fact that audio description can enhance the enjoyment of a film.

One way that AD can bring out the aesthetic value of a film is by reflecting its camerawork. By using different types of shots, camera angles, camera movements, or lighting techniques, film creators guide the attention of the viewers, build up tension, or convey the emotions experienced by the protagonists in a film (e.g., Bordwell and Thomson 2013). For example, close-ups can signify intimacy, whereas slow motion can help create suspense. And although most of the time viewers do not have to be aware of the different techniques to appreciate a given film, sometimes—especially in films where the filmic language is rich and meaningful—awareness can influence film reception. According to Jerzy Płażewski (2008), filmic language should be learned in order to fully understand and recognize the worth of filmic art. He even talks about "filmic illiteracy" and stresses that not every film is meant for an average viewer in the same way that not every literary work is meant for all readers. We have already mentioned that filmic language can be described in an AI and thus better prepare the viewer (both sighted and visually impaired) for the aesthetic experience ahead of them.[18] But filmic language can also be reflected in the audio description itself, for example, by using filmic terms such as "a close-up," "a panoramic view," or "the camera draws closer." And although the jury is still out as to whether sighted viewers are willing to welcome such terms in AD (Fryer and Freeman 2012), in the case of more artistic films, AD can be a tool that helps the sighted audience to access the rich visual layer of such works.

Another way to account for camerawork in AD is to reflect it in the language of the description. For example a close-up could be conveyed by placing what is being focused on by the camera in the subject position of a sentence (e.g., "A hand packs cookery books into a box"). A good example of a film in which AD integrates filmic language is *Maska* [*The Mask*] (2010), a 23-minute digital animation based on a short story under the same title by Stanisław Lem, Poland's best known science fiction writer. The film—set in a technologically advanced yet feudal world—is very visual, and most of the shots are dark and repetitive, with flashes of white light. It is woven around the monologue of the main character, who, at the beginning of the film is being born (transformed) in front of the viewers' eyes. The Polish audio description, for which there is ample time (because the film contains little dialog), actually sounds like it was originally part of the film, and does enhance its somewhat psychedelic visual layer. The approach of the audio describer is to convey the rich filmic language, not by using filmic terms (such as "a close-up"), but by reflecting it in the very language of the AD. It should be noted that Polish, with its elliptical structures and flexible word order, renders itself better than, for example, English (with the rigid subject-verb-object order), for such purposes. To provide one illustration of this approach, the repetitive filmic sequences have been reflected using repetitive language structures, as in the following example:

> She raises her hands from hips to breasts, from hips to breasts. She raises her hands from hips to breasts. She raises her head. She raises her head.
>
> *Maska* (AD) 2010

The description is read out by a professional actor who varies the tone of his voice and the intonation: as the camera draws closer to the female protagonist, his voice becomes louder and his reading becomes faster. He in fact sounds like a narrator in the film, and it can be safely assumed that the experience of some of the sighted viewers would be greatly enhanced by his presence, both in terms of explaining and complementing the complex visual and verbal layers of the film.[19]

The aesthetic dimension of a film or a theater play could potentially also be augmented using alternative methods of describing such as "auteur audio description." Traditional AD "focuses on the description of what is seen—the set, actors' movements, and lighting—rather than on what is meant to be seen—the director's vision" (Udo and Fels 2009: 179). Auteur AD, on the other hand, "incorporates the director's creative vision in the AD scripts" and is aided by a screenplay, interviews, or reviews, thus giving the audio describer "the artistic license to depart from the dictate of objectivism" (Szarkowska 2013: 383). Such audio description does not shy away from subjective interpretations; it may include metaphors, descriptions of emotions, and allusions to filmic language. When the AD is screenplay-based, it may feature the auteur-director's idiolect or reflect his writing style. It may also be replete with neologisms, unconventional similes, or stylistically marked vocabulary (Szarkowska and Wasylczyk 2014: 49). For example, Raimunda, the lead female character in Almodóvar's *Volver* (2006), played by Penelope Cruz, was described in the Polish AI to the film as "firmly grounded by her luscious rounded bottom and her bosom," words taken verbatim from the screenplay (Szarkowska 2013: 384). And although the primary aim of such an AD is to "immerse spectators who are blind or have low vision in the story world created by the film's director" (Szarkowska 2013: 383), it can be assumed that, thanks to such a description, sighted viewers are also offered an opportunity to better experience the aesthetic world created by the director. Another example of such experimental AD is a description of a cartoon show titled *Odd Job Jack* (2003–2007). The description is written from the vantage point of, and told by the main character. In the comparison to a standard version of the show, blind and vision impaired viewers chose the version with AD as more entertaining (Fels et al. 2006). A similar solution was applied in the audio description of a popular German children's movie, *Bibi Blocksberg* (2002), in which the audio describer adopts the voice of the father of the title character. The audio describer/father tells the viewers what happens to the little girl, but also shares his emotions with the audience, thus serving more as a narrator than an audio describer. This allows both sighted and blind children to enjoy the film even more (Benecke 2017). Finally, John Patrick Udo and Deborah Fels (2009) report on an alternative audio description that was created for *Hamlet*, which is delivered, not only from the point of view of one of the characters, Horatio, but also written using the iambic pentameter, a type of metrical line characteristic of Shakespeare's work. The following description of the set is an illustration of the technique:

> A home is now transformed into a maze
> As Hamlet passes through the castle halls;
> Upstairs to landings leading to more stairs
> Through secret chambers into hidden rooms.
>
> Udo and Fels 2009: 181

Again, such a description could be appreciated by sighted and blind spectators alike, as it is a work of art in itself.

Finally, sports AD is yet another area where persons without sight loss can have their experience augmented through audio description. When it comes to soccer, for example, the sighted fans who cannot watch a given game, whether live at a stadium or in the comfort of their own homes in front of the TV, usually listen to a live radio commentary. The genre, which has been successfully used by soccer fans for years, often favors "color commentary" over "action or play-by-play commentary," meaning that in addition to mentioning shots, passes, and fouls, commentators fill in the pauses with "more discursive and leisurely speech" (Holmes 2001: 247). Such "color commentary" usually includes random facts about the teams, players, and game officials. Moreover, radio commentaries often allow for silent pauses and can be quite emotional, with a high level of excitement expressed by the commentators. And although soccer audio describers do not shy away from either expressing their emotions or giving ample background information, their commentary—being primarily targeted at visually challenged fans—gives a more accurate description of the action, the field, the players, including their gestures and facial expressions, or even the stands and the fans at the stadium.[20] Furthermore, the descriptions are far from dry or clinical. They are often very lively, vivid, and colorful, as can be seen in the following example from the EURO 2012 game between the Czech Republic and Portugal:

> Fabio Coentrao got stabbed with Rezek's hip, did a double spin up in the air, and fell onto the grass, most likely, with a loud thud.
>
> Michalewicz 2014: 158

All in all, sports AD can be an effective alternative to traditional sports commentary in that the sighted fans receive the best of both worlds: On the one hand, they receive an accurate verbal rendition of the action on the field. On the other hand, they can tune into the energy and atmosphere at the stadium through the emotions shared by the audio describers-cum-commentators.

3.1.4 Social benefits

When discussing social benefits of AD, the first characteristic that normally comes to mind is the social integration of VIPs alongside sighted viewers and listeners (e.g., Cronin and King 1990; Pearson and Evans 2009; Piety 2004; Schmeidler and Kirchner 2001). Thanks to this mode of audiovisual transfer, they can participate in the social and cultural life, be it by watching TV alongside their sighted family members, going to the movies or the theater to enjoy a film or a play using closed AD via headphones, laughing or crying at exactly the same moments that their sighted companions do, cheering at a soccer game in sync with the rest of the fans, or going to the museum and using the available AD audio guide and then discussing the art and sharing their impressions from the exhibition.

But the situation could be reversed, and all of the above-mentioned situations could apply to a sighted person who might want to take along their visually impaired friend or family member to see a movie, a theater performance, or an exhibition in order to share experiences and create common memories. When it comes to museums, the idea of inclusivity is stressed by Giansante who remarks that the same audio tours for persons with and without visual impairments create "an inclusive experience with blind and sighted people enjoying an exhibition together" (Giansante n.d.). This view is echoed by the creators of the Open Art multimedia guide app meant for museum visitors both with and without sensory impairments:[21]

> Our goal is to enable different types of viewers, with or without hearing or visual impairments, to visit the museum together, without the need to attend special AD tours or sign language tours, which by definition target one group of visitors only.
>
> Szarkowska et al. 2016: 305

According to Eraldo Busarello (2013),[22] it is now still quite common for sighted persons and VIPs to watch films separately. Alternatively, the visually impaired watch films without AD alongside their sighted companions. However, based on the results of her study, Perego concludes that "AD does not seem to interfere much with [sighted] viewers' comprehension, memory and appreciation of the film," and that "mixed viewing situations where VIPs and sighted users enjoy the same film with AD are feasible" (Perego 2016: 437–439).

It is estimated that the biggest group among the visually impaired is over the age of sixty-five. The reason is the aging of society and age-related degenerative eye diseases such as macular degeneration or glaucoma (e.g., ADLAB 2012: 12). It is thus highly probable that having a VIP within the family circle will become a reality for most. It is then thanks to AD, especially and preferably in its universal design form, as discussed below, that sighted persons will be able to continue to spend time with their visually impaired close ones, sharing a social and cultural life.

4. Universal design in audio description

Given all the ways in which audio description can benefit sighted people as well as those with visual impairments, a question arises as to whether it can be integrated into products or works of art from their very inception, providing all users—irrespective of their physical or cognitive well-being—a choice as to whether to use it or not. After all, "AD is about democracy" (Snyder 2005: 16) and is meant to diminish the barriers between those with and without visual impairments. This is in line with the Social Model of Disability, which differentiates between a physical impairment (such as loss of a limb, or loss of sight in our case) and disability, which is defined as:

> [T]he disadvantage or restriction of activity caused by a contemporary social organization which takes little or no account of people who have physical impairments and thus excludes them from participation in the mainstream of social activities.
>
> Oliver 1996: 22, as quoted in Shakespeare and Watson 2001: 3–4

According to the model, it is the society that makes impaired people disabled through physical barriers such as stairs or high curbs, which make buildings or streets difficult or impossible to navigate by wheelchair users. Lack of audio description could also be construed as such a barrier, in this case to the visual world otherwise inaccessible to those with impaired sight. Gian Maria Greco (2014) even goes as far as suggesting that audio description could be considered a human right per se rather than a mere accessibility tool:

> In the case of accessibility and persons with disabilities, it would mean that accessibility is a right for persons with disabilities because they have disabilities, not because they are human beings. They have the right to accessibility because of their disability, not because of their humanity.
>
> Greco 2014: 20

Treating AD as a human right could therefore help lessen the "ghetto effect," whereby visually impaired populations are being excluded from society, and by the same token ensure a more inclusive society (Greco 2014: 20).

Such inclusivity could be achieved through Universal Design (UD; also known as "inclusive design," "accessible design" or "design for all"), a paradigm which assumes "the design of products, environments, programs and services to be usable by all people, to the greatest extent possible, without the need for adaptation or specialized design" (Ostroff 2011: 1.3). It is based on seven main principles (NDA 2018):

1. Equitable Use.
2. Flexibility in Use.

3. Simple and Intuitive Use.
4. Perceptible Information.
5. Tolerance for Error.
6. Low Physical Effort.
7. Size and Space for Approach and Use.

The goal of UD is not to create a "one-size-fits-all" solution, but rather one that can accommodate the needs of as many potential users as possible already at the design stage, which would help to avoid the usually high costs of retrofitting (Ellis 2016: 42). For example, a ramp or an elevator in a building will serve not only wheelchair users, but someone who has to carry a heavy suitcase as well. Similarly, the idea that curb cuts will make the lives of cyclists or mothers pushing strollers easier gave rise to a concept of equity known as the "Curb Cut Effect."

Although, originally, UD was mainly applied to the design of urban landscapes, it now has broadened its scope of application and can also be successfully used in audio description. Rather than being an afterthought (i.e., inserted at the postproduction stage, which is usually the case), AD could be accounted for from the very beginning of the production process and should involve the entire creative team, including the director. John Patrick Udo and Deborah Fels (2010a and 2010b) have applied the seven principles of UD to theater audio description. They stress that "[t]heatre directors are in a unique position [...] as they have a more direct access to audiences and adjustments can be made during a show's run" (Udo and Fels 2010b: 200). They point out that their film and television counterparts are less privileged in this respect, as they are detached from their audiences, and once a film is released it cannot be modified. Nonetheless, Pablo Romero Fresco (2013) demonstrates that UD (which he prefers to call "accessible filmmaking"[23]) is also feasible in film. He calls for making films accessible from the very beginning of the production process. By accessibility, Romero Fresco is not only referring to audio description or subtitling for the deaf and hard of hearing, but also translations into various target languages, all in collaboration with the film's creative team (Romero Fresco 2013: 218). He demonstrates that this is feasible both through the example of a 12-minute documentary he directed himself, and by referring to other independent and mainstream films in which the idea of accessible filmmaking has been applied successfully.

Another area where UD can be successfully employed is museum audio description. A case in point is the Open Art project. A part of this project, already mentioned above, is a multimedia guide app for selected Polish museums. The app serves visitors both with and without sensory impairments (hearing and visual; Szarkowska et al. 2016). The idea behind the project is that the needs of various audiences would be accommodated already at the app's design stage and its elements (including the description of a given work of art itself), balanced in such a way so that they would not be overwhelming for any of the audiences concerned. The app—which can be used on mobile devices—includes short videos along with audio narration, subtitles, and sign language interpreting. Its content is expandable, as museums can add new information, in new languages, if this is what a given museum needs or desires. It thus complies with most of the UD principles, including the principles of physical effort, size, equitable use, and perceptible information.

To sum up, the idea of UD, as applied to audio description, can prove to be an effective tool for ensuring equal access to visual media for VIPs, and for making AD optional for sighted persons.

5. Discussion and conclusion

In the sections above, a number of possible benefits that could be drawn from AD by sighted viewers have been discussed. This section will focus on discussing possible challenges in implementing an "AD for all" approach. It seems that whereas AD could be quite welcome by sighted persons at sports events or museums, where they are already used for some kind of commentary, either by a sports commentator or an (audio) guide, they may find it difficult to accept an additional narration track in a film, a TV show, or a theatrical performance.

First, some viewers may think that audio description interferes with or distorts the original vision of the film director or creator. Moreover, this view could possibly be shared by the authors of the works concerned.

Second, different audiences (both sighted and visually impaired) may have different expectations as to the degree of detail or the style of AD. For example, congenitally blind persons may require more narrative descriptions, whereas viewers with low vision may expect the AD to be more descriptive, as it assists them with recognizing images which they cannot see clearly or which they can only see a part of. Both challenges could however be addressed—at least to some degree—using the above-mentioned UD or accessible filmmaking approaches aimed at a middle-of-the-road solution catering to the tastes of as many target viewers as possible, and involving the authors of a given work from the very start in AD creation (though, admittedly, there may be a need for bespoke ADs created for specific target groups, such as the discussed autistic children who may need a tailor-made AD that would fulfill a therapeutic function).

Third, some sighted persons may find it distracting to have visual information "repeated" verbally (despite the possible cognitive and linguistic benefits discussed above). Although a group of full vision study participants who had been watching AD programs with VIPs for a year reported that they found it unobtrusive (Cronin and King 1995), findings by Perego (2016) and Fryer and Freeman (2012) indicate that persons without visual impairment achieve greatest engagement levels when watching films without AD. According to the latter scholars, a lesser preference for audio described programs may in fact be the result of repetition of information and cognitive overload:

> Sighted people were less immersed when visual information was replicated verbally, challenging them to compare what they saw with what they were being told by the describer. These multiple sources of information may have added to their processing load, with a negative effect on presence.
>
> Fryer and Freeman 2012: 19

In addition, the authors explain that the sighted participants could have been distracted by visual information from the surroundings (which is not the case for blind viewers or even those with low vision who usually sit close the screen). Further, what could have an impact on the results was sound level reduction, which was applied in order to accommodate the AD commentary and the resultant loss of some auditory details.

Finally, and perhaps most importantly, "verbal commentary is not a normal part of 'reality' for sighted people" (Fryer and Freeman 2012: 19). On the other hand, Perego (2016), concludes that despite the slight preference of sighted participants in her study for a film clip with no AD, "the addition of AD does not dramatically affect the overall satisfaction of the film experience and the effort required to follow it" and that "[o]verall, the results reinforce the view that watching a film is a cognitively effective process that is not affected by the addition of extra semiotic stimuli [e.g., in the form of] oral texts inserted between dialogues" (Perego 2016: 438–439). As the above findings are inconclusive, more studies should be conducted on the effect of AD on the cognitive load of its recipients (both sighted and visually impaired).

The above notwithstanding, it seems that the mentioned limitations and challenges could be mitigated, at least to some extent. For example, the cognitive load could be lessened if the descriptions were more balanced, not too wordy or detailed, and thus not too taxing for the viewers. This again would require experimental studies in order to determine the amount of description that might be excessive, or how much detail can be provided without overloading the cognitive capacities of the audience and risking that their concentration will lapse several minutes into a film (e.g., Fresno et al. 2014). Another important consideration is the proper mixing of the AD commentary with the existing dialogs and soundtrack in terms of timing and sound level so that AD does not interfere with important sounds, and is neither too loud nor too soft. Also significant are the voices reading out audio description, which should always be pleasant to listen to. The enunciation should be impeccable, and the reading should match film genre, style, and tempo. The AD narration should not conflict with the voices already present in a film, and audio description should allow the film (and the audience) to breathe, which means that not all pauses should be talked over. The end result should be an audiovisual product in which AD blends in so smoothly with the existing sounds that after some time the viewer becomes unaware that they are watching a production with an additional narration track.

A possible remedy to some of the problems mentioned above would be greater exposure of sighted persons to audio description, assuming that if they watched more productions with AD, they would be more open to this form of audiovisual transfer, in line with the "Mere-exposure Effect," according to which people develop a preference for the formats they are familiar with (Zajonc 1968).

To conclude, unlike people with visual impairment, sighted persons do not *need* audio description, but they may *want* to enjoy the cognitive, linguistic, experiential, or social benefits it offers, ranging from noticing minute but significant details in a film, acquiring new vocabulary, whether in the mother tongue or in a foreign language, "watching" a game of soccer in their mind's eye while driving, or touring an exhibition with their visually impaired friend and sharing their impressions about the paintings they both "have seen." As AD is a fairly novel solution, it will surely be opposed by some sighted persons, but they should have the choice to turn it on while watching a film at home (similar to the way in which they switch on subtitles in their native tongue), to listen to it via wireless headphones in a theater, to borrow an AD audio guide set at a museum, or download an AD app onto their mobile phones. It is thanks to the UD approach—catering to the needs and expectations of as many users as possible—that this choice could be made available.

Glossary

Audio Description (AD): Making visual media accessible to visually impaired persons by means of a verbal commentary.

Universal Design (UD): A paradigm which assumes designing buildings, products, and environments that are usable by all people, to the greatest extent possible, without the need for adaptation.

Visually Impaired Person (VIP): A person with a decreased ability to see to a degree that causes problems that cannot be corrected with usual means (e.g., glasses or contact lenses); the term also covers persons with complete or nearly complete loss of vision.

Visual Media: A term covering works or events that require visual competence in order to be engaged, such as films, television programs, theatrical performances, opera, athletic events, paintings, sculptures, etc.

Notes

1 See, for example, Fryer (2016: 4).
2 Also see Hollins (1985), as quoted in Fryer and Freeman (2012: 2).
3 We will return to the topic of vocabulary retention in section 3.1.2. on linguistic benefits.
4 Unless indicated otherwise, all translations from Polish sources are mine.
5 On intercultural communication in translation see e.g., Katan 2004.
6 "Cultural Bumps" is a part of the title of Ritva Leppihalme's book (Leppihalme 1994).
7 For a classification see Díaz Cintas and Remael (2007: 201).
8 Also see Mazur (2018) for a discussion of crisis points in AD and the proposed strategies.
9 All translations from this source are by Szarkowska and Jankowska (2015).
10 See section 3.1.2. on linguistic benefits for more examples of culturemes in AD.
11 See sections 3.1 and 3.1.1.
12 See sections 3.1 and 3.1.1 as well as the paragraph below.
13 See section 3.1.
14 Also see section 3.1.1 for cultural references in AD.
15 In places that the title is not translated, the same title is used in the English language version.

16 See section 3.1.1.

17 See section 3.1.1 for more examples.

18 See section 3.1.1.

19 For more examples of camerawork reflection in AD see Chmiel and Mazur 2014: 195–252.

20 For a comparison between sports AD and sports commentary also see Kulak (2014).

21 See section 4.

22 As quoted in Perego (2016: 427).

23 "Accessible filmmaking" is a part of the title of Romero Fresco's article (Romero Fresco 2013).

References

A Separation (2011), [Film] Dir. Asghar Farhadi, Iran: Filmiran (Iran) and Sony Pictures Classics (US).

ADLAB (2012), Report on user needs assessment. Report no. 1, ADLAB (Audio Description: Lifelong Access to the Blind) project.. Available online: http://www.adlabproject.eu/ (accessed January 8, 2018).

ADP (2009), "Audio Description Standards: A Work in Progress," *Audio Description Project*. Available online: http://www.acb.org/adp/ (accessed December 7, 2017).

Afonia i pszczoły [*Afonia and the Bees*] (2009), [Film] Dir. Jan Jakub Kolski, Poland: Argomedia Production Lambros Ziotas.

Benecke, B. (2017), "Can you Believe it? An Experiment with 'Subjective AD' for Children." Paper presented at the 6th Advanced Research Seminar on Audio Description ARSAD, 16–17 March, 2017, Barcelona, Spain.

Bibi Blocksberg (2002), [Film] Dir. Hermine Huntgeburth, Germany: Constantin Film.

Bordwell, D. and K. Thompson (2013), *Film Art. An Introduction* (10th edition), New York: McGraw Hill.

Busarello, E. (2013), "Cos'è la Cooperativa Senza Barriere Onlus." Paper presented at the AD Day Seminar, University of Trieste, April 19, 2013, Trieste, Italy.

Chopin. Pragnienie miłości [*Chopin. A Desire for Love*] (2002), [Film] Dir. Jerzy Antczak, Poland: ITI Cinema.

Chmiel, A. and I. Mazur (2014), *Audiodeskrypcja* [*Audio Description*], Poznan: Wydział Anglistyki UAM.

Cronin, B.J. and S.R. King (1990), "The Development of a Descriptive Video Service," *Journal of Visual Impairment and Blindness*, 84 (10): 503–506.

Díaz Cintaz, J. (2005), "Audiovisual Translation Today: A Question of Accessibility for All," *Translating Today*, 4: 3–5.

Díaz Cintas, J. and A. Remael (2007), *Audiovisual Translation: Subtitling*, St. Jerome Publishing: Manchester.

Ellis, G. (2016), "Impairment and Disability: Challenging Concepts of 'Normality,'" in A. Matamala and P. Orero (eds.), *Researching Audio Description: New Approaches*, 35–45, London: Palgrave Macmillan.

Fels, D.I., J.P. Udo, P. Ting, J.E. Diamond, and J.I. Diamond (2006), "Odd Job Jack Described—A First Person Narrative Approach to Described Video," *Journal of Universal Access in the Information Society*, 5 (1): 73–81.

Frazier, G. and I. Coutihno-Johnson (1995), *The Effectiveness of Audio Description in Processing Access to Educational AV Media for Blind and Visually Impaired Students in High School*, San Francisco: Audio Vision.

Fresno, N.J. Castellà and O. Soler (2014), "Less is More. Effects of the Amount of Information and its Presentation in the Recall and Reception of Audio Described Characters," *International Journal of Sciences: Basic and Applied Research (IJSBAR)*, 14 (2):169–196.

Fryer, L. (2016), *An Introduction to Audio Description,* London and New York: Routledge.

Fryer, L. and J. Freeman (2012), "Audio Description and its Potential for Virtual Reality Applications," *Journal of Cyber Therapy and Rehabilitation*, 5 (1): 15–23.

Fryer, L. and J. Freeman (2013), "Cinematic Language and the Description of Film: Keeping AD Users in the Frame," *Perspectives: Studies in Translatology*, 21 (3): 1–15.

Fryer, L. and P. Romero Fresco (2014), "Audiointroductions," in A. Maszerowska, A. Matamala and P. Orero (eds.), *Audio Description: New Perspectives Illustrated*, 11–28, Amsterdam and Philadelphia: John Benjamins.

Giansante, L. (n.d.), "Writing Verbal Descriptions for Audio Guides." Available online: http://www.artbeyondsight.org/mei/verbal-description-training/writing-verbal-description-for-audio-guides/ (accessed January 10, 2018).

Greco, G.M. (2014), "On Accessibility as a Human Right, with an Application to Media Accessibility," in A. Matamala and P. Orero (eds.), *Researching Audio Description: New Approaches*, 11–33, London: Palgrave Macmillan.

Hollins, M. (1985), "Styles of Mental Imagery in Blind Adults," *Neuropsychologia*, 23: 561–566.

Holmes, J. (2001), *An Introduction to Sociolinguistics*, Essex: Pearson Education Limited.

Ibáñez Moreno, A. and A. Vermeulen (2013), "Audio Description as a Tool to Improve Lexical and Phraseological Competence in Foreign Language Learning," in D. Tsagari and G. Floros (eds.), *Translation in Language Teaching and Assessment*, 41–65, Newcastle: Cambridge Scholar Press.

Ibáñez Moreno, A. and A. Vermeulen (2018), "The ARDELE Project: Audio Description as a Didactic Tool to Improve (Meta)linguistic Competence in Foreign Language Teaching and Learning," in J. Díaz Cintas and K. Nikolić (eds.), *Fast Forwarding with Audiovisual Translation*, 195–211, Bristol: Multilingual Matters.

ITC Guidance on Standards for Audio Description (2000). Available online: http://www.ofcom.org.uk/static/archive/itc/itc_publications/codes_guidance/audio_description/index.asp.html (accessed December 3, 2017).

Jakobson, R. (1966), "On Linguistic Aspects of Translation," in R.A. Brower (ed.), *On Translation*, 233–239, Cambridge: Harvard University Press.

Katan, D. (2004), *Translating Cultures: An Introduction for Translators, Interpreters and Mediators* (2nd edition), Manchester and Kinderhook: St Jerome.

Krejtz, I., A. Szarkowska, A. Walczak, K. Krejtz and A. Duchowski (2012), "Audio Description as an Aural Guide of Children's Visual Attention: Evidence from an Eye-tracking Study," in *ETRA'12 Proceedings of the Symposium on Eye Tracking Research and Applications*, 99–106, NY, USA: ACM New York.

Krejtz, K., I. Krejtz, A. Duchowski, A. Szarkowska, and A. Walczak (2012), "Multimodal Learning with Audio Description: An Eye Tracking Study of Children's Gaze During a Visual Recognition Task," in *Proceedings of the ACM Symposium on Applied Perception* (SAP '12), 83–90, NY, USA: ACM New York.

Kulak, M. (2014), "Audio Description versus Live TV Commentary of Football Games—a Comparative Study," MA diss., Faculty of English, Adam Mickiewicz University in Poznan, Poznan, Poland.

Künstler, I. (2017), personal communication, September 27, 2017.

Leppihalme, R. (1994), *Culture Bumps: On the Translation of Allusions*, Helsinki: University of Helsinki.

Marie Antoinette (2006), [Film] Dir. Sofia Coppola, Japan/France/United States: Pricel, Tohokushinsha, American Zoetrope, Pathé.

Maska [*The Mask*] (2010), [Film] Dir. Stephen Quay and Timothy Quay, Poland: Se-ma-for Studios.

Matchpoint (2005), [Film] Dir. Woody Allen, United Kingdom/Luxemburg: BBC Films, Thema Production and Jada Productions.

Mazur, I. (2018), "Audio Description Crisis Points: The Idea of Common European Audio Description Guidelines Revisited," in J. Díaz Cintas and K. Nikolić (eds.), *Fast Forwarding with Audiovisual Translation*, 127–140, Bristol: Multilingual Matters.

Memoirs of a Geisha (2005), [Film] Dir. Rob Marshall, USA: Columbia Pictures.

Michalewicz, I. (2014), "Audiodeskrypcja po Euro 2012—zawrotne tempo akcji, czy para w gwizdek? [Audio description after Euro 2012]," *Przekładaniec*, 28: 153–162.

Midnight in Paris (2011), [Film] Dir. Woody Allen, USA/Spain: Sony Pictures Classics.

NDA (2018) "The 7 Principles," *National Disability Authority*. Available online: http://universaldesign.ie/What-is-Universal-Design/The-7-Principles/ (accessed March 2, 2018).

Odd Job Jack (2003–2007), [Television show] Dir. Adrian Carter and Denny Silverthorne Jr., Canada: The Comedy Network.

Ofcom Code on Television Access Services (2010). Available online: http://stakeholders.ofcom.org.uk/binaries/broadcast/other-codes/ctas.pdf (accessed November 21, 2017).

Oliver, M. (1996), *Understanding Disability: From Theory to Practice,* Basingstoke, UK: Macmillan.

Ostroff, E. (2011), "Universal Design: An Evolving Paradigm," in W.F.E. Preiser and K.H. Smith (eds.), *Universal Design Handbook* (2nd edition), 1.3–1.6, New York: McGraw-Hill.

Paivio, A. (1986), *Mental Representations: A Dual Coding Approach,* Oxford: Oxford University Press.

Palomo López, A. (2008), "Audio Description as Language Development and Language Learning for Blind and Visually Impaired Children," in R. Hyde Parker and K. Guadarrama García (eds.), *Thinking Translation. Perspectives from within and without,* 113–134, Boca Raton, FL: Brown Walker Press.

Peli, E., E.M. Fine and A.T. Labianca (1996), "Evaluating Visual Information Provided by Audio Description," *Journal of Visual Impairment and Blindness,* 90 (5): 378–385.

Pearson, R. and E.J. Evans (2009), "Boxed Out: Visually Impaired Audiences, Audio Description and the Cultural Value of the Television Image," *Perceptions: Journal of Audience and Reception Studies,* 6 (2): 373–402.

Pedersen, J. (2011), *Subtitling Norms on Television. An Exploration Focusing on Extralinguistic Cultural References,* Amsterdam and Philadelphia: John Benjamins Publishing Company.

Perego, E. (2016), "Gains and Losses of Watching Audio Described Films for Sighted Viewers," *Target,* 28 (3): 424–444.

Piety, P. (2004), "The Language System of Audio Description: An Investigation as a Discursive Process," *Journal of Visual Impairment and Blindness,* 98 (8): 453–469.

Płażewski, J. (2008), *Język filmu* [*Film language*] (3rd edition), Warsaw: Książka i Wiedza.

Remael, A., N. Reviers, and G. Vercauteren (eds.) (2014), *Pictures Painted in Words. ADLAB Audio Description Guidelines.* Available online: http://www.adlabproject.eu/ (accessed December 6, 2017).

Romero Fresco, P. (2013), "Accessible Filmmaking: Joining the Dots Between Audiovisual Translation, Accessibility and Filmmaking," *The Journal of Specialised Translation,* 20: 201–223.

Schmeidler, E. and C. Kirchner (2001), "Adding Audio Description. Does it Make a Difference?" *Journal of Visual Impairment and Blindness,* 95 (4): 197–212.

Shakespeare, T. and N. Watson (2001), "The Social Model of Disability: An Outdated Ideology?" in S. Barnarrt and B.M. Altman (eds.), *Exploring Theories and Expanding Methodologies: Where are we and where do we need to go? Research in Social Science and Disability* (Vol. 2), Amsterdam: JAI.

Snyder, J. (2005), "Audio Description. The Visual Made Verbal Across Arts Disciplines— Across the Globe," *Translating Today,* 4: 15–17.

Snyder, J. (2007), "Audio Description: The Visual Made Verbal," *The International Journal of the Arts in Society,* 2 (2): 99–104.

Starr, K.L. (2017), "Thinking Inside the Box: Bespoke Audio Description for Cognitively Diverse Audiences." Paper presented at the 6th Advanced Research Seminar on Audio Description ARSAD, 16–17 March 2017, Barcelona, Spain.

Szarkowska, A. (2013), "Auteur description—From the Director's Creative Vision to Audio Description," *Journal of Visual Impairment and Blindness*, 107 (5): 383–387.

Szarkowska, A. and A. Jankowska (2015), "Audio Describing Foreign Films," *The Journal of Specialised Translation*, 23: 243–269.

Szarkowska, A. and P. Wasylczyk (2014), "Audiodeskrypcja autorska," *Przekładaniec*, 28: 48–62.

Szarkowska, A., A. Jankowska, K. Krejtz, and J. Kowalski (2016), "Open Art: Designing Accessible Content in a Multimedia Guide App for Visitors with and without Sensory Impairments," in A. Matamala and P. Orero (eds.), *Researching Audio Description: New Approaches*, 301–320, London: Palgrave Macmillan.

The Wedding Planner (2001), [Film] Dir. Adam Shankman, United States: Columbia Pictures.

Udo, J.P. and D.I. Fels (2009), "Suit the Action to the Word, the Word to the Action: An Unconventional Approach to Describing Shakespeare's *Hamlet*," *Journal of Visual Impairment and Blindness*, 103 (3): 178–183.

Udo, J.P. and D.I. Fels (2010a), "The Rogue Poster-children of Universal Design: Closed Captioning and Audio Description," *Journal of Engineering Design*, 21 (2–3): 207–221.

Udo, J.P. and D.I. Fels (2010b), "Universal Design on Stage: Live Audio Description for Theatrical Performances," *Perspectives: Studies in Translatology*, 18 (3): 189–203.

Volver (2006), [Film] Dir. Pedro Almodóvar, Spain: Sony Pictures Classics.

Wadjda (2012), [Film] Dir. Haifaa al-Mansour, Saudi Arabia/Germany/Jordan/The Netherlands/The United Arab Emirates/The United States: Koch Media.

Walczak, A. (2016), "Foreign Language Class with Audio Description: A Case Study," in A. Matamala and P. Orero (eds.), *Researching Audio Description: New Approaches*, 187–204, London: Palgrave Macmillan.

Walczak, A. and W. Figiel (2013), "Domesticate or Foreignize? Culture Specific Items in Audio Description." Paper presented at Intermedia 2013 conference, 22–23 November 2013, Łódź, Poland.

Walczak, A. and M. Rubaj (2014), "Audiodeskrypcja na lekcji historii, bilogii i fizyki w klasie uczniów z dysfunkcją wzroku [Audio description in history, biology and physics classes for visually impaired learners]," *Przekładaniec*, 28: 63–79.

Walczak, A. and A. Szarkowska (2012), "Text-to-speech Audio Description to Educational Materials for Visually-impaired Children," in S. Bruti and E. di Giovanni (eds.), *Audiovisual Translation across Europe*, 209–233, Bern: Peter Lang.

WHO (2017), "Vision Impairment and Blindness," World Health Organization. Available online: http://www.who.int/mediacentre/factsheets/fs282/en/ (accessed December 8, 2017).

Zajonc, R.B. (1968), "Attitudinal Effects of Mere Exposure," *Journal of Personality and Social Psychology*, 9 (2, Pt. 2): 1–27.

7

Translating Translation

Editor's Introductory Note

Chapter 7 introduces the intricate representation of language in multilingual films within an ideal context: a country that recognizes eleven official languages. In the context of the contemporary South African linguistic landscape, it is easy to recognize the unique features of multilingual representation in film: every choice of the language of a dialog, code-switching, code-mixing, or attributing languages to particular characters, is a loaded statement about identity, culture, social hierarchy and political affiliation. The chapter is at once a fascinating tour of South Africa today, and of the complex use of its many languages in films that reflect its social, political, and economic realities.

The chapter goes on to explore this complexity when films are either subtitled or dubbed in French. Can either the subtitled or dubbed version preserve the multiple layers of meaning that are present in the original? Through an erudite and extensive study, the chapter examines the different techniques that are used to convey the complexities of multilingual films. The translator's choices are impacted by the challenge of linguistic choices that are not only a text in a foreign language to be translated. The translator must take into account that the alternation between languages is an imagined representation of a linguistic setting, and that the portrayal of the exchange between speakers of different languages is an evocative representation of intercultural translation.

Translating Multilingual Films in a
South African Context

Zoë Pettit

1. Introduction

Multilingual communities and societies are a common feature of today's globalized world. It is therefore no surprise that this multilingual reality is represented through film more and more frequently, presenting additional challenges and perhaps even opportunities for the audiovisual translator. As Jorge Díaz-Cintas and Aline Remael (2007: 230) point out: "Since film is a 'hybrid text of globalization' par excellence, films increasingly reflect the world's linguistic evolutions and mixes." Lukas Bleichenbacher (2008) offers an interesting analysis of the representation of multilingualism in Hollywood films, examining this growing phenomenon in depth. His focus is on different languages rather than variation in terms of dialect or register (Bleichenbacher 2008: 3), but he also considers code-switching which features in the films that are referred to here.

Multilingualism is fundamental to the South African context in a country which recognizes eleven official languages in its constitution. This chapter will explore a series of films which showcase the multilingual reality that is present in South Africa. Code-switching and code-mixing both feature highly and the particular variety that is South African English is an additional factor to consider as part of the translation process. What are the effects that are created in the original and do they have an impact on the French subtitled and dubbed versions? Which strategies are employed to allow the viewer to access these multiple layers of meaning that are present in the complex audiovisual text? The dialog and imagery recreate the South African context and multilingualism serves an important function. This study analyzes the role of multilingualism in the original films, the potential effect this may have on meaning, and the manner in which this impacts the choices that are made with regards to translation. Montse Corrius and Patrick Zabalbeascoa (2011: 113) propose that in addition to the language of the source text and that of the target text, first language (L1) and second language (L2) respectively, there is a third language (L3) in multilingual films. The third language in the source text is referred to as L3ST; and in the target text, or translation, the L3 is referred to as L3^{TT}:

> The third language is a feature of multilingual texts and communication acts. Each language (L1, L2, and any number of different L3ST and L3^{TT}) may be a distinct, independent language or an instance of relevant language variation, sufficient to signal more than one identifiable speech community being portrayed or represented within a text. Thus, L3ST may be a language variety (e.g., a dialect) of L1, (likewise for L3^{TT} with regard to L2). L3, then, may be either the representation or portrayal of a natural, living language, dialect or variety, or a fictitious, invented, language (e.g., Cityspeak).
>
> Corrius and Zabalbeascoa 2011: 114

Corrius and Zabalbeascoa refer to a corpus of eleven audiovisual texts (films and television series) to explore the various solutions that are available to the audiovisual translator. This includes examples where the original is unchanged, neutralized, or adapted (Corrius and Zabalbeascoa 2011: 120). The current analysis will examine the consequences of a multilingual source text in the translation processes of South African film, in an attempt to establish the different trends that can be mapped in relation to translation strategies.

In a subtitled version, the viewer hears when a different language is being used, although as Anna Vermeulen (2012: 311) points out in her article on audiovisual translation and heterolingualism, it would be worthwhile to test this observation. Following her analysis of a subtitled and dubbed Belgian film from Dutch into Spanish she concludes: "It would be interesting to investigate whether the Spanish viewers really detect code-switching in subtitled versions. Or are they so focused on reading the subtitles that they forget to listen?" (Vermeulen 2012: 311). We take it for granted that the viewers hear the change in language, but for some viewers who do not have a good command of the source text L1, code-switching may not be recognized. Is there any additional indication in the subtitles at the level of translation choice? In a dubbed version, the new soundtrack replaces the audio cues which indicate a shift in language. Is a different dubbing actor used? A different dialect? To what extent and how is the multilingualism of the original version retained? Are there any instances where it is not and why? Christine Heiss also proposes that there will be differences in approach depending on the type of film:

> In the case of auteur films that focus on a linguistic minority, even during the production phase, an attempt is usually made to reach an equivalence in the

multilingual depiction. This attempt must be made, since the multilingual reality must remain perceptible and believable in the translated version of the film. This would be possible (in many cases) even with dubbing. In this case, the target audience must be ready to change its attitude towards the languages that are represented in the dubbed film. In the dubbed version, the language spoken in the depicted county is replaced with the language spoken in another immigrant country in which the film is supposed to be dubbed. This requires the target audience to mentally accommodate this change, in a peculiar kind of "suspension of disbelief" (*Illusionspakt*).

> Heiss 2014: 21

This final point is of particular significance in that watching a dubbed film already requires suspension of disbelief. The audience listens to a dialog that has been transposed onto the actions, gestures, and image of the original film. Where the audiovisual text is situated within a multilingual reality, this creates further complexities regarding this notion of suspending disbelief. In an article that explores Italian dubbing of code-switching in a selection of British and American films, Silvia Monti (2014: 165) concludes that the strategies used "seem to highlight a new trend that privileges a more faithful rendering of the otherness of foreign languages and cultures. Code-switching gives vital clues about the immigrant characters' socio-linguistic hybrid identities and, as such, it is a very important feature of the filmic text." To what extent does this hold true for the films that form part of the current study?

All the South African films which are referred to in this chapter examine elements of South Africa's past with references to the journey of a new democracy in light of its troubled history. This is symbolized in phrases such as "The Rainbow Nation" or "The New South Africa." In a country with eleven official languages, it is unsurprising that multilingualism and code-switching occur frequently in everyday life. This is replicated and showcased in the films chosen for analysis. Throughout this discussion, the extracts will be considered in relation to the particular situation that is the multimodal audiovisual text with reference to French subtitled and dubbed versions.

2. The films: A multilingual reality

Sequences for analysis are drawn from the French DVD versions of four films: *Hijack Stories* (2002), *In My Country* (2007), *District 9* (2009), and *Invictus* (2009). The degree of multilingualism varies across the films and the viewer encounters a variety of (South African) English dialects, various African languages, and even invented speech in the case of *District 9*. The translation strategies are analyzed to establish the potential effects on the viewer.

The South African gangster subculture permeates *Hijack Stories*. Sox Moraka, a successful young actor from a wealthy suburb in Johannesburg (Rosebank), auditions for a popular television series, playing the role of a Sowetan gangster. *District 9* is a science fiction thriller, shot in the style of a documentary and parodies the apartheid regime. Aliens who have been forced to live in District 9, a violent shantytown situated outside Johannesburg, face imminent eviction by "Multi-National United," the organization responsible for containing the aliens. Whilst carrying out research on alien technology and their weapons, the main protagonist is exposed to a virus. This alters his DNA and during the course of the film he transforms into an alien himself. The eviction is reminiscent of events which occurred during the apartheid era when residents were forcibly removed from District Six in Cape Town. *In My Country* is based on a semi-autobiographical novel, *Country of my Skull* by Antjie Krog, which refers to historical facts. The film is a drama which is set shortly after the 1994 democratic elections and focuses on the Truth and Reconciliation Commission hearings which were organized to find justice for the human rights violations that occurred during the apartheid era. If perpetrators step forward to confront victims and tell the truth they may be granted amnesty. The female protagonist is a poet, Anna Malan, played by Juliette Binoche and loosely based on Krog. The last film which forms the basis of this study is *Invictus*. This film recreates events leading up to the 1995 Rugby World Cup in South Africa, with Nelson Mandela as the first black South African president. The main language of *Invictus* is English, but multilingualism does feature.

The dialog and imagery in the films recreate the South African context which includes multilingual citizens. The translator needs to consider the effect of code-switching and code-mixing in the original and make decisions as to whether it is necessary to retain code-switching in some form, or whether there are other more important elements which should drive the translation choices. This paper attempts to address two guiding questions:

1. Where multilingualism features in the original, what are the effects and do they have an impact on the French subtitled and dubbed versions?
2. Which translation strategies are adopted to allow the viewer to access the multiple layers of meaning that are created by multilingualism in the source text?

Each of the films depict South Africa's linguistic variety through dialogs that represent the different languages and the manners in which they merge through code-switching and mixing. Different English accents can be heard, and the dialog includes terms and concepts that are specific to the South African context, some of which may only be accessible to a South African audience. It is the translator's role to render the original audiovisual text accessible to a foreign and international audience. However, meaning exists at different levels. When a speaker switches to another language, this can also signify something other than what is actually being said. For example, it may indicate solidarity between two groups, as the speakers identify with a particular region or subset of society. At the level of translation strategy, Corrius and Zabalbeascoa (2011:127) explain that the translators "(or their commissions) decide the degree to which the third language is to be identifiable in the translation, which ranges from not marking it (invisibility) to clearly distinguishing between the in-group and the out-group by means of language variation." This is reminiscent of Lawrence Venuti (1995) and his seminal work on the invisibility of the translator, where the concepts of foreignization and domestication are presented. The former aligns the target text with the source language and culture, whereas the latter is closer to the target language and target culture.

3.　Translation choices

The examples which follow present the potential consequences of the translation choices. Looking more closely at the strategies in each of the films where multilingualism occurs, is it possible to identify any similarities or differences between their approaches? Have those involved in the translation or adaptation processes considered the effect that is created by having an additional language(s) appearing in the original film? Elena Voellmer and Patrick Zabalbeascoa (2014: 243) identify eight options in dubbing multilingual features present in the source text: 1) interlingual translation where the L3 is removed; 2) "transference" where an accent is used to imply that there is a shift; 3) "neutralisation" where the L3 is untranslated or deleted and therefore cannot be identified; 4) compensatory devices such as pronunciation or vocabulary; 5) verbatim transcription (a repetition of the original text in L3); 6) highlighting the ethnicity or nationality of a character through the use of specific vocabulary or non-native pronunciation; 7) adaptation where the L3 in the dubbed version is actually the same as the

L1 used in the rest of the film; and finally 8) adaptation where the L3 in the translated version is not one of any of the languages that appear in the original. Some of these options appear in the sequences chosen for analysis. The selected extracts have been divided into two broad sections to differentiate between instances where the multilingual elements present in the original have been removed, and others, where they have been retained.

3.1 Removal of multilingual elements from the target text

In the examples which follow, the multilingual source text and code-switching are not overtly indicated, although it could be argued that the informal register and slang used in the translated versions help to maintain the tone of the original.

In this example (Table 1) from *Hijack Stories*, people are lining up for an audition. The director's assistant steps out of the studio to ask them whether they have any forms or documents. He speaks to them in Sesotho, making sure everyone has understood the instruction. The subtitle offers a translation (Do you have a dossier?) and the audience is left to ascertain the language shift through the soundtrack. In the dubbed version, French dialog is added rather than inserting subtitles or using a different language to indicate the switch. This is an example in which the source language could have been retained as the meaning is clear from the visual clues. In the dubbed version, barely audible dialog is inserted which adds nothing in terms of what is actually said whilst simultaneously removing all traces of code-switching.

Table 1 Multilingualism removed (*Hijack Stories*)

Original version	Fr Sub	Fr Dub
Assistant: [in Sesotho] Mphe ta ma form, doc. [Give me your form, document.] English subtitle inserted: Hey, do you have all the forms?	Assistant: Vous avez tous un dossier ? [Do you all have a dossier?]	Hé, vous avez tous un script . . . [Hey, do you all have a script. . .]

In the next extract (Table 2), the speaker switches between English and languages used in Soweto, a township on the outskirts of Johannesburg:

Table 2 Multilingualism removed (*Hijack Stories*)

Original version	Fr Sub	Fr Dub
Sox: Hi Uncle, I'm Sox. Sox Moraka.	Bonjour, l'oncle. Je suis Sox Moraka. [Hello Uncle. I am Sox Moraka.]	Bonjour mon oncle. Je suis Sox, Sox Moraka. [Hello, my Uncle. It's Sox, Sox Moraka.]
Uncle Dan: [switches to Afrikaans] Ek kan sien. [I can see.] English subtitle inserted: I see . . .	Je vois bien. [I can see that.]	J'ai des yeux. [I have eyes.]
Jy lyk not soos daai mbomla Ou-Lady van jou. [You don't look like that ugly mother of yours.] English subtitle inserted: You look like that ugly mother of yours.	Tu es aussi laid que ta mère. [You're as ugly as your mother.]	Tu es aussi laid que ta pauvre mère dans ses mauvais jours. [You are as ugly as your poor mother on her bad days.]
My boy,	Mon fils, [My son,]	Mon fils, [My son,]
There's only one way to understand township life	Pour comprendre la vie au ghetto [to understand life in the township.]	Il n'y a qu'une seule solution pour comprendre la vie au ghetto [There is only one solution to understand township life]
That is to live township life.	il faut vivre au ghetto. [you have to live in the township]	C'est de venir vivre au ghetto. [that's coming to live in the township.]
Sox: But you see Uncle D for me to get this role	Mais oncle, pour avoir ce rôle [But Uncle, to get this role]	Mais tu sais oncle, je vais décrocher ce rôle [But you know, Uncle, I'm going to land this role]
My feelings are . . . I, I have to study it.	je sens que je dois l'étudier. [I feel like I have to study it.]	Et je me dis qu'il y a des choses à étudier. [And I tell myself that there are things to study.]
Uncle Dan: Well you learn by survival, that's all.	On apprend en survivant, c'est tout. [You learn by surviving, that's it.]	On les apprend en survivant, c'est tout. [You learn them by surviving, that's it.]
You don't survive, you don't learn.	Tu survis pas, t'apprends pas! [You don't survive, you don't learn!]	Tu survis pas, t'apprends pas! [You don't survive, you don't learn!]
Sox: Come on now Uncle Dan	Allons Uncle Dan [Come on Uncle Dan]	Je t'en prie Oncle Dan [I'm begging you Uncle Dan]

You've been one of these guys	tu as été un de ces hommes [you were one of these men]	tu as été un de ces hommes [you were one of these men]
Just show me things, you know.	Montre-moi les trucs. [Show me your stuff.]	qui . . . montre-moi les gestes c'est tout. [who. . . show me the moves, that's all.]
Uncle Dan: Ah [switches to Afrikaans] my laaitie, [switches back to English] I'm trying to forget that stuff. [my boy I'm trying to forget that stuff.]	Mon fils, j'essaie d'oublier ces choses. [My son I try to forget these things.]	Oui, mais petit, je me force d'oublier ces choses maintenant. [Yes, but young one, I now make myself forget these things.]
I used to be a bootlegger, used to drive liquor to the shebeens when it was illegal.	J'étais passeur d'alcool pour des bars, quand c'était illégal. [I smuggled alcohol for bars when it was illegal.]	J'étais dans le trafic d'alcool, mon truc c'était de fournir les bars du temps où c'était illégal. [I used to be involved in alcohol trafficking, my thing was to supply bars when it was illegal.]
I used to carry a gun.	Je portais un flingue. [I carried a gun.]	Je portais un flingue. [I carried a gun.]
But I'm not a gangster.	Mais je suis pas un gangster. [but I'm not a gangster.]	Mais je suis pas un gangster. [but I'm not a gangster.]
Just a businessman.	Juste un businessman. [Just a businessman.]	Juste un businessman. [Just a businessman.]
[switches to Afrikaans] Jy verstaan? [You understand?]	Tu comprends? [You understand?]	Tu comprends? [You understand?]
Sox: Yeah but how did it feel?	Mais tu éprouvais quoi? [But what did you feel?]	Mais dis-moi, qu'est-ce que tu éprouvais? [But tell me, what did you feel?]
How did you walk?	Tu bougeais comment ? [How did you move?]	Comment tu bougeais? [How did you move?]
What were your moves?	Tu opérais comment ? [How did you operate?]	Et comment tu faisais? [What did you do?]
Uncle Dan: [switches to Afrikaans] Jy sien, die ding is so . . . as jy een van die ouens is in die kasie [You see, the thing is like this, if you are one of guys in the township] English subtitle inserted: The thing is, if you're one of the guys in the township	Le truc, [The thing is] si t'es un homme du ghetto, [if you're a township man]	C'est important l'allure [The look is important.] Dans le ghetto, il faut faire reconnaître qui tu es. [In the township, you have to make a name for yourself]

Original version	Fr Sub	Fr Dub
Dan carry jy so . . . [Then, carry yourself like this.] English subtitle inserted: you walk like this.	tu bouges comme ça. [you move like this.]	Regarde. Je vais te montrer. [Look, I'll show you.]
–	–	Il y a les pas. Tu vois ça? Ça glisse. [There are steps. You see that? Gliding along.]
Man: Bra Dan! [Brother Dan] An English subtitle is not inserted.	–	Tout dans le rythme. [Rhythmically.]
–	–	Oui, en douceur, oui. [Yes, gently, yes.]
(Uncle Dan pretends to stab Sox while he is distracted by the dancing)		

All the switching between languages in this sequence is removed from the dubbed version. There are some colloquialisms, but for the most part the richness of the linguistic features in the original is diluted. The viewer of the dubbed version will have no idea that the speaker is switching from one language to another as French dialog is inserted throughout the dubbed version. The venue is a bar in a South African township, and we follow a conversation between an uncle and his nephew who is trying to understand township life. As the uncle immerses himself into this specific South African context, far removed from the affluent suburb where his nephew lives, the code-switching becomes all the more relevant. Different worlds collide and the way in which the code-switching is used here is a symbolic representation of the cultural tension in the film. Of course it is also part of the everyday South African reality where languages frequently come into contact and even merge to create pidgins such as Fanagalo, based on Zulu and Afrikaans, or the urban, township slang, Tsotsitaal, which mixes Zulu, Sotho, Tswana, Xhosa, Afrikaans, and English (Pettit 2011). The following extract from Table 2 illustrates this:

> *Jy lyk not soos daai mbomla Ou-Lady van jou.*
> You don't look like that ugly mother of yours.

"Jy lyk" (you look) is Afrikaans, "not" is English; "soos daai" (like that) is Afrikaans; "mbomla" is Zulu, which literally means "pumpkin," but is used in township slang to refer to an ugly person. "Ou-Lady," where "ou" (old) is Afrikaans and has been combined with "lady," which in township slang refers to mother; and "van jou" (of yours) is Afrikaans. The translations also reduce the implied irony by removing the negative construction: "You don't look like that ugly mother of yours," a back translation of the original, becomes "You look like that ugly mother of yours" (Original version), "You're as ugly as your mother" (Fr Sub), and "You are as ugly as your poor mother on her bad days" (Fr Dub). Another interesting example of code-switching and mixing occurs towards the end of the dialog, when Uncle Dan says: "Dan carry jy so." "Dan" (then) is Afrikaans, followed by "carry" in English, and then goes back to Afrikaans again with "jy" (you or yourself in this context) and "so" (like this or in such a way). Referring more generally to this sequence, the subtitled version chooses not to translate the Afrikaans dialog and uses a colloquial register that corresponds appropriately to the context. Towards the end of the extract, the dubbed version moves a step further and inserts dialog where there is none to translate. As the character dances, the French version describes his actions:

> *Dans le ghetto, il faut faire reconnaître qui tu es. Regarde. Je vais te montrer. Il y a les pas. Tu vois ça ? Ça glisse. Tout dans le rythme. Oui, en douceur, oui.*
> In the township you have to recognize who you are. Look. I'll show you. There are steps. You see that? Gliding along. Rhythmically. Yes, gently, yes.

This is an example which shows that the translator considered it necessary to add a dialog, even though, in reality, there is no need to do so. The actions are clear and the camera is not in close-up on the actor's face, so there is no specific need for lip synchronization. The additional dialog is therefore superfluous. However, it would have been appropriate to indicate the code-switching in other parts of the dialog as it corresponds to the physical location of the scene.

Similarly in the next extract from *Hijack Stories* (Table 3), the gangster character, Zama, switches to Afrikaans, as he says: "verstaan" (understand). In the original, this adds a menacing tone, an order that the protagonist must obey or disobey at his peril. In the previous table, "jy verstaan?" (you understand?) has a phatic function and the tone is conversational. In Table 2, removing "jy" (you) turns the utterance into an imperative. Again, the use of Afrikaans is deliberate. As a language formerly associated with oppression and the police force during apartheid (Silva 1997), this switch potentially carries these additional meanings with it. This is replicated to a certain extent in the French subtitled version with the very brief "compris" (understood). This effect is attenuated in the dubbed version with "C'est compris?" (Is it understood?):

Table 3 Multilingualism removed (*Hijack Stories*)

Original version	Fr Sub	Fr Dub
Zama: Never go near my family again.	Appoche plus jamais ma famille. [Don't ever go near my family.]	N'approche plus jamais de ma famille, t'entends? [Don't ever go near my family, you hear?]
I don't trust you and I never will.	J'ai pas confiance. J'aurai jamais confiance! [I don't trust you. I will never trust you.]	J'ai pas confiance. J'aurai jamais confiance! [I don't trust you. I will never trust you.]
[switches to Afrikaans] Verstaan? [Understand?] English subtitle inserted: Understand?	Compris? [Understood ?]	C'est compris? [Understood ?]
Sox: Look all I wanted . . .	Tout ce que je veux . . . [All I want. . .]	Ca m'a . . . [It. . .]
Zama: Heh! [Switches to Afrikaans] Verstaan? [Understand?] [English subtitle not inserted]	Compris? [Understood ?]	C'est compris ? [Is it understood ?]
Sox: Yes, yes (nods).	–	Oui, oui. [Yes, Yes]
Zama: OK.	–	OK.

In Table 4, a translation is also provided when the switch occurs:

Table 4 Multilingualism removed (*Hijack Stories*)

Original version	Fr Sub	Fr Dub
Sox: My name is Sox. They call me Sox.	Je m'appelle Sox. [My name is Sox.]	Je m'appelle Sox. Appelle-moi Sox. [I'm called Sox. Call me Sox.]
Gangster: Hey [switches to Zulu] wena, don't know any Sox here. [Hey you, don't know any Sox here] English subtitle inserted: I don't know any Sox around here.	Je ne connais pas de Sox. [I don't know a Sox.]	Ta gueule. Je ne connais pas de Sox sur terre. [Shut up. I don't know any Sox on this earth.]

[switches to Xhosa] U ngc weva? [You hear?] No English subtitle inserted.	D'où tu sors? [Where have you come from?]	Où elle est ta vie? [Where is your life?]
Gangster: Heh where do you come from? **Sox**: Oh, I stay in Rosebank.	– D'où tu es ? – J'habite à Rosebank. [Where are you from? I live in Rosebank]	– Où elle est ta maison ? – Ah, je crèche à Rosebank. [Where is your house? – Ah, I doss down in Rosebank.]
Gangster: Oh Rosebank. Get the fuck out back to Rosebank. [switches to Afrikaans] Voetsak, voetsak! [Get lost, get lost!] English subtitle inserted: Fuck off! Fuck off !	Retourne mourir à Rosebank! Casse-toi ! [Go back and die in Rosebank! Piss off!]	À Rosebank. Retourne t'en faire baver à Rosebank. Va chier, va chier. Casse-toi! [In Rosebank? Go back and have a hard time in Rosebank. Fuck you, fuck you. Piss off!]

Here we see that Sox does not actually understand the question. He is an educated, middle-class character who is trying to learn the way of gang members in order to appear in a television show. He is removed from a context in which slang and code-switching are the norm. English has become his main language. In this extract, a different strategy would have been possible. As the protagonist does not understand the question due to the switch in language and slang usage, it would have been perfectly reasonable to omit a translation. The viewer would then have been placed in the same situation as the character. The odd construction, "Où elle est ta vie" (Where is your life?) in the dubbed version, compensates for the fact that the language switch is not indicated. Code-switching also occurs in the original with the offensive Afrikaans term, "voetsak" (go away or get lost). The informal register is maintained in both subtitled and dubbed versions.

Up until this point, we have seen examples where the code-switching is not clearly indicated in the translations although there may be certain compensatory devices such as the particular use of colloquialisms and slang. What happens when code-switching occurs in the original and there is no accompanying translation in the original film? In *Invictus*, another film that forms a part of this study, there is a scene in which the L3 is not intended to be understood by the other characters. This is maintained in both versions. The exchange is not translated so that the target viewer is placed in a similar situation as in the original (Table 5):

Table 5 Multilingualism present but untranslated (*Invictus*)

Original version	Fr Sub	Fr Dub
[Detectives discuss between themselves in Afrikaans] Nou wanneer moet ons slaap? [When must we sleep] ...voor ons tande borsel. [...for brushing our teeth]	–	–
Black detective: What did he just say?	Il a dit quoi? [What did he say?]	Qu'est ce que tu viens de dire? [What did you just say?]
White detective: He asked when we're supposed to sleep.	Il demande quand on est supposés dormir. [He's asking where we're supposed to sleep]	Il a demandé quand nous étions censés dormer. [He asked when we're expected to sleep.]

This example indicates that both subtitled and dubbed versions have sought to achieve the same effect as the original. This is not always the case as will become evident in some of the examples that will be analyzed in the next section, which also includes sequences where multilingualism is either maintained or implied in the French versions.

3.2 Inclusion of multilingual elements in the target text

In *District 9*, street interviews are carried out, adopting the style of a documentary. Some interviewees speak in an African language, or Afrikaans, rather than English, which is the language used in most of the film. In these instances, the dialog fulfills an informative function and is therefore translated in both the subtitled and dubbed versions. In the dubbed version, the translation appears either in the form of French subtitles where the original dialog is retained, or dubbed dialogs are inserted. The former occurs in one example where the interviewee is speaking Tswana. She does not appear elsewhere in the film, so there are no challenges to overcome in relation to continuity. Regarding the latter, where the street interviews are dubbed, the switch in language is reinforced through the use of different accents or dubbing actors (Table 6):

Table 6 The use of accents (*District 9*)

Original version	Fr Sub	Fr Dub
1) **Young African Man 1** [South African accent]: I think they must fix that, that ship and they must go.	Qu'ils le réparent et partent. [They must fix it and leave.]	Je pense qu'ils devraient réparer leur vaisseau et foutre le camp d'ici. [French African accent] [I think that they should fix their ship and get the hell away from here.]
2) **Young African Man 2** [South African accent]: If they were from another country we might understand. But they are not even from this planet at all.	D'un autre pays, d'accord, mais pas des aliens. [From another country, OK, but not aliens.]	S'ils étaient de notre pays on peut comprendre mais ils sont même pas de la même planète que nous. [French African accent] [If they were from our country we can understand but they are not even from the same planet as us.]

Using both strategies contributes to the effect created by the variety of opinions that are expressed by the interviewees. The strategies help to reinforce this sense of variety. South Africans have different accents due to their L1 and this is brought to the fore in these scenes. Whilst the strategies are different, inserting subtitles or adding accents, the overall effect is the same in that the multilingual context is represented in the subtitled and dubbed versions.

The extract in Table 7 from *In My Country* shows Dumi, a black sound engineer, going to buy some beer from an Afrikaans shopkeeper:

Table 7 Multilingualism retained (*In My Country*)

Original version	Fr Sub	Fr Dub
Dumi: I'm back!	Me voilà! [Here I am.]	C'est moi! [It's me!]
[switches to Afrikaans] Hey Maurice, jy is die man! So hoe vier? [Hey Maurice, you're the man! So how much?] English subtitle inserted: Hey Maurice, you're the man! So how much?	Maurice! T'es champion. Combien? [Maurice! You're a champion. How much ?]	[switches to Afrikaans, same original dialog but no inserted subtitles]

Original version	Fr Sub	Fr Dub
Maurice: [still in Afrikaans]	39 rands, comme les autres. [39 rands, like the others.]	
Nege en dertig rande. Selfde as die laaste twee kratte.		
[Thirty-nine rands. Same as the other two crates.]		
English subtitle inserted: R39, same as the last two crates.		
Dumi: [still in Afrikaans] Hier is veertig rande. Hou die kleingeld. [Here is forty rands. Keep the change.] English subtitle inserted: Here's R40—keep the change.	Voilà 40 rands, garde la monnaie. [Here's 40 rands, keep the change]	

This scene takes place in the Orange Free State, a region characterized by a high proportion of Afrikaners and Afrikaans-speaking South Africans. The Orange Free State is one of the four South African provinces (1910–1994) that were established as part of the Union of South Africa in 1910 when the two Boer Republics (Transvaal and Orange Free State) were combined with the former British colonies (Cape Colony and Natal Colony) to create four provinces: the Cape Province, Natal, the Orange Free State, and Transvaal. It is now one of nine South African provinces and, after the first democratic elections in 1994, it has been renamed Free State. In this sequence, Dumi switches to Afrikaans as he speaks to the shopkeeper. The image provides the viewer with sufficient information to understand the shopkeeper/customer situation. Therefore, the Afrikaans dialog is not translated in the dubbed version. The code-switching is significant here. On the one hand, this is an indicator of the geographical region where Afrikaans is widely spoken. However, it is also symbolic of a newly democratic South Africa, post-1994, where we see Dumi, a black South African, happily conversing with the Afrikaans shopkeeper. This exchange embodies the multilingual reality of South Africa's citizens. Dumi switches to Afrikaans with good humor and there is no resentment or insistence on carrying on the conversation in English or Xhosa, or indeed another South African language. The subtitled version relies on the fact that the soundtrack allows the viewer to hear the change in language. This could have been reinforced perhaps, through italicized subtitles. The dubbed version, however, chooses to recognize the code-switching in the original, allowing the dialog to switch from French to Afrikaans. That said, subtitles are not inserted so the viewer is not given an insight into what is actually being said. Perhaps it is sufficient that the viewer will understand from the image that the character is purchasing items from a shopkeeper. The vocal tone and pitch of the dubbing actor has been matched to the original actor, which eases potential problems relating to continuity.

In another example from *In My Country* (Table 8), there are diverging approaches to this situation in the dubbed and subtitled versions. Towards the middle of the film, the black American journalist (Langston), the black SABC sound engineer (Dumi), and the white South African poet (Anna Malan) are stranded somewhere in the Orange Free State due to a punctured tire. The characters manage to reach the nearest small town in the middle of the night. Anna knocks on the door of a local Bed and Breakfast and is answered by a middle-aged Afrikaans woman who initially has a room to rent and then swiftly changes her mind when she sees Dumi and Langston behind her. Anna improvises and says that the two men are Americans and that they know Oprah Winfrey. She says all this in Afrikaans. This exchange is subtitled in the French version but not in the dubbed version, where the original dialog and soundtrack is heard. In fact, the dialog is spoken by an Afrikaans dubbing actor, and Juliette Binoche, who plays Anna Malan, lip syncs the dialog. There are no challenges in terms of continuity as the vocal pitch and tone of the dubbing actor in the original film match the voice of the dubbing actor in the dubbed version. However, the different strategies change the viewer's point of view in each respective case. In the subtitled version, the viewer interprets the situation through Anna's eyes, understanding what is said with the help of subtitles. However, in the dubbed version, the viewer is placed in the same situation as Langston, the American journalist, who does not understand Afrikaans. When they are admitted, Langston enquires: "Did she ask you if I was married to Oprah?" The wry humor of the original is retained in the subtitled version due the fact that the Afrikaans dialog has been translated. Without a translation in the dubbed version, the French viewer would not have picked up the additional nuances that are present in the source text and which are included for comic effect. This scene is important as it provides the viewer with momentary relief from the film's serious and traumatic subject matter. It also serves to remind the viewer that in spite of the 1994 elections, prejudices will take longer to erase. The two black men are only admitted because the B&B owner thinks that they know Oprah Winfrey.

Table 8 Multilingualism retained (*In My Country*)

Original version	Fr Sub	Fr Dub
[switch to Afrikaans and English subtitles inserted]	Désolée de vous réveiller.	[switch to Afrikaans and no dubbed dialogs or subtitles are added]
Anna: Verskoon my, tannie. Ek het tannie wakker gemaak. Maar, het tannie, miskien 'n kamer te huur?	Vous n'auriez pas une chambre? [Sorry to wake you. Would you have a room?]	Verskoon my, tannie. Ek het tannie wakker gemaak. Maar, het tannie, miskien 'n kamer te huur?
[Excuse me auntie for having woken you, auntie, but does auntie perhaps have a room to rent?]		[Excuse me auntie for having woken you, auntie, but does auntie perhaps have a room to rent?]
English subtitle inserted: Excuse me auntie, Sorry to wake you. But do you have a room?		
B&B Lady: Maar sekerlik kind, kom in. Dis mos al baie laat. [But of course child, come in. It's already very late.]	Oui, entrez mon enfant, il est tard. [Yes, come in my child, it's late.]	Maar sekerlik kind, kom in. Dis mos al baie laat. [But of course child, come in. It's already very late.]
English subtitle inserted: Certainly child. Come in, it's very late.		
Anna: Maar dankie, tannie. Daar is drie van ons. Hulle wag daar buite. [But thank you, auntie. There are three of us. They are waiting outside.]	Merci, nous sommes trois. Ils attendent là-bas. [Thanks. There are three of us. They are waiting over there.]	Maar dankie, tannie. Daar is drie van ons. Hulle wag daar buite. [But thank you, auntie. There are three of us. They are waiting outside.]
English subtitle inserted: Thank you. There are three of us ma'am. They are waiting over there.		
[looks at Langston and Dumi]		
B&B Lady: O, nee ek dink nie so nie. [Oh, I don't think so] English subtitle inserted: No, I don't think so.	Ça n'ira pas. [It won't work.]	O, nee ek dink nie so nie. [Oh, I don't think so.]

Anna: Tannie, hulle is Amerikaners. [Auntie, they are Americans.] English subtitle inserted: Auntie, they are Americans.	Ce sont des Americains! [They are Americans!]	Tannie, hulle is Amerikaners. [Auntie, they are Americans.]
Daardie ou, hy ken vir Oprah! [That guy, he knows Oprah!] English subtitle inserted: That chap . . . he knows Oprah.	Ce type-là, il connait Oprah! [That chap over there, he knows Oprah!]	Daardie ou, hy ken vir Oprah! [That guy, he knows Oprah!]

In the next example (Table 9), both the subtitled and dubbed versions retain the same dynamic as the original, by omitting a translation of the additional language:

Table 9 Multilingualism retained (*In My Country*)

Original version	Fr Sub	Fr Dub
Woman: [in Zulu] Ngifuna ti zano Anna Malan ebale khle [switches to Afrikaans] en dan [switches back to Zulu] funa te, te naye. [I want advice from Anna Malan to do a good thing and then to look for a lady with her.]	–	–
Dumi: [in Zulu] Oh, oh. Ma,–ma, ma, ma, ma, ma, ma. Ezolile, ezolile, bheka buya phansi ukhona. Uxbani, uxbani. [Calm down, calm down, settle down, don't worry.]		–
Anna . . . Anna.	–	Anna . . . Anna.
It's for you, some woman, she listens to you on the radio	Pour toi, une femme qui t'écoute à la radio. [It's for you, a woman, who listens to you on the radio.]	C'est pour toi, c'est une femme qui t'écoute à la radio. [It's for you, a woman, she listens to you on the radio.]
And she won't talk to anyone else.	Elle veut parler qu'à toi. [She only wants to talk to you.]	Elle veut parler avec personne d'autre. [She doesn't want to speak with anyone else.]

Original version	Fr Sub	Fr Dub
Anna: Hello, [in Afrikaans] ja. [yes.]	–	Allo, oui. [Hello, yes.]
Woman: I have something bad	J'ai une mauvaise chose [I have a bad thing]	(accent) J'ai une chose mauvaise [I have a bad thing]
For you please.	pour vous. [for you.]	pour vous, Madame. [for you, Madame.]
Anna: What?	Quoi? [What?]	Quoi? [What?]

There is no need to understand what the woman is saying to Dumi as all will be revealed in the sequence that follows (Table 10). Both the subtitled and the dubbed versions retain the original soundtrack, which is appropriate in terms of strategy. Those responsible for the translations have correctly resisted the temptation to try and translate everything and have let the original speak for itself. This character does not speak at other times in the film and so there is no dubbing actor for her dialog. There is therefore no concern about continuity.

As an aside, it is worth mentioning that the film narrative of *In My Country* refers to the fact that there are several languages operating in the South African context:

Table 10 Film narrative and a multilingual reality (*In My Country*)

Original version	Fr Sub	Fr Dub
Anna: All the words they use	Les mots qu'ils employaient [The words that they use]	Tous les mots qu'ils employaient [All the words that they used]
to humiliate people	pour humilier les gens [to humiliate people]	pour humilier les gens [to humiliate people]
the orders to kill people,	les ordres de les tuer, [the orders to kill them]	les ordres pour tuer les gens, [the orders to kill people]
to torture people …	de les torturer … [to torture them]	les torturer … [to torture them]
were given in my own language	étaient donnés dans ma langue [were given in my language]	étaient donnés dans ma propre langue [were given in my own language]

Afrikaans	l'afrikans [sic.] [Afrikaans]	l'Afrikaans [Afrikaans]
the language of my heart	la langue de mon coeur [the language of my heart]	c'est la langue de mon coeur [it's the language of my heart]
the language in which I wrote about	la langue de mes écrits [the language of my writings]	c'est la langue dans laquelle j'ai écrit pour parler [it's the language in which I write to speak about]
love, beauty . . .	sur l'amour, la beauté . . . [on love, beauty]	d'amour et de beauté . . . [love and beauty]
tenderness.	la tendresse. [tenderness.]	de tendresse. [of tenderness.]
What does that make me?	Ça fait quoi de moi ? [What does that make me?]	Qu'est-ce que je suis maintenant? [What am I now?]

This means that in terms of the overall translation strategy, the dubbed version has to indicate at some level that various languages are being used, including Afrikaans, which is referred to explicitly in this scene. Therefore, a foreignizing strategy is adopted which is not usually the case in dubbed versions where domesticating strategies tend to be more prevalent. In her study on Italian dubbed versions, Vincenza Minutella (2012: 330) makes a similar observation, albeit in relation to a different film corpus: "Although the dubbed versions resort—to some extent—to domestication and adaptation, thus diminishing the importance of multilingualism, foreignizing strategies are also chosen and sociolinguistic variation is often conveyed."

A comparable situation arises in which two South African terms are borrowed in the subtitled and dubbed versions of *In My Country*: *Ubuntu* (compassion, humanity) and *gamadoelas* (in the middle of nowhere) (Table 11). As the speaker explains what these terms mean to the American journalist, and as they form an integral part of the film narrative, it makes sense to borrow the terms. Also, this film is clearly based on historical fact and retraces South Africa's path towards a democratic future. Therefore, it makes sense for the dubbed version to avoid diluting the specificity of the South African context by not choosing equivalent terms in French. A similar approach is apparent in *Invictus*, as the

Table 11 Film narrative and a multilingual reality (*In My Country*)

Original version	Fr Sub	Fr Dub
1) **Anna**: You mean the American journalist hasn't heard of Ubuntu?	Le journaliste américain sait-il ce qu'est l'Ubuntu ? [Does the American journalist know what Ubuntu is?]	Vous voulez dire que le journaliste américain n'a aucune idée de ce qu'est l'Ubuntu? [You mean to say that the American journalist has no idea what Ubuntu is?]
2) **Anna**: Great, stuck in the bloody gammadoelas.	Super! Plantés en pleine gammadoelas. [Super! Stuck in the middle of the gammadoelas.]	Voilà. Super! Coincés en pleine gammadoelas. [Super! Stuck in the middle of the gammadoelas.]
Langston: Stuck in the what?	Dans quoi? [In what?]	En plein quoi? [In the middle of what?]
Dumi: The bloody gammadoelas. The back of beyond. The bloody middle of nowhere.	En pleine brousse, au milieu de nulle part! [Right in the bush, in the middle of nowhere!]	Le gammadoelas. La pleine brousse, le plein milieu de nulle part. [The gammadoelas. Right in the bush, in the middle of nowhere.]

maid hands something to Mandela on a tray which the viewer assumes to be the *muti* (medicine) that she refers to (Table 12):

Table 12 Multilingualism retained (*Invictus*)

Original version	Fr Sub	Fr Dub
Maid: Here's your muti Madiba.	Voilà votre *muti*, Madiba.	Votre muti Madiba.

Whilst the non-South African viewer may not necessarily know exactly what the speaker is referring to, it is enough, perhaps, to understand that something is given to Mandela with his warm milk. One may argue that this is not sufficient given that he falls ill later in the film, but in terms of this sequence, italicizing *muti* in the subtitle is appropriate and takes account of the specific context. The strategy of foreignization, as opposed to domestication, is the correct approach in each of the examples in tables 11 and 12.

In the final extract (Table 13) in which multilingualism is retained, this time from *District 9*, invented speech appears. Simultaneously we hear the MNU agents trying to force their way in:

Table 13 Multilingualism retained (*District 9*)

Original version	Fr Sub	Fr Dub
Alien: This place is swarming with MNU. [Invented speech. English subtitle inserted]	[French subtitles are inserted in italics:]	[French subtitles are inserted in italics to translate the alien invented speech:]
MNU: Open up!	*Ce sont les agents du MNU.* [It's the agents from the MNU] [French subtitles are inserted in italics:]	*Ce sont les agents du MNU.* [It's the agents from the MNU.] [French subtitles are inserted in italics to translate the alien invented speech:]
Alien 1: I will be searched. [Invented speech. English subtitle inserted]	*Ils me fouilleront.* [They will search me.]	*Ils me fouilleront.* Nous sommes du MNU. Ouvrez-nous. Il y a quelqu'un? [They will search me. We are from the MNU. Open up. Is anyone there?]
I must get back to my son. [Invented speech. English subtitle inserted]	[French subtitles are inserted in italics:] *Je rejoins mon fils.* [I'm going back to my son.]	[French subtitles are inserted in italics to translate the alien invented speech:] *Je rejoins mon fils.* MNU … [I'm going back to my son. MNU…]
Alien 2: Don't make them angry – be polite! [Invented speech. English subtitle inserted]	[French subtitles are inserted in italics:] *Les énerve pas, sois poli!* [Don't annoy them. Be polite!]	[French subtitles are inserted in italics to translate the alien invented speech:] *Les énerve pas, sois poli!* On vient vous notifier de votre avis d'expulsion. [Don't annoy them. Be polite! We have your eviction notice.]
MNU: MNU agents. Open the door, please.	MNU, ouvrez la porte! [MNU, open the door!]	MNU, ouvrez-nous s'il vous plaît! [MNU, open up please.]

The alien's speech is subtitled and italicized in both versions, so the switch in language is marked typographically in addition to the fact that the viewer hears the aliens speak.

4. Concluding remarks

This paper attempts to illustrate the effects that are created in the original film by multilingualism and the extent to which the same impact is transferred to subtitled and dubbed versions in French. Multilingualism provides information about the characters in the film. It may tell the viewer something about the context, the region, or milieu, and the relationship between speakers. The function of multilingualism in the source text may shape and determine the resulting translation strategy. Multilingualism automatically adds different nuances in meaning. Therefore, it cannot be dismissed out of hand and needs to be considered alongside other elements that contribute to meaning in an audiovisual text. As Voellmer and Zabalbeascoa (2014: 246) point out with reference to dubbing multilingual films, the audiovisual translator needs to take account of "the presence of L3 in [audiovisual texts]." They conclude that: "Recognising that L3 is part of an author's particular style – a deliberate choice in view of achieving certain effects and not something alien from the rest of the text – is an important first step."

After having established the role played by multilingual features, the translator needs to decide whether to remove or retain them. This is the first stage in the decision-making process. Then it is a question of deciding on an appropriate strategy. A number of possibilities are referred to in the selected examples. In the examples selected here, the audiovisual translator may choose to borrow, omit, neutralize, alter the register to match the image, italicize subtitles, or use different dialects or accents (in the case of dubbing). As Corrius and Zabalbeascoa maintain:

> Translating an audiovisual text with one or more L3s, for instance, is not necessarily more constrained than other forms of translation insofar as the third language is simply a textual feature that translators have to deal with (like metaphors, proper nouns, symbolism and many others).
>
> Corrius and Zabalbeascoa 2011: 121

In the selected examples in which the multilingual features in the source text were not transferred to the target text, one can note that, although there were some

Table 14 Summary of examples where multilingualism has been removed

Selected film	Fr Sub	Fr Dub	Comparison of Translation Strategy
Table 1: *Hijack Stories*	Equivalent translation in French.	Barely audible French dialog added.	Different
Table 2: *Hijack Stories*	Equivalent translation in French.	Adaptation. French dialog added to describe the visual signs.	Different
Table 3: *Hijack Stories*	Equivalent translation.	Equivalent translation.	Same
Table 4: *Hijack Stories*	Equivalent translation.	Colloquial register used as a compensatory device.	Different

differences in strategy between the subtitled and dubbed versions, on a number of occasions, the same strategies were adopted. Whilst subtitling and dubbing may opt for different solutions that are specific to the relative constraints or opportunities of each audiovisual translation mode (for example, condensing the dialog for subtitling and lip synchronization for dubbing), at times it is possible for similar strategies to be used. Table 14 summarizes the examples where multilingualism is not indicated in the translations. In one example (in Table 15), the entry for Table 5, the subtitled and dubbed version adopt the same strategy.

The same observation is apparent in the examples in which the multilingual features have been retained. Similar strategies have been employed in both the subtitled and the dubbed version. This indicates that it is not always the audiovisual translation mode, in this case subtitling or dubbing, that is a deciding factor in the translation choices.

Multilingualism appears in a film for a specific reason: "In multilingual films, a meaningful element is represented by the fact that the viewers are confronted with what is foreign to them, and this must not be lost in the translation" (Heiss 2004: 218). The role that multilingualism plays in relation to a single scene, a longer sequence, and indeed the film as a whole, needs to be fully understood and appreciated. Once this has been established, the various translation strategies and potential choices can be identified and implemented. The audiovisual text is a moving, dynamic text, comprised of verbal and non-verbal elements, audio and visual components that contribute to the meaning-making processes, and

Table 15 Summary of examples where multilingualism has been retained

Selected film	Fr Sub	Fr Dub	Comparison of Translation Strategy
Table 5: *Invictus*	Untranslated.	Untranslated.	Same
Table 6: *District 9*	Equivalent translation.	Equivalent translation and dubbing actors with a French African accent.	Different
Table 7: *In My Country*	Equivalent translation.	Untranslated. Original soundtrack without subtitles.	Different
Table 8: *In My Country*	Equivalent translation.	Untranslated. Original soundtrack without subtitles.	Different
Table 9: *In My Country*	Untranslated. Original soundtrack without subtitles.	Untranslated. Original soundtrack without subtitles.	Same
Table 11: *In My Country*	Terms borrowed.	Terms borrowed.	Same
Table 12: *Invictus*	Term borrowed.	Term borrowed.	Same
Table 13: *District 9*	Translations italicized.	Translations italicized.	Same

the target viewers' interpretation of the film. The L3 that appears in the original is an additional feature to take into account when deciding upon an appropriate translation strategy.

Glossary

Code-Switching and Mode-Mixing: Situations in which a speaker switches to another language and then returns to the original language within the same dialog. This is a common feature of multilingual communities.

Compensatory Mechanisms or Devices: Features of the translation or target text that compensate for aspects that have been omitted in the process of translation.

Domestication: A translation that aligns the target text closely with the target language and culture, erasing and replacing words, grammatical structures, names, and other feature that highlight the origins of the text.

Foreignization: A translation that aligns the target text closely with the source language and culture, using words, grammatical structures, names, and other features that highlight the origins of the text.

Interlingual and Intralingual Translation: Interlingual translation involves a translation from one language to another. Intralingual involves a translation (or adaptation) between different formats, registers, and dialects within the same language. A common use of Intralingual translation involves subtitling for the deaf and hard-of-hearing.

References

Bleichenbacher, L. (2008), *Multilingualism in the Movies. Hollywood Characters and their Language Choices,* Tübingen: Francke Verlag.

Corrius, M. and P. Zabalbeascoa, (2011), "Language Variation in Source Texts and their Translations: The Case of L3 in Film Translation," *Target*, 23(1): 113–130.

District 9 (2009), [DVD] Dir. Neill Blomkamp, London: Sony Pictures Home Entertainment. J. Díaz-Cintas and A. Remael, (2007), *Audiovisual Translation: Subtitling.* Manchester: St. Jerome Publishing.

Heiss, C. (2014), "Multilingual Films and Integration? What Role Does Film Translation Play," in D. Abend-David (ed.), *Media and Translation: An Interdisciplinary Approach*, 3–24. New York: Bloomsbury Academic.

Heiss, C. (2004), "Dubbing Multilingual Films: A New Challenge?," *Meta*, 49, (1): 208–220.

Hijack Stories (2000), [DVD] Dir. Oliver Schmitz, South Africa: Momentum Pictures.

In My Country (2006), [DVD] Dir. John Boorman, London: Sony Pictures Home Entertainment.

Invictus (2010), [DVD] Dir. Clint Eastwood, USA: Warner Home Video.

Minutella, V. (2012), "'You Fancying Your Gora Coach is Okay with Me': Translating Multilingual Films for and Italian Audience," in A. Remael, P. Orero, and M. Carol (eds.), *Audiovisual Translation and Media Accessibility at the Crossroads*, 313–334, Amsterdam/New York: Rodopi.

Monti, S. (2014), "Code-switching in British and American Films and their Italian Dubbed Version," *Linguistica Antverpiensia, New Series. Themes in Translation Studies*, 13: 135–168.

Pettit, Z. (2011), "Translating *Tsotsi* for the Screen," in A. Serban, A. Matamala and J.M. Lavaur (eds.), *Audiovisual Translation in Close-Up*, 75–91, Bern: Peter Lang.

Silva, P. (1997), "South African English: Oppressor or Liberator?" in *The Major Varieties of English*, Papers from MAVEN 97, Vaxjo, 20–22. November 1997.

Venuti, L. (1995), *The Translator's Invisibility: A History of Translation*. London and New York: Routledge.

Vermeulen, A. (2012), "Heterolingualism in Audiovisual Translation: De Zaak Alzheimer/La Memoria del Asesino," in A. Remael, P. Orero, and M. Carol (eds.), *Audiovisual Translation and Media Accessibility at the Crossroads*, 295–312, Amsterdam/New York: Rodopi.

Voellmer, E. and P. Zabalbeascoa, (2014), "How Multilingual can a Dubbed Film Be? Language Combinations and National Traditions as Determining Factors," *Linguistica Antverpiensia, New Series. Themes in Translation Studies*, 13: 232–250.

Translation and Localization in Advertisement

Editor's Introductory Note

Chapter 8 does not speak directly about the representation of translation. On the contrary, it presents a well-argued antithesis in relation with the collection's theme: When it comes to advertisement translation, the focus is on domestication, or—to use a term that is more popular among advertisers—localization. Translators must take into account the target audience's values, needs, desires, and interests. Of course, this strategy cannot be absolute, and translators are either consciously or subconsciously influenced by the original advertisement as well as its original linguistic and cultural features. Some features of the original language might "invade" the target language along with some of the cultural references and values of the original text. Moreover, the foreign nature of the product might provide some exotic and prestigious appeal as well. In this sense, the representation of translation is found in the tension between localization and the fetishization of foreign language and culture. Needless to say that in the background of this chapter there is some discussion between the author and the editor, traces of which the reader can find between the lines. And, of course, it is left to the reader to judge both in a longstanding debate between domestication and foreignization, and a relatively new debate as to what constitutes a translation that is not entirely about transmitting content, but is rather a representation of translation.

Localization Strategies in English–Chinese Advertisement Translation

Ying Cui and Yanli Zhao

1. Introduction

Advertising is a type of "paid persuasive communication that uses non-personal mass—as well as other forms of interactive communication—to reach broad audiences" (Wells et al. 2006: 5). The major function of advertising is to persuade the target audience to accept a product or service. Advertising texts and their translations are designed to attract the audience's attention and arouse their interest and desire in order to serve the final purpose of promotion. The practice of advertisement translation is also flexible and creative, and in some cases it can be regarded as a process of rewriting or re-creating (Cui 2008). Many experts in the area of global marketing and advertising object to the employment of translators in translating advertisements, and they believe that "using translators is one of the pitfalls in preparing advertising campaigns" (Ho 2004: 238). As a result, professional translators are seldom assigned to translate advertising texts (Torresi 2010: 8), and it is suggested that advertising texts be produced by "native speaker copywriters or copywriter/translators whose expertise goes beyond straight translation" (Smith and Klein-Braley 1997: 175). This does not mean that translators are never hired to translate advertisements. Instead, this view demonstrates the importance of adjusting or localizing advertisement translations in keeping with the target audience's needs or expectations so that the translations can function better in the target context. In this sense, translators do not only translate advertisements from one language into another; they play a more active role in designing translations that suit the target audience. And the translations, which are often adapted and therefore different from the original texts in meaning and/or form, can be seen as products of localization. This research aims to explore the representation of translation in advertisements which, on the one hand, localize the original content for the target audience and, on the other hand, are influenced and sometimes purposely retain the original advertisement and original linguistic and cultural characteristics.

2. Localization and advertisement translation

Traditionally, it was believed that most advertising in one language could be transferred to another via translation (De Mooij 2004: 196). This view has changed, as it has been realized that translating advertising texts requires that "the translator should closely co-operate with the copywriter/art director team, and not only translate, but also advise about culture-specific aspects of both languages" (De Mooij 2004: 196). Translators of advertisements are therefore seen as cultural mediators. In other words, if advertising texts can be translated at all with various kinds of help such as copywriters' and art directors' instructions, such translation does not have the same implications as the term "translation" suggests, and "the position of the translator as a cultural mediator implies an active role as an expert" (Adab and Valdés 2004: 164–165). In a nutshell, translators of advertisements play an active and creative role, and they have to take into account the target audience's cultural and linguistic background when translating the advertising texts.

2.1 Models of marketing

Three major models of international marketing are summarized by Ronald W. Lane and Thomas Russell (2001: 312–313), and involve different degrees of localization: First, standardization means that advertising "is handled globally with copy translated but few changes in creative or other elements of a campaign" (Lane and Russell 2001: 312). In this model, one advertising agency is entrusted with the "centralized responsibility to interface with client counterparts" (Lane and Russell 2001: 312). Second, pattern standardization means that a global advertising agency controls overall strategies or approaches, while execution is handled locally or regionally, and each country tailors the advertising campaigns to meet local needs. Third, there is localization, which means that each country decides its own execution of advertising campaigns with a local focus. The least freedom to carry out an independent advertising campaign can be found in the first model. Comparatively speaking, the second and third models grant more freedom to local agencies to carry out advertising campaigns in different cultural contexts.

2.2 Models of advertisement translation

Advertisement translation is a complex process, and there are many constraints to be considered, as "various aspects of advertisements are closely bound up with cultural phenomena" and intercultural comparisons have to be made in translation (Jettmarova et al. 1997: 187). The strategies of advertisement translation can be classified into three major categories, which correspond to the three marketing models outlined in section 2.1: first, complete transfer preserves the image and semantic content of the original and highlights its exotic features; second, translation with minimum changes or partial adaptation allows various degrees of departure from the original; and third, adapted translation or complete adaptation transforms the original text and image to appear more alluring to the target audience (Jettmarova et al. 1997: 187). In the first marketing category of standardization, advertisement translation is straightforward. It presents a complete transfer. The second category is partially localized and translation is more flexible, but the central idea remains controlled. This category therefore corresponds with the partial adaptation model. The third category is the most flexible: both ideas and forms of expression can be adjusted. This is effectively a process of localization or rewriting as we have mentioned above. This study is more concerned with the flexible treatment of advertisement translation, or the second and third categories of localization. We are going to investigate these two levels of localization in advertisement translation, including the adaptation in terms of the content of advertising texts and adaption in terms of the textual devices used to organize advertisement translations.

3. Corpus

The examples to be analyzed in this study are chosen from the bilingual advertisements collected by Li Kexing (2010), which are regarded as the "epitome of bilingual advertisements in Greater China for the past twenty years or so" (Li 2010: 1). Altogether, 158 bilingual advertisements are selected for this research according to two criteria: First, the advertisements are authentic in the sense that they are used in actual marketing. Second, we have chosen examples that cover a relatively comprehensive categorization of products or services such as cars, cosmetics, clothes, cell-phones, computers, wine, juice, taxis, watches, jewelry, magazine, banking, government, university, subway, airlines, recruitment, tourism, supermarket, and restaurants. The initial analysis of the corpus shows that localization is common. For ninety-nine advertisements, the Chinese translations are adapted either in terms of content, wording, or both, accounting for 62 percent of the total. To be more specific, the content of English advertisements is often localized for the Chinese audience in relation to their aesthetic standards, traditional values, and conceptualization of images; the wording of English advertisements can be localized with reference to the Chinese four-character structure and Chinese songs or poem, and the original wording may also be simplified in translation. Typical examples of the localization strategies will be discussed in sections 4 and 5 to demonstrate the manner in which adjustment is made in advertisement translation as well as the effects achieved by such adaptation and provide reference for the practice of advertisement translation.

4. Localization of content

The content of the original advertisement is often adapted in translation. Sometimes information that is not present in the original text is added to the translation. Similarly, information that is present in the original text can be deleted in translation. It is also possible that certain information in the original text is replaced with something else in the translation. Such adaptation regarding the content of advertising texts, which is designed to better suit the target audience's needs and arouse their interest and desire, is justified in the case of advertisement translation because the key function of translated advertisements is to promote a product or service. It is argued that advertisement translations should be assessed "for what they do rather than what they are, or for how well they affect the reader rather than how close they are to the original" (Torresi 2010: 1). It can be seen that the emphasis is placed upon the effect of the translation rather than faithfulness to the original text. To achieve the expected effects, "cultural adaptation of the copy is always necessary, to varying extent, on more or less obvious points, in more or less subtle ways" in the practice of advertisement translation (Coclet 1985: 40). The analysis of our corpus shows that there are three major types of cultural adaptation or localization regarding the content of advertising texts in the case of English–Chinese advertisement translation. These types of adaptation are discussed below.

4.1 Adaptation with reference to Chinese aesthetic standards

The content of English advertisements is often localized to fit Chinese aesthetic standards, which is the case with the following two advertisements of cosmetics:

Slogan:

Makeup so brilliant, skin radiates sheer light.

亮肌智慧粉妆, 诱发肌肤绽放美透<u>白</u>光彩.

Back translation of the Chinese version:

liang ji zhi hui fen zhuang, you fa ji fu zhan fang mei tou bai guang cai.

bright and brilliant makeup stimulates the skin to give off its light of beauty, clearness, and <u>fairness</u>.

Product:

Shiseido

Li 2010: 41

Slogan:

The Temptation of *Natural Pinkish.*

粉红 <u>白皙</u> 的诱惑.

Back translation of the Chinese version:

fen hong bai xi de you huo.

the temptation of pinkish, <u>fair</u> complexion.

Product:

Natural Pinkish Skin and Lip Color Refreshing Cream

Li 2010: 42

In the first example, the English version lists several effects that can be achieved or enhanced by the makeup, such as the skin's brilliance, purity, and light. The Chinese version, however, has added another function of the makeup, namely a whitening effect, as shown via the underlined Chinese character " 白 (*bai*; white, fair)". The same addition is found in the second example, in which the English version gives prominence to being natural and pinkish, and the Chinese version emphasizes being white/fair as illustrated via the underlined Chinese characters " 白 皙 (*bai xi*; fair)." With the addition of one word, the content of the two English advertisements is adjusted in their translations for the Chinese audience by laying emphasis on the whitening effect of the makeup. The preference for white/fair complexion is typical of Chinese aesthetic standards. Chinese people "are attracted to fair complexion" ("Chinese Culture"). Having a fair complexion is not only a preference or fashion, but also a belief "strongly embedded in Chinese culture" that "white is gorgeous and right," and that it is a sign for "prominence and fame" ("Beauty Tips"). In contrast, tanned skin is preferred in Western culture, which has become a trend and a symbol of fashion, health, and luxury ("Sun Tanning"). To summarize, English–Chinese bilingual advertisements are intended to promote the same products for different audiences. When translated into Chinese, the content of the English original advertisements is often adjusted to suit the

Chinese audience's aesthetic standards. In the two examples above, it is apparent that the Chinese audience's preference for white/fair complexion has been taken into account. Therefore, in the Chinese translations of these two advertisements, the whitening effect of the makeup is foregrounded, while it is not even mentioned in the English advertisements. Such adjustments in terms of the content of advertisements in translation help to address the Chinese audience's needs better and allows translations to function better in the Chinese context.

4.2 Adaptation with reference to traditional Chinese values

The content of the original advertisements can also be localized in English–Chinese translation with reference to traditional Chinese values:

Slogan:

New age Volvos.

Age old wisdom.

For Balance. For Life.

我们让您在新生代Volvo体内悟尽古人和谐之道为了和谐之道，为了长相守.

Back translation of the Chinese version:

wo men rang nin zai xin sheng dai Volvo ti nei wu jin gu ren he xie zhi dao, wei le he xie zhi dao, wei le chang xiang shou.

We will let you experience the harmony of the ancients to the full within the new generation of Volvo, for harmony, for lifelong companionship.

Product:

Volvo

Li 2010: 96–97

Slogan:

Ericsson: Taking you forward.

爱立信：以爱立信，以信致远.

Back translation of the Chinese version:

ai li xin: yi ai li xin, yi xin zhi yuan.

To establish trust with love and to go far with trust.

Product:

Ericsson

Li 2010: 7

In the first advertisement, the English version refers to wisdom and balance, which are related to the concept of harmony in Chinese culture. But it does not explicitly mention harmony, while the Chinese version specifies "和谐 (*he xie*;

harmony)" and repeats it twice. The unity of Heaven and man has been greatly emphasized in traditional Chinese culture, and the Chinese mentality is characterized by the pursuit of harmony and unity ("Harmony: A Precious Element in Traditional Chinese Culture"). In the second example, the English version only mentions that the brand will take users forward, which implies that users will have new experiences as a result of using the product. In the Chinese version, the message is mediated and three aspects are emphasized: love, trust, and going far. The relation between love and trust, as well as between trust and going far, is clarified in the slogan, which says that trust is established through love, and that only with trust can one really go far. The emphasis on love and trust can be attributed to "Five Cardinal Virtues" ("The Five Constant Virtues of China") in Confucianism, which are of great significance in Chinese culture. They include "仁 (*ren*; benevolence)," "义 (*yi*; righteousness)," "礼 (*li*; propriety)," "智 (*zhi*; wisdom)," and "信 (*xin*; fidelity)." Among them, benevolence involves love and compassion for people, and fidelity concerns righteousness and trust. To summarize, within the two examples, the original content has been localized for the Chinese audience by catering for its traditional values: harmony, love, and trust.

4.3 The addition of local imagery

It is also common for English advertisements to be localized for the Chinese audience via the establishment of local images in Chinese translations:

Slogan:
Skin Beauty
绝色美肌，倾国倾城.
Back translation of the Chinese version:
jue se mei ji, qing guo qing cheng.
Peerlessly beautiful skin, overthrowing states and cities.
Product:
IPSA

Li 2010: 88

Slogan:
REMY MARTIN XO Exclusively Fine Champagne Cognac
人头马一开，好事自然来.
Back translation of the Chinese version:

ren tou ma yi kai, hao shi zi ran lai.
Once you open Remy Martin XO, something good will come naturally.
Product:
REMY MARTIN XO

Li 2010: 11

In the first example, the English version merely mentions the beauty of skin, which does not present any specific image beyond a fine skin. The message is translated into Chinese with the addition of the expression "倾国倾城 (*qing guo qing cheng*; overthrowing states and cities)". In Chinese culture, the phrase originally refers to women whose beauty captivated emperors to such an extent that the latter neglected state affairs and, in the end, lost their countries. This image leaves consumers with a vivid impression and guides them to visualize the beauty and perfection of skin.

In the second example, the English version merely mentions the brand Remy Martin and its product, Champagne Cognac. The Chinese translation of the slogan is more specific: it claims that once one opens a bottle of Remy Martin XO, something good will happen. The advertisement is localized for the Chinese audience that is disposed to choose expressions of good fortune and to avoid unlucky expressions (Chan and Huang 2001: 232). The Chinese translation associates Remy Martin with the image of "好事 (*hao shi*; something good)". The reliance on images in Chinese translations can be partly attributed to the fact that Chinese native speakers tend to encode verbal information in a "visual mental code" (Chan 2007: 13), and it is easier for the Chinese to "recall information when visual memory is accessed" (Carroll and Luna 2007: 224).

5. Localization of wording in advertisement translation

In addition to the localization of the content of English advertising texts in translation, the textualization of original advertisements is frequently adjusted to design translations that can enhance the Chinese audience's memory and arouse its interest and desire. In many cases, the wording in the English advertisement is difficult to reproduce directly in Chinese due to linguistic differences. It is therefore natural that translators try to make use of the devices available in Chinese in order to reproduce similar effects to those of the original. There are three major types of localization in terms of the wording of advertisements within our corpus. These types of localizations are discussed below.

5.1 Use of the four-character structure

The original text of English advertisements is often packed into four-character expressions which are often rhymed. Four-character expressions are popular in Chinese and extensively used in Chinese advertisements. This is the case with the following two examples:

> Slogan:
> The Future of the Automobile.
> 领导时代 驾驭未来.
> Back translation of the Chinese version:
> *ling dao shi dai, jia yu wei lai.*
> Leading the times, and steering the future.
> Product:
> Mercedes-Benz
>
> Li 2010: 18

> Slogan:
> We care to provide service above and beyond the call of duty.
> 殷勤有加 风雨不改
> Back translation of the Chinese version:
> *yin qin you jia, feng yu bu gai.*
> Highly attentive, and neither wind nor rain can change it.
> Product:
> UPS
>
> Li 2010: 21

In the first advertisement, the English version is a noun phrase which claims that Mercedes-Benz represents the future of automobiles. The Chinese translation also mentions the times and the future, but the message is packed into two four-character expressions: The Chinese translation "领导时代， 驾驭未来(*ling dao shi dai, jia yu wei lai*; Leading the times, and steering the future.)" is made out of two parts, each with four Chinese characters. The two parts of the Chinese version have a similar rhythm, and both of them bear the structure of a two-Chinese-character verb phrase and a two-Chinese-character noun phrase. To be more specific, the first part, "领导时代 (*ling dao shi dai*; Leading the times)", is made out of the verb phrase "领导 (*ling dao*; leading)" and the noun phrase "时代 (*shi dai*; the times)". The second part "驾驭未来 (*jia yu wei lai*; and steering the future)" is made out of the verb phrase "驾驭 (*jia yu*, steering)" and the noun phrase "未来 (*wei lai*, the future)".

In the second advertisement, the English version stresses the efforts that UPS workers make to provide customers with the best services. Its Chinese translation also emphasizes the workers' highly attentive attitude. Similar to the first advertisement, the Chinese translation is presented via the four-character structure. The Chinese version "殷勤有加，风雨不改 (*yin qin you jia, feng yu bu gai*; Highly attentive, and neither wind nor rain can change it.)" is, again, made out of two phrases, each containing four Chinese characters. The two parts of the Chinese version have the same structure. And, as in the previous example, the first part, "殷勤有加 (*yin qin you jia*; Highly attentive)", is composed of "殷勤 (*yin qin*; attentive)" and "有加 (*you jia*; highly)". The second part "风雨不改 (*feng yu bu gai*; neither wind nor rain can change it)" is composed of "风雨 (*feng yu*; wind and rain)" and "不改 (*bu gai*; not change)." The use of the four-character structure enhances the regularity and rhythm of the advertisements, which is in line with readers' aesthetic needs, provides them with amusement, and serves the final purpose of promotion.

There are inherent reasons for the popularity of four-character expressions in Chinese advertisements. The four-character structure is "something unique about the Chinese language" (Mo 2003: 54). It embodies the traditional Chinese mentality of harmony, balance, symmetry, and order (Gong 2009: 128), and Chinese users have always liked this phonological form (Mo 2003: 55). A survey conducted by the Modern Chinese Dictionary shows that four-character expressions account for 8 percent of the vocabulary (Zhou 2004: 40). Four-character phrases have many advantages: they are concise, they are of aesthetic value thanks to their orderly structure and rhythm, and they are flexible, being able to express various ideas via four Chinese characters (Liu and Zhan 2012: 99). The Chinese language is regarded as "the briefest language," as it is able to "convey the most information with the least efforts" (Gong 2009: 130), and four-character expressions are "Chinese of Chinese and king of kings" (Gong 2009: 130); they are "independent linguistic units" (Wang 2007: 58), including all the essential elements of a sentence, with a subject, verb, and object compacted into four Chinese characters. To a great extent, the four-character structure is "the cream of the Chinese language" and part of "the quintessence of Chinese culture" (Gong 2009: 128), and it materializes language users' mastery of Chinese (Wang 2007: 58). Four-character expressions applied in Chinese advertisements have the practical benefit of saving space, particularly in print advertisements, and enhancing the musical and rhythmical beauty of the texts (Tao 2004: 40). To summarize, it is a prominent feature in English–Chinese advertisement translation to localize the wording of English advertisements via the four-character structure for the Chinese audience.

5.2 Use of Chinese idioms or poems

Within our corpus, English advertisements are also localized in translation via the application of Chinese idioms or classical poems:

> Slogan:
> Overexposed.
> 身在危中不知危.
> Back translation of the Chinese version:
> *shen zai wei zhong bu zhi wei.*
> One is in danger, yet they have not realized how dangerous it is.
> Product:
> Friends of the Earth (HK)
>
> Li 2010: 98

In the above example, the English version is composed of one word, "overexposed," which is concise and helps to attract the audience's attention. As no other details are provided, it can arouse the audience's curiosity about what the advertisement means and guide them to think about the possible implications. In terms of the semantic meaning, saying that the earth is overexposed implies that too many plants have been destroyed, the earth is exposed without protection, and people need to be concerned about environmental problems and try to save the earth which is already in danger. If translated according to the original wording of the advertisement, the Chinese version would be "过分暴露 (*guo fen bao lou*; overexposed)" or "过度裸露 (*guo du luo lou*; overexposed)". However, in this example, the Chinese translation does not follow the original advertisement verbatimly. Instead, it is localized for the Chinese audience, and a Chinese idiom is applied here with some adjustment. There is a popular saying in Chinese: "身在福中不知福 (*shen zai fu zhong bu zhi fu*; one is happy, yet they are not aware of how happy they are)". The Chinese character "福 (*fu*; happiness or prosperity)" is repeated twice in the idiom, which enhances its rhythm. In the Chinese translation of the advertisement, the syntactic structure of the idiom is applied, but the Chinese character "福 (*fu*; happiness or prosperity)" is replaced with "危 (*wei*; danger)", which is also repeated twice. Like the original idiom, the translation is rhythmic. In addition, such flexible adaptation can attract the audience's attention and arouse their interest. To summarize, while succinct wording is applied in the English version, the advertisement is localized in the translation in line with the Chinese audience's linguistic and cultural background. And while the textualization in the two versions is different, they can both achieve the effect of arousing audiences' awareness concerning the urgency to protect the earth.

In addition to applying Chinese idioms in translation, the English advertisements in our corpus are frequently localized with reference to Chinese classical poems, which is the case with the following example:

Slogan:
Dare to Dream Higher!
深信，既有的骄人成就，总可以更上层楼.
Back translation of the Chinese version:
shen xin, ji you de jiao ren cheng jiu, zong ke yi geng shang ceng lou.
we firmly believe that, with the achievement that we have already accomplished
    and are so proud of, we can always climb higher.
Product:
Lexus

Li 2010: 96

In this advertisement, the English version, "Dare to Dream Higher," is related to the song "Dare to Dream" (Olivia Newton-John) , which was the theme song of the 2000 Olympics. This reference helps the target audience to associate the product with the popular song. In the Chinese context, some of the audience may not be familiar with the English song and would not be able to make the same association. Therefore, the wording is localized in relation to a Chinese classical poem that is well-known by the Chinese audience. The Chinese translation of the advertisement, "既有的骄人成就，总可以更上层楼 (*ji you de jiao ren cheng jiu, zong ke yi geng shang ceng lou*; with the achievement that we have already accomplished and are so proud of, we can always climb higher)," is based on the famous Chinese classical poem "登鹳雀楼 (*deng guan que lou*; on the stork tower)." The original wording of the poem is: "欲穷千里目，更上一层楼 (*yu qiong qian li mu, geng shang yi ceng lou*; in order to see a thousand miles further, you need to ascend to another level)" ("Deng Guan Que Lou"), which means that one needs to climb higher in order to see further. Accordingly, the Chinese expression, "更上一层楼 (*geng shang yi ceng lou*; ascending to another level)", means that one has made or will make great progress. Therefore, the Chinese version of the advertisement, "总可以更上层楼 (*zong ke yi geng shang ceng lou*; can always climb higher)," conveys the implication that the brand has achieved a great deal and that its products and service will become even better. In summary: the English advertisement is based on a popular song, which helps the audience to associate the product with achievement. The Chinese translation is localized in relation to a famous Chinese classical poem in keeping with the Chinese audience's linguistic and cultural background to realize the same effect.

5.3 Simplification of wording

English advertisements that use special rhetorical devices such as puns, or refer to particular English songs or poems, may pose a problem for the Chinese audience. In such cases, the original wording is often simplified in translation, which is also a type of localization. Such simplification of wording is seen in the following two examples:

Slogan:
Give fur the cold shoulder.
双肩的冻及不上它们的痛，请不要穿毛皮.
Back translation of the Chinese version:
shuang jian de dong ji bu shang ta men de tong, qing bu yao chuan mao pi.
The coldness of your shoulders is not comparable to their pain, and please do
  not wear fur.
Product:
PETA (People for the Ethical Treatment of Animals)

Li 2010: 98

Slogan:
Wherever you are. Whatever you do. The Allianz Group is always on your side.
安联集团，永远站在你身边.
Back translation of the Chinese version:
an lian ji tuan, yong yuan zai ni shen bian.
The Allianz Group is always on your side.
Product:
Allianz Group

Li 2010: 86

In the first example, the English version applies the expression of "giving someone the cold shoulder," which metaphorically means treating someone with antagonism. But in this context, it literary means that one should keep their shoulders cold in order to spare the animals and not take their fur. Such play on words helps to attract the audience's attention, make them think about the implications of the advertisement, and deepen their impression. However, there is no equivalent expression in Chinese, and the direct translation of "cold shoulder" in Chinese does not have the same implication or even make sense to the Chinese audience. Therefore, the wording of the English advertisement is simplified in translation, and the play on words is deleted. The Chinese translation is more explicit, pointing out the pain of the animals and calling on people not to wear fur (even if their shoulders remain cold).

In the second example, the English version is designed with reference to a well-known love song: "Right Here Waiting." In the lyrics, the line "Wherever you go, whatever you do, I will be right here, waiting for you" ("Bryan Adams") is repeated several times and forms the climax of the song. The second-person pronoun "you" is repeated three times, which helps in involving the listeners. The words "wherever" and "whatever" are alliterated and rhymed. The two clauses: "Wherever you go" and "whatever you do", have the same syntactical structure and form a rhythmic couplet. Such wording can provide pleasure for the audience and involve their emotional response. The wording of the English advertisement is similar to the lyrical line: "Wherever you are, whatever you do." The syntactical structure is also applied here and the second-person address, "you" or "your," is used in each clause. The adaptation of the song in the English version helps to attract the target audience's attention and arouse their interest. As the song is popular, those who are familiar with the song can remember the advertisement easily. Besides, "The Allianz Group is always on your side" personifies the Group, and the expression "on your side" renders it closer to the audience, which helps to win their trust and deepen their impression. In the Chinese context, an equivalent song is unavailable, and some of the target audience may not be familiar with the English song. Accordingly, the Chinese translation does not imitate the original, and its wording is simplified. The Chinese version is localized for the Chinese audience and only keeps the personification in the English version: "安联集团，永远站在你身边 (*an lian ji tuan, yong yuan zai ni shen bian*; The Allianz Group is always on your side.)." Within this line, the last words of the two parts are rhymed, "团 (*tuan*; group)" and "边 (*bian*; side)." This preserves some of the features of the original advertisement, as the reading of the Chinese line is rhythmical and easy for the Chinese audience to remember.

6. Further discussion

As shown in sections 4 and 5, translators of advertisements play a creative role as cultural mediators, as what they do is more than transferring messages or words from one language into another, and localization for the target audience is common in advertisement translation. We analyze the various manners in which translators localize the content of English advertisements according to the Chinese audience's aesthetic standards, traditional values, and preference for images. And we demonstrate that translators often adjust the wording of English advertisements via the use of the Chinese four-character structure, the application of Chinese idioms, songs or poems, and the simplification of wording. Such aspects of localization show the creativity and flexibility of advertisement translators. However, this does not mean that translators enjoy unlimited freedom and can design translations at will. On the contrary, they have to take into account a number of restrictions.

First, the adaptation in translation is not done randomly, as translators are supposed to take into account the target audience's values, needs, desires, and interests. Since advertising texts and their translations are intended to attract audiences' attention, arouse their desire, and persuade them to spend money on the product or service that is being advertised, the target audience's role in realizing the functions of advertising is essential. In other words, advertising texts and their translations need to be acceptable and attractive to the target audience.

Second, translators work on the basis of the original advertisements, and either consciously or subconsciously, they are influenced by the original advertisement as well as its original linguistic and cultural features. In the case of English–Chinese advertisement translation, the impact of the English advertisements is obvious, even in the examples of localization which we analyze in sections 4 and 5. While the Chinese translations are flexible, they convey the same message as the English advertisements do. In addition, the wording of the Chinese translations is closely related to their English originals. For example, in the PETA advertisement that is analyzed in section 5.3, the Chinese version mentions "shoulders," which is related to the expression "the cold shoulder" in the English version. However, Chinese do not normally say this: "双肩的冻 (*shuang jian de dong*; The coldness of your shoulders)". Chinese native speakers would say "我很冷 (*wo hen leng*; I am cold)", and if they are specific about which part of the body feels cold, it is common to mention hands or feet, "我手冷 (*wo shou leng*; my hands are cold)" or "我脚冷 (*wo jiao leng*; my feet are cold)", but rarely shoulders. In other words, while the Chinese audience can understand the meaning of the translation, its wording is not genuinely Chinese and it is apparently influenced by the diction of the English advertisement. This is also the case in the Ericsson advertisement that is analyzed in section 4.2. In this advertisement, the Chinese version lays emphasis on trust and love, which is not even mentioned in the English advertisement. However, the Chinese brand name "爱立信 (*ai li xin*; love establishes trust)" is a transliteration of the English version. The pronunciation of the Chinese brand name is similar to the original sound ["eriksn"]. It can be seen that while the Chinese brand name has new meaning added, it actually follows the original pronunciation. Besides, the meaning of the Chinese advertisement is also related to the English version. The English advertisement claims that the brand will take users forward, and the Chinese translation mentions going far. Therefore, it can be seen that however free and creative translators of advertisements can be, their translation practice is still restricted by the original text, language, and culture.

7. Conclusion

In this study, we investigate the phenomenon of localization in English–Chinese advertisement translation with reference to a corpus which is composed of 158 bilingual advertisements. The necessity of localization, the major models of localization, and the common strategies of localization that are often applied in English–Chinese advertisement translation are discussed in this chapter in the hope of deepening translators' understanding of the importance of being flexible and creative in the translation process.

Advertisement translation involves more than the transference of semantic information between languages, as it is intended to achieve the ultimate purpose of communication: the promotion of products or services. In this sense, translators need to take into account the possible influence of their translation strategies on the realization of the final purpose when making decisions in the process of translation. In order to produce translations that can achieve the expected effects in the target context, translators have to consider the target audience's conditions, because the target audience are active participants in the reception of advertisement translations and make the purchase decision. In other words, advertisement translation is eventually dependent upon the target audience who actually decides whether to buy the product. This is the main reason that advertisements are often localized in translation for the target audience. As discussed in sections 4 and 5, both the content and wording of advertisements can be adapted in translation, and translators are supposed to be familiar with the target audience's linguistic and cultural background. Three types of content localization and three types of textual localization in English–Chinese advertisement translation are generalized in this study based on our corpus. We are aware that there are many more specific strategies of localization other than those covered in this study. In future research, a bigger corpus can be analyzed; the strategies of location in advertisement translation that are summarized in this research can be tested and substantiated; more subcategories of localization can be explored; and the inherent linguistic and cultural differences can be further investigated.

Meanwhile, as discussed in section 6, localization does not mean that the practice of advertisement translation is completely free, and the original advertisements as well as the original linguistic and cultural characteristics also have an impact on the translation. In other words, the translations are always closely related to their original advertisements in one way or another. This relationship between the translation and the original should be taken into account in the exploration of localization.

Glossary

Harmony: A traditional Chinese perception of humans as an integral part of nature.

Image: In this study, images are not necessarily visual or concrete; they can also be abstract.

Localization: The adaptation of a text in consideration of the target audience's needs, values, and expectations.

Rewriting: A method of translation that does not follow the original wording.

Simplification: A method of translation that deletes the rhetorical devices of the original text and merely presents the original message.

References

Adab, B. and C. Valdés (2004), "Introduction," in B. Adab and C. Valdés (eds.), *The Translator: Key Debates in the Translation of Advertising Material (special issue)*, 161–177, Manchester: St. Jerome.

"Beauty Tips," Available online: http://www.beautytipshq.com/ (accessed April 25, 2011).

Carroll, R. and D. Luna (2007), "Dual Language Processing of Marketing Communications," in T. Lowery (ed.), *Psycholinguistic Phenomena in Marketing Communications*, 221–246, Mahwah, NJ: L. Erlbaum.

"Bryan Adams," Available online: http://www.justsomelyrics.com/1697437/Bryan-Adams-where-ever-you-go-whatever-you-do-Lyrics (accessed April 26, 2011).

Chan, A.K.K. and Y.Y. Huang (2001), "Chinese Brand Naming: A Linguistic Analysis of the Brands of Ten Product Categories," *Journal of Product and Brand Management*, 10 (2): 103–119.

Chan, B.Y. (2007), "*Brand Naming: A Study on Brand Name Translation in China: U.S. Brands Translated into Chinese and Chinese Brands Translated into English*," BA diss., Hong Kong Baptist University, Hong Kong.

"Chinese Culture," Available online: http://www.mapsofworld.com/china/china-culture/ (accessed April 25, 2011).

Coclet, M. (1985), "Translating Advertising Copy: Problems and Solutions," in P.E. Newman (ed.), *American Translators Association Conference, 1985: Proceedings of the 26th Annual Conference of the American Translators Association*, 39–41, Medford, NJ: Learned Information.

Cui, Y. (2008), "Rewriting Strategy in Advertisement Translation – Analysis from the perspective of presupposition," *Perspectives: Studies in Translatology*, 16 (1 and 2): 21–35.

De Mooij, M. (2004), "Translating Advertising: Painting the Tip of an Iceberg," in B. Adab and C. Valdés. (eds), *The Translator: Key Debates in the Translation of Advertising Material (special issue)*, 179–198. Manchester: St. Jerome.

"Deng Guan Que Lou," Available online: http://www.stmsxx.com/Article_Show.asp?ArticleID=125&jdfwkey=mgmwp (accessed April 26, 2011).

Gong, X. (2009), "Influence of Foreignized Translation on Four-character Idioms and the Inherent Cultural Implications," *Crazy English*, 2009 (1): 128–131.
[龚晓斌. (2009). 异化翻译对汉语四字成语的影响及其文化透视, 2009 (1): 128–131].

Ho, G. (2004), "Translating Advertisements across Heterogeneous Cultures," in B. Adab and C. Valdés (eds), *The Translator: Key Debates in the Translation of Advertising Material (special issue)*, 211–244, Manchester: St. Jerome.

Jettmarova, Z., M. Piotrowska, and I. Zauberga (1997), "New Advertising Markets as Target Areas for Translation," in M. Snell-Hornby, Z. Jettmarova, and K. Kaindl (eds.), *Translation as intercultural communication: Selected papers from the EST Congress, Prague 1995*, 185–194, Amsterdam; Philadelphia: J. Benjamins.

Lane, W.R. and J.T. Russell (2001), *Advertising: A Framework* (1st edition), Upper Saddle River, NJ: Prentice Hall.

Li, K. (2010), *Advertisement Translation: A Theoretical and Practical Approach*, Beijing: Beijing University Press.

Liu, Y. and W. Zhan (2012), "Analysis of the Structures of Four-Character Idioms,"

Literature and Art, 2012 (5): 99. [刘阳，　詹务本. (2012). 四字格套语结构浅析文学艺术, 2012 (5): 99].

Mo, P. (2003), "The 'Four-Character Form' and Idiom Rhetoric," *Journal of Changzhou Institute of Technology*, 16(3): 53–58. [莫彭龄. (2003). "四字格"　与成语修辞. 常州工学院学报, 16(3): 53–58].

Olivia Newton-John, Available online: http://www.smartlyrics.com/Song409419-Olivia-Newton-John-Dare-to-dream-lyrics.aspx (accessed April 26, 2011).

Smith, V. and C. Klein-Braley (1997), "Advertising – A Five-stage Strategy for Translation," in M. Snell-Hornby, Z. Jettmarova and K. Kaindl (eds.), *Translation as intercultural communication: Selected papers from the EST Congress, Prague 1995*, 173–184, Amsterdam; Philadelphia: J. Benjamins.

"Sun Tanning," Available online: http://en.wikipedia.org/wiki/Sun_tanning (accessed April 25, 2011).

Tao, Y. (2004), "A Study on the Chinese-English Translation of an Advertisement with Four-Character Idiom," *Journal of Inner Mongolia Radio and TV University*, 2004 (2): 40–41. [陶源. (2004). 从一则广告看汉语四字格并列结构的英译. 内蒙古电大学刊, 2004 (2): 40–41].

"The Five Constant Virtues of China," Available online: http://www.foreignercn.com/index.php?option=com_content&view=ar ticle&id=5047:the-five-constant-virtues-of-china&catid=1:history-and-culture&Itemid=114 (accessed December 2, 2016).

"Harmony: A Precious Element in Traditional Chinese Culture," Available online: http://www.visiontimes.com/2018/01/26/harmony-a-precious-element-in-traditional-chinese-culture.html (accessed September 7, 2018)

Torresi, I. (2010), *Translating promotional and advertising texts*, Manchester, UK; Kinderhook, NY: St. Jerome.

Wang, T. (2007), "Evolution of the Unique Chinese Form of Four-Character Idioms," *Journal of Beijing Vocational College of Labour and Social Security*, 2007 (1): 58–60. [王天虹. (2007). 独特的汉语四字格形式发展探析. 北京劳动保障职业学院学报, 2007(1): 58–60].

Wells, W., S. Moriarty, and J. Burnett (2006), *Advertising: Principles and Practice* (7th edition), Upper Saddle River, NJ: Pearson/Prentice Hall.

Zhou, J. (2004), "On the Formation of Four-Character Phrases," *Chinese Journal*, 2004 (1): 40–46. [周荐. (2004). 四字组合论. 汉语学报, 2004(1): 40–46].

9

The "Non-Translation"

Editor's Introductory Note

The final chapter in this collection examines the representation of translation in multilingual films from three perspectives: the inclusion of a scene in which the language that is used is different from the primary language of the film; a reversed translation, as the scene is originally written in the primary language of the film and translated by an expert; and a reversed-reversed translation, as the translated scene is fitted with captions that re-translate the text for the benefit of the viewer. In examining the tension between the original script, the translated scene, and the re-translation of the scene within captions, this chapter borrows Dirk Delabastita's theory about the dramatic function of translation to consider the reasons for the inclusion of a secondary language, and the many ways in which the purpose of translation can be either partially or entirely divorced from the communication of a verbal text.

The chapter complicates further the discussion of multilingual films by exploring the Yiddish Prologue to Joel and Ethan Coen's film, *A Serious Man*. Using a language that is spoken by a few people (of whom a large portion of speakers do not watch popular media), Joel and Ethan Coen unearth a complicated historical and political facet of Jewish-American life that could hardly have been included in the film through a different method without turning it into a documentary. Moreover, the chapter makes an argument for an interdisciplinary study of multilingual films. The vast critical response to the film by scholars in a wide array of fields is examined, making the argument that the discussion of a multilingual film requires simultaneously a background in film studies, the languages that are used in the film, and the cultures and the histories that are represented by these languages. Here, the chapter contains a serious political error: critics who are likely to discuss multilingual films with the benefit of one of two of these three elements are also the ones who are likely to read, evaluate, and review this chapter. The reader is therefore asked to keep an open mind: rather than considering this chapter a harsh judgment of previous research, the reader is asked to consider it as a suggestion for making future research even better.

Yiddish, Media and the Dramatic Function of Translation—or What Does It Take to Read Joel and Ethan Coen's film, *A Serious Man?*

Dror Abend-David

1. Introduction

Multilingual usage in film, summoning a variety of languages, is not new. Already in *The Longest Day* (1962), viewers are met with full dramatic scenes in French and in German, accompanied by subtitles. A more recent example on a similar theme that was the subject of a great deal of theoretical response is *Inglourious Basterds*. In this film from 2009, the dialog is divided generously between English, French, German, and Italian. Examples abound, and not only in Central European languages, but also in Mandarin, Hindi, Arabic, and even in Yiddish. In the 1970s, director Mel Brooks inserted a Yiddish dialog in *Blazing Saddles* (1974) and director Robert Aldrich has done this (to a greater extent) in *The Frisco Kid* (1979). Since then, Yiddish has been making repeated appearances, both in films and on television, from *M*A*S*H* (1972–1983) to *The Nanny* (1993–1999).

The beginning of the twenty-first century, however, presents a new trend both in terms of the quantity, quality, and variety of foreign dialog. Moreover, such representation is often self-aware, ironic, and acutely conscious of the dramatic function of translation (Delabastita 2004) and multilingualism (Delabastita and Hoenselaars 2015). Films such as Coppola's *Lost in Translation* (2003) and Pollack's *The Interpreter* (2005) actually address issues related to translation, presenting some thoughtful doubts and observations about the limits and potentials of translation (and interpretation). And even when not considering translation critically, films such as *East Side Sushi* (2014) feature dialog in two or more languages, which is both fluent and credible, and is situated in the midst of a complicated cultural exchange. Most of all, such films reflect on the extent towards which linguistic and cultural diversity has become an inseparable part of contemporary reality. In *East Side Sushi*, a cultural language is presented as a zone of comfort and intimacy for the different characters, but it also marks an identity politics that infringes on the prospects of a Hispanic woman who wishes to become a sushi chef.

On television, translation and secondary languages in television drama can be quite ironic as well. One example includes the use in *Brothers & Sisters* of Chinese (Season 2, Episode 11; February 10, 2008) and of French (Season 4, Episode 4; October 18, 2009): Chinese and French remain untranslated, highlighting the fact that Sarah (Rachel Griffiths) is ignorant of these languages, while the men that she is involved with speak them fluently. In *House M.D.* (Season 7, Episode 7; November 15, 2010), the main character, Dr. Gregory House (Hugh Laurie), prefers the translation of an online Dutch stripper to the services of a professional translator, which can be construed as a comment on the nature of translation as a profession...

This trend does not skip the realm of online and off-line commercials,[1] sometimes with surprising twists in plot. While it might not seem surprising that Japanese is used in a car commercial on prime-time television, it becomes quite a surprise when this is done to sell the Chrysler 200 (an American car) (*2015 Chrysler 200 Commercial Japanese Quality*). Yiddish, by comparison, has made a foray into the world of television commercials—but so far only in Israel, where it has been used to sell fruit-drinks (*Primor BeYidish* 2015), crackers (*Beygl, Beygl, Dakim BeTeamim* 2011), and satellite television services (*Yes Pirsomet Kharedim* 2012).

In the United States, both on television and in film, Yiddish has been used creatively and quite significantly on two occasions: in a 2002 opening scene of episode 11 of the fourth season of *The West Wing* (December 11, 2002),[2] and in the opening scene of Joel and Ethan Coen's 2009 film, *A Serious Man*.[3] These scenes are significant because prior use of Yiddish in media is, almost without exception, comic and stereotypical. These prologues are important dramatic scenes that are carried fluently and professionally in Yiddish with subtitles—and with an important role within the entire plot. Moreover, as a language almost without speakers (leaving some enthusiasts and certain Ultra-Orthodox populations that do not watch movies), the use of Yiddish must be read outside any functionality for a prospective foreign language audience, and addresses only the symbolism, atmosphere, references, emotional appeal, and political significance of what is essentially a "pure language" (Benjamin 1970), completely abstract and divorced from a speech community—and yet of great emotional appeal.

From the point of view of Translation Studies, the use of Yiddish in media is important for two reasons: The first reason is that it serves to highlight the extent to which the use of foreign language in media has become widespread, inclusive, and authentic. The second reason is that—because Yiddish in the media does not serve a particular speech community—the use of Yiddish serves to demonstrate that either translation or foreign language in the media is not utilitarian, assisting those who might not understand the source language, but rather serves in various ways a dramatic function of translation. From the point of view of Jewish Studies, the use of Yiddish in media marks an opportunity to utilize a fresh theoretical approach that will provide a new cultural, social, and political perspective to modern Jewish history.

However, *A Serious Man*, to date an epitome of Yiddish usage in popular media both in terms of quality and of content, points to a theoretical gap that renders the discussions of Translation and Yiddish and of Yiddish and Media difficult. Translation has been a topic of some interest in Yiddish Studies in the past two decades as the field has been taking its first steps towards applying a theory of translation.[4] An important phenomenon in this respect is the work of Albert Waldinger who, since 1996, has published several articles on Yiddish translation as well as translation in general, both in Journals of Jewish and Translation Studies. From the perspective of Translation Studies, however, with few exceptions,[5] there has been little interest in Yiddish Translation. There has been, of course, a great deal of research about Media and Translation.[6] But as far as work on Yiddish and Media is concerned, it is a limited venue.[7] Despite their considerable chronological gap, the stereotypical view of Yiddish in this respect is not very different from Latin: that it is too old (and too dead) to be a good subject for media research.

This chapter utilizes an approach that combines a background in Media, Jewish and Translation Studies—not only to understand better the purpose of the Yiddish Prologue in *A Serious Man*, but to suggest a new way of discussing the use of Yiddish speech and translation in contemporary media.

2. Critical responses to *A Serious Man*

A Serious Man is the subject of a great deal of critical response, both in academic and non-academic sources (such as film reviews)—so much so that it is difficult to summarize. Three of the most recent scholarly contributions in this field, by Russell J.A. Kilbourn in *Adaptation*, Timothy Stanley in *Bible and Critical Theory*, and Peter Mathews in *Cultura-International Journal of Philosophy of Culture And Axiology* (Kilbourn 2014, Mathews 2014, Stanley 2014), are indicative of two main trends in the discussion. The first trend is of a religious discussion that often sees the film as a modern adaptation of the book of *Job*, as is done by

Carol Linnitt in an early article from 1999 in *Journal of Religion and Film*, and by David Tollerton and Norman M. Cohen in two later articles in the same Journal published in a single issue in 2011 (Cohen 2011, Linnitt 2009, Tollerton 2011). Added to the same venue are the articles of J.M. Tyree in *Film Quarterly* (2010) and Alan A. Stone in *Psychiatric Times* (2010). The second trend is a contextualization of the film within a number of literary and cultural traditions. Given the ambivalent social representation in the film, one is not surprised by the title of Ido Lewit's article in *Journal of the Kafka Society of America*: "The Kafkaesque Cinematic Language of the Coen Brothers' *A Serious Man*" (Lewit 2009). In 2013, the *Jung Journal-Culture & Psyche* published a "blockbuster" cluster of four articles that contextualize *A Serious Man* in relations to various texts stretching from *The Tempest* to the Grimm Brothers' fairy tales (Naifeh, S. 2013, Naifeh, K. 2013, Rubin 2013, Zemmelman 2013).

In 2011, the *AJS Review* (Association of Jewish Studies) published a "blockbuster" of its own, with five articles about *A Serious Man* (Boyarin J. 2011, Ginsburg 2011, Lang 2011, Riv-Ellen Prell 2011, Shandler 2011). This "printed symposium" followed a session about the film that was presented at the previous AJS annual conference, and addressed various perspectives that are related to Jewish Studies. Three of these articles even address the Yiddish prologue to film (Ginsburg 2011, Shandler 2011, Boyarin J. 2011).

In most cases, even when scholars mention the Yiddish prologue to *A Serious Man* (Stone 2010, Tyree 2010, Boyarin J. 2011), they do not attempt to decipher either the significance of the scene for the rest of the plot, or the use of Yiddish in a complete dramatic scene in a manner that is very different from prior usage of Yiddish in the cinema. The two exceptions are the articles of Shai Ginsburg and Jeffrey Shandler, which devote a great deal of attention to the prologue. Unlike critics who conclude that, as Tyree writes: "some puzzlement attends the curious Yiddish prologue of *A Serious Man*" (Tyree 2010: 37), Ginsburg insists that the short prologue is essential to the plot. He repeats the notion of other critics that the story of the prologue might be "merely an absurd story" or a private joke on behalf of the directors, but adds that "jokes often point at a painful reality" (Ginsburg 2011: 364). Ginsburg makes an important point when he ties the prologue with the uncertainty principle that the main character (Larry Gopnik, played by Michael Stuhlbarg) teaches to his students at the beginning of the film. Moreover, Ginsburg argues convincingly that there is some similarity between the character of the stabbed Rabbi (Rabbi Groshkover, played Fyvush Finkel) who may or may not be a *dibek* (a possessing spirit)—and the famous theoretical Schrödinger's Cat, who may or may not have been stabbed to death (Ginsburg 2011: 358). He concludes that the Coen Brothers use the "Schrödinger's Rabbi" (my phrase) to hint at the need to accept one's uncertainly in life, both in the spiritual and the practical realm. At this point, however, Ginsburg abandons the discussion of Yiddish, and takes his work in the direction of quantum mechanics (which the main character is teaching in the film) rather than translation theory. Shandler pays attention both to the prologue and to the fact that it is delivered in Yiddish. Moreover, he discusses the translation and provides a good deal of information about the process through which the scene was produced. He also makes the important point that the scene presents a "reversed translation"[8]—as the scene was first written out in English, and only later translated into Yiddish and fitted with English subtitles. This, among other issues, is an important point when coming to evaluate the accuracy of the "translation" in this scene—which I discuss below. Shandler does not, however, attempt to explain the significance of either the events or the language that is used in this part of the film. Why was it necessary to create this prologue? And why was it essential that it will be performed in Yiddish? Ginsburg provides a possible answer to the first question. This article attempts to answer the second.

3. An interdisciplinary approach to *A Serious Man*

With all the interdisciplinary work that has been done in the past two decades in Yiddish, Media and Translation, it is still a challenge to discuss a complicated cultural text such as *A Serious Man*, which demands at once a "serious" take on films, translation, and Jewish history.

The first step, as I already mention above, involves Dirk Delabastita's work on the dramatic function of translation. Grounded in Shakespearean drama, this theory claims that when translation is inscribed in drama, it rarely bares the utilitarian task of explaining the text to the audience (which otherwise could simply be presented in the target language). The dramatic function of translation, according to Delabastita, is rather to motivate the plot, and to infuse the drama with social, political, and historical meaning, while the "comprehension of the original text is not an issue at all" (Delabastita 2004: 39). In relation to *A Serious Man*—which opening scene is pronounced an incomprehensible mystery by some of the film's puzzled critics—Delabastita provides an excellent key for reading a scene (and what it might mean in the context of the entire plot) in a language that few viewers would either comprehend or use as a first language: the sound of the foreign language in the scene (which could be easily replaced with an English dialog); it's emotional significance; and it's tone and vitality, are as important than the words that are being said.

A second step (which I take in the next section) into deciphering the conundrum of *A Serious Man* is provided by a historical note on Jewish-American history, and the tension between Hebrew and Yiddish during the first half of the twentieth century. I refer to a number of sources that describe the impression of this tension on Jewish-American literature and culture (Finkelstein 2001, Fredman 2001, Zukofsky 1978). But my purpose—like that of Joel and Ethan Coen—is not to teach a lesson about Yiddish and Hebrew, but to explore the cinematic technique through which the juxtaposition between Yiddish and English (and short sequences in Hebrew) replaces what would otherwise necessitate a lengthy historical footnote. The abrupt move in the film between languages helps the viewers to feel, rather than understand, the tension between what the different languages represent—not only in relation to Jewish-American communities in the 1960s—but in relation to contemporary popular religion in the United States as well.

Finally (in section 5), I contextualize the use of Yiddish in this scene within a growing use of secondary language in contemporary American Media. In doing so, I suggest that Yiddish is an important part of this trend, and that a study of the use of Yiddish in Media can make an important contribution to contemporary Yiddish and Jewish Studies as well as to Translation Studies.

4. What does the Yiddish prologue to *A Serious Man* mean?

The opening scene of *A Serious Man* is an improvement, perhaps even a perfection of the aforementioned Yiddish prelude to a *West Wing* episode in 2002. One should take into account of course the different contexts and perhaps the different resources available for a television episode and for a film production. But it also seems that the pioneering endeavor of *The West Wing* (1999–2006) laid the foundations, both thematically and aesthetically, to what is likely the best Yiddish scene in the English-speaking American cinema to date. The scene is played superbly by Allen Lewis Rickman, Yelena Shmulenson, and Fyvush

Finkel. And the reconstruction of the snow-covered East European village transports the viewers who are shivering in their seats as Rickman is struggling against the freezing darkness of nineteenth-century Russia.

While Alan Stone (2010) is able to appreciate the technical qualities of this scene, critics are almost universally puzzled as to its meaning. In this prologue, Velvel (Allen Lewis Rickman) returns home with great news: the honorable Rabbi Groshkover (Fyvush Finkel) is coming to visit them. But his wife, Dora (Yelena Shmulenson), is not happy at all. She has heard through trustworthy gossip that Rabbi Groshkover died three years ago of typhus. The only logical conclusion, therefore, is that the visitor is a *dibek*, a possessing spirit. She therefore stabs the supposed specter of the honorable Rabbi with an ice pick. At first nothing happens and the *dibek* bursts out in horrible laughter. But then a spot of blood that spreads over its white shirt leaves room for the possibility that this was in fact the poor Rabbi Groshkover who had recovered from typhus only to be murdered by a superstitious housewife. The scene leaves the viewers as confused about whether Rabbi Groshkover was a *dibek*, as to what this might all mean—when they are transported to a recitation of Hebrew grammar in a 1967 Hebrew School in Minnesota.

This abrupt move from the Yiddish speech of Eastern Europe to the Hebrew class in Minnesota seems arbitrary, but it isn't. It's related to Jewish-American politics, and the struggle between Yiddish and Hebrew, which has concluded in the 1940s and 1950s with an overwhelming preference of Hebrew in Jewish communities across the United States. The viewers are not supposed to be aware of this issue, of course, but through a sharp transition from one language to another, they must sense the main difference between the two: that the first was a living language that encompassed all walks of daily life, while the other is a stilted tongue of little emotional significance. More importantly, to the community of Jews in Bloomington, Minnesota, Hebrew is not the language of their ancestors.

One quality that highlights the vitality of Yiddish in contrast with Hebrew in the film is the use of idiomatic language that is delivered with great passion. As already mentioned above, the scene uses a "reversed translation," as the scene was first written in English, and then translated into Yiddish, with the original script as the subtitles. As a result, while the subtitles essentially deliver the same information—the performance in Yiddish includes various idioms and linguistic conventions that have been added to create a fluent and authentic delivery. For example, when Dora claims that only one of Rabbi Groshkover's cheeks is shaved because the devil has snatched his body before the other could be tended to—she declare with wide dramatic gestures: "Holy Sabbath; Happy Holiday... the dead man is gone!" The English subtitle simply reads: "You were already gone!" This is not a matter of "good" or "bad" translation, as it is not completely clear what is being translated into which language. The function of subtitles is to deliver meaning clearly and succinctly,[9] which is certainly done in this case, and which probably could not be done while retaining various cultural terms and expressions (taking into account, among other considerations, the number of characters and the time during which the title flickers on the screen). The idiomatic quality of the scene, however, is felt even by viewers who do not speak English, but are impressed by the vitality and passion with which the dialog is delivered.

In fact, the notion that the characters in the film have been cut off from the language of their ancestors, and that it has been forgotten along with its entire tradition of folk-stories and cultural heritage, is felt even by critics who do not devote a great deal of attention to the use of Yiddish in the film. Stone[10] describes this notion well in relation to the representation of Hebrew in a number of scenes:

> And then there is the bar mitzvah at which Danny is so stoned he has trouble finding and focusing on the part of the Torah... Danny is having a drug trip, not a religious experience. Jews who have gone through similar rituals will know that Danny (like most American Jews) has no idea what the Hebrew words he is reading mean. He has been taught to chant, not to understand.
>
> Stone 2010: 33

Part of the effectiveness of the Yiddish dialog has to do with what Daniel Boyarin refers to in *Unheroic Conduct* as "Jewissance": a sense of validation that the (Jewish) viewer feels when a reference to "a world of memory, intimacy and connectedness" appears on the screen (Boyarin D. 1997: xiii). One might argue of course that a similar "*jouissance* [pleasure]" is felt by anyone who's ethnic or religious origins are reflected in popular media. However, my claim is that the use of either Hebrew or Yiddish produces different types of validation; that Hebrew corresponds to one set of Jewish values, references, and associations, while Yiddish corresponds to another. Within modern Jewish history, the choice between Yiddish and Hebrew has often been an aesthetic, cultural, and ideological choice that comprised a great deal of the meaning of the text in addition to its actual content.

The different symbolism, and, in fact, the tension between Hebrew and Yiddish is pervasive to modern Jewish life, stretching back to the Czernowitz Conference of 1908—where Hebrew was identified as the language of the Zionist project, while Yiddish was identified with diasporic life and the attempt to create a cultural Jewish identity in several locations. A significant facet of this tendency is the creation of a vibrant secular Yiddish culture in the Soviet Union—where creation in Yiddish was encouraged and supported by the authorities, while Hebrew was banned as a reactionary, religious tongue in the service of Jewish merchants and clergymen.[11] In Palestine, at the same time, the Zionist Jewish community has functioned in Hebrew while ostracizing Yiddish and removing it from the public sphere. This was a time of great ideological zeal and harsh choices. And those who attempted to benefit both from the ancient splendor of Hebrew and the oral vitality of Yiddish, were at risk of being shunned by both Hebraists and Yiddishists.[12]

In the United States, with mass immigration of Jews from various locations and with different ideologies, the tension between Yiddish and Hebrew was often less severe—and seldom the subject of either legal or communal restrictions. However, the choice of either Hebrew or Yiddish—particularly where cultural production was involved—had a specific social and artistic significance. For Jewish-American writers during the first half of the twentieth century, the choice between Hebrew and Yiddish had very little to do with a consideration of Zionism or other political venues. It had more to do with class issues within the Jewish-American community. Hebrew was grasped as elitist, often Rabbinical, and in opposition to an impertinent initiative in film and drama, poetry and prose of young creators who wanted to establish a Modernist Jewish tradition alongside, and often at the inspiration of writers such as T.S. Eliot, Ernest Hemingway, and Eugene O'Neill. In 1928, poet Louis Zukofsky parodied in his poem, *A-4*, the intolerance of Hebraists towards *jargon*, the pejorative namesake of Yiddish:

> Wherever we put our hats is our home
> Our aged heads are our homes,
> Eyes wink to their own phosphorescence,
> No feast lights of Venice or The Last Supper light
> Our beards' familiars; His
> Stars of Deuteronomy are with us, Always with us,
> We had a Speech, our children have evolved a jargon.

> Zukofsky 1978: 12

As both critics Stephen Fredman and Norman Finkelstein argue (Fredman 2001: 125–126, Finkelstein 2001: 41–42), the reference to Yiddish as a senseless jargon is ironic. The old male Hebraists, half sorcerers adorned with hats and with beards, are described as fanatics who shut their ears to the voices of a new and creative cultural production. While others might have seen Hebrew, particularly after the Holocaust, as a secular language of national rejuvenation—in this formula Hebrew takes its chronological place as the older language, and Yiddish is presented as the language that is both new and innovative. In Zukofsky's case, he presents himself as a young avant-garde who is knocking at the gates of an old Hebraist elite. Fredman and Finkelstein add that Zukofsky had his own ax to grind with the editors of *Menorah*, a journal of Jewish Literature which had no interest in either his translations from Yiddish or his essays about Yiddish Literature. However, the tension between Zukofsky's native Yiddish and an elitist Hebrew tradition is typical of Jewish-American intellectuals at the time, who were more comfortable writing either in Yiddish or (later) in English—and who found little room within a "serious" Hebraist tradition for their individual thoughts and aspirations.

Over the years, however, the social and political functions of Hebrew and Yiddish in the United States became more symbolic than practical. Writing in 1941, Samuel (Charney) Niger observes that many second-generation Jews in the United States speak neither Hebrew nor English (Niger 1990). Niger relates this communal "amnesia" to the historical trauma of war and immigration, as immigrant parents were too occupied with the daily struggle for livelihood to teach these languages to their children. In fact, the aim of poor immigrants was to learn English and to assimilate into American society as soon as possible. Writing this a short time before the Second World War, Niger is optimistic that American Jews will overcome the trauma of the Great War of 1914–1918 and regain both the scholarly and religious heritage of Hebrew, and the cultural traditions of Yiddish.

The events of the Second World War, the Holocaust, and the establishment of Israel, however, triggered a very different linguistic development. At the aftermath of the Holocaust, the prospect of sovereign Jewish Nationality was naturally seen as the appropriate response to the feeling of loss, helplessness, and frustration over the massacre of six million Jews. Hebrew, the language of Jewish nationalism, was consequently adopted in synagogues and Hebrew Schools—not only as a religious language, but as a rite of identification with the State of Israel and a Zionist cause. Hebrew was now seen as a "new" language of national and cultural rejuvenation, while Yiddish was identified with a dark past that few wanted to preserve, much less to explore. At the same time, Yiddish was the language of one's grandparents, rife with memories, songs, stories, and anecdotes. And while Hebrew had become an official Jewish language related to all serious matters of religion, scholarship, and national identity—Yiddish still lurked beneath the surface with a great deal of mysticism and apocrypha, filled with magic, charms, demons, angels, righteous men and women, and of course—*dibeks*. It offered funny words that triggered memories of one's ancestors, and it has been a source of funny stories, anecdotes, and comedy—which is also the way in which Yiddish has been represented in popular media during the second half of the twentieth century. Despite the sad fate of European Jewry, Yiddish has remained a part of the Jewish collective memory—and while Hebrew has become associated with formal communal matters, Yiddish has come to represent the personal: the *Bobe* [grandmother], her endearing *chutzpah* [audacity] and her delicious *Cholent* [stew]. It has become laced with tragedy, humor, memories, and a great deal of emotions.

This historical exegesis already provides some insight to the namesake of the film, which was translated into Hebrew (for projection in Israel) as *Yehudi Tov* [*A Good Jew*]. The "good" or serious tradition is that of Hebrew, consisting of Hebrew School lectures, memorization, and religious ritual. But this serious, good, and Hebraist tradition is also opaque, leaving the Minnesota flock, and particularly the main character of Larry Gopnik, spiritually abandoned and confused. And when facing an opaque and humorless universe, one must search for moral, mystical, and supernatural explanations to what cannot be comprehended otherwise. Gopnic, turning in desperation to the three Rabbis of his community, seeks a mystical explanation to what seems an inexplicable and unbearable load of unhappiness that is thrown into his lap: his impending divorce; his fear that he might not receive tenure; and the incorrigible behavior of his gambling, unemployed, and very annoying brother.

But is this mystical search worthwhile? Will Gopnic find a spiritual explanation and perhaps even a remedy to his problems? The answer to these questions is found in the opening scene, presented in the language and the context of a tradition that Gopnic and his generation have abandoned. Our attitude towards Gopnic's mystical search depends on whether or not we believe that the appearance of Rabbi Groshkover in the opening scene was truly that of a *dibek*, and that Dora has done well to stab it with an ice pick. If so, we might conclude that Joel and Ethan Coen endorse our inclination towards spirituality and mysticism. If not, we might conclude that Dora's attempt to protect her home from evil spirits through her limited knowledge of the *Sitrah Akhra* [a traditional reference to the realm of the devil; literally: the other side] is a dangerous inclination that might lead to illogical and sometime criminal behavior.[13]

A clue for reading this scene is provided for the viewers at the beginning of the film by a short motto. Just before the opening scene, a saying by Rabbi Shlomo Itzhaki (*Rashi*) flickers across the screen: "Receive with simplicity everything that happens to you." These words do not only help us decipher the opening scene, but also what at first seems like Gopnic's Job-like conundrum: the plight of a good man who is plagued by an outrageous fortune. The biblical character of Job is raised in relation with Gopnic by a number of critics. But, on reflection, his bitter fate, consisting of an unstable marriage, an annoying and parasitical family, and the trials and tribulations of attaining tenure in an academic institution, is far from unique (even when these problems appear in unison). It certainly does not merit a supernatural explanation.

The Rabbis try to tell him so in their different ways. Junior Rabbi Scott (Simon Helberg) comes closest to the words of Rabbi Itzhaki when he advises Gopnic to "look at the parking lot" and find his answers within everyday occurrences. Rabbi Nachtner (George Wyner) tells Gopnic a more elaborate story about a non-Jew who was found to have a message in Hebrew inscribed in his teeth. The story "must" mean something, but it doesn't. And the senior Rabbi Marshak (Alan Mandell), who knows that Gopnic will not be convinced, simply refuses to see him. But he does present to his son, Danny, the wise words of Jefferson Airplane:

When the truth is found to be lies and
all the joy within you dies don't you
want somebody to love?

Love, simple human interaction, be it even with the gorgeous hash-smoking nude sunbather next door (Mrs. Samsky, played by Amy Landecker), is the best spiritual remedy that the wise Rabbi can recommend.

The film therefore develops a clear anti-mystical theme. The answer to Gopnic's trouble is not found in a secret combination of sacred and incomprehensible Hebrew letters. Gopnic must face up realistically to his trouble, and a logical and methodical approach might solve them—or perhaps it will not. It is also entirely possible, as the end of the film implies, that greater problems such as a serious illness or a tornado might serve to put Gopnic's "horrible" predicament in perspective.

Of course, the criticism in the film of mysticism as a substitute for taking responsibility for one's life is not limited to American Jews, as the film is not intended only for a Jewish audience. The film is set in a Jewish community in Minnesota in the late 1960s to create a fable with sufficient distance from the daily lives of most viewers. However, they might recognize in Gopnic's story a growing tendency towards mysticism in a contemporary society that renders people increasingly less autonomous and less capable of either comprehending or controlling their fate.

5. Some contemporary context

While the film takes place in 1967, it is produced in 2009—and responds to an existing context in Yiddish Studies, Translation, Media, and contemporary culture.

In terms of Yiddish Studies and the image of Yiddish in contemporary society, it is difficult to separate the choice of the Coen Brothers to produce an opening scene in Yiddish from a certain Yiddish renaissance that has been taking placing since the 1990s in various academic institutions and centers of Jewish activity. Over the past three decades, Yiddish has regained popularity and interest in institutions such as Columbia, Harvard, Penn State, and Ohio State, and overseas at the School of Oriental and African Studies in London, Oxford, Trier, Düsseldorf, and even at Bar Ilan University in Israel. Among other venues, Yiddish has been introduced as a vital means for studying and reevaluating the life of European Jews in Eastern Europe before the Holocaust, and a vital— sometime radical—means for studying Jewish secular culture, literature, music, theater, drama, and even a vibrant Jewish film industry at the beginning of the twentieth century. From a political point of view, Yiddish Studies offer students an opportunity to explore their roots without considering a Zionist ideology. And with popular trends such as Klezmer-Jazz and Fringe Theater, Yiddish offers a very "hip" cultural venue. This trend certainly affected a great change in various sub-disciplines within Jewish Studies. The increased tangibility of Yiddish instruction, scholarship, and sources means that one can no longer study Jewish history in Eastern Europe, Jewish immigration, and perhaps Jewish culture in general without knowing and using original documents in Yiddish. Similarly, in popular culture, Yiddish is beginning to necessitate a certain "seriousness" of its own—which is expressed through the highly invested and meticulously performed prologue of *A Serious Man*. For one thing, Yiddish is no longer seen as an anecdotal, often comic *Shtick* that demands a minimal investment and effort in order to "get a laugh." More importantly, this "seriousness" points out to Yiddish as an important cultural source of Jewish history and culture which, as this is represented in the film, has been sorely missed in Jewish-American lives.

Another important context is the development of Jewish representation in the cinema since the 1990s. In *The New Jew in Film*, Nathan Abrams claims that over the past twenty-five years, the representation of Jewish characters in the American cinema (and the representation of Jewish masculinity in particular) has transcended a few prescribed stereotypes, and opened up a wide array of representations, including "Jews who are stoned, solitary, nasty, brutish, short, unprofessional, working class, and more" (Abrams, 2011: 21). Among the many compelling examples of this phenomenon which Abrams provides, he writes:

> The Coen Brother's post-1990 films manifest many of the trends that will be discussed in this book. Indeed, they are essential to understanding contemporary Jewish cinema.
>
> Abrams, 2011: 24

Of these, the character of Walter Sobchak (John Goodman) in *The Big Lebowski* (1998) serves to demonstrate that the character of a Jew can be represented as neither stereotypically Jewish in appearance, nor particularly squeamish or moral. And, among other traits, the character of Larry Gopnik in *A Serious Man* demonstrates—in opposition to previous stereotypes—a healthy sexual appetite. Most importantly, since the character of the "new Jew" in cinema can be just about anyone—Jewish identity is tied to a new sense of responsibility, as it is no longer enforced from the outside, but depends on one's active cultivation. For Gopnic, who "does not know what a *get* (religious divorce) is," and who prefers easy mystical solutions to a "serious" study of Jewish sources, an existential crisis is inevitable (Abrams, 2011: 25–36, 83, 150). Indeed, the Jewish cinema creates a new reality in which a crooked nose, a trite anecdote and a few words in either Hebrew or Yiddish, are no longer enough to create credible Jewish representation. Gopnic's character seems to try to retreat back into a comfortable stereotype, but that refuge is no longer available. His family, his co-workers, his sexy neighbor, and even the Rabbis, force him out of his comfort zone and he is left to his own devices, without either divine guidance or inspiration.

Finally, this new seriousness, both in terms of Jewish representation and the use of Yiddish in popular media, fits well both within the context of global communication, and of recent developments within Translation Studies. The complex and highly invested representation in *A Serious Man*, both in terms of the Yiddish prologue and of Jewish life in Minnesota in the 1960s, meets the growing demand in the media for authentic and well-researched presentation: neither of an English dialog that is colored with an assumed foreign accent; nor of a token representation of ethnic identity—but a thoughtful and well-researched performance. More importantly, while in comparison with a film such as *The Interpreter*, *A Serious Man* does not address specifically some of the concerns of translators and translation scholars—it fits well with themes that have been developed over the past three decades, and the growing sense of scholars that translation is not only about the dissemination of information, but that it is a complex cultural, political, and psychological process. Particularly within a global reality, where national and ethnic languages are undermined by few all-encompassing lingua-francas—languages take on a particularly emotional role. The latter, as Michael Wood explains in "The Languages of the Cinema" (Wood 2005), is not only expressed verbally, but also in terms of scenery, music, props, and various cultural elements that enhance the meaning of the dialog and are often tied with ethnic and national representation. In the opening scene of *A Serious Man*, the reconstruction of the Jewish town, the East European landscape, and the Yiddish theme song that is repeated throughout the film—enhance the meaning of the prologue, very much in the manner that Wood describes in relation with Grigori Konzinsev's 1971 cinematic adaptation of *King Lear*.

It is therefore the context of a number of fields: Jewish Studies, Communication, and Translation Studies, that the Coen Brothers respond to a growing "seriousness" about ethnic representation, linguistic performance, and identity formation. Larry Gopnik, by the same token, is asked to become "a serious man" by realizing that such identity is not inherent, but requires an active involvement and personal responsibility.

6. Conclusion (or: Why is this important?)

Translation and foreign language are not only (and sometime not at all) about communicating information, but a part of the performance, and an integral part of the message in the text. In *A Serious Man*, the Yiddish prologue calls on the characters in the film—and perhaps on some of the viewers—to regain a lost tradition while placing it within a wider cultural and historical context. To add to Delabastita's notion of the dramatic function of translation, I suggest that the increased use of a secondary language in American Media serves to demonstrate cultural and political issues with particular effectiveness, and in circumstances under which more explicit exposition might be inappropriate.

In *A Serious Man*, the use of Yiddish (and some Hebrew) helps to guide the viewers through a film that is rife with references to Jewish culture. There are probably few other ways of exposing most viewers to the tensions between Hebrew and Yiddish without boring them with a historical explanation. And the swift transition from Yiddish to Hebrew in *A Serious Man*, as well as the depiction of the Hebrew School classroom, tells the viewers, even if they are not Jewish, everything that they need to know about the contemporary use of Jewish languages in the United States: that Jewish congregants are cut off from their cultural past (in Yiddish), and that many of them practice a religion (in Hebrew) that is incomprehensible to them.

But, to return to the beginning of this essay, there is a remaining question as to what an "interdisciplinary" study means in this context, and whether one even agrees that an interdisciplinary effort is required in order to read texts such as *A Serious Man*. When it comes to Media and Translation, there is simply no other choice. In addition to the two obvious fields of Media and Translation, at least one national/ethnic language lurks in the background with its history, geography, culture, and literature intact. This means that Media and Translation have a great deal to teach about Yiddish and vice versa. Where media can show, rather than tell, the strong emotional, social, and political effects that the move from one language to another entails, it provides effective means for cultural communications that lengthy historical and ethnographic accounts cannot replace. At the same time, cultural and historical knowledge are essential for those who want to create and to theorize about translation and the use of foreign language in media.

Glossary

Dibek (**Yiddish**): A malicious possessing spirit believed to be the dislocated soul of a dead person. It supposedly leaves the host body once it has accomplished its goal, sometimes after being helped.

Schrödinger's Cat: A thought experiment, sometimes described as a paradox, devised by Austrian physicist Erwin Schrödinger in 1935. It illustrates what he saw as the problem of the Copenhagen interpretation of quantum mechanics applied to everyday objects.

Hebraists and Yiddishists: Two social movements at the end of the nineteenth and the beginning of the twentieth century, often overlapping in themes and participants, that strived to create a national modern Jewish culture either in Hebrew or in Yiddish.

***Sitrah Akhra* (Aramaic):** *Sitrah Akhra* literally means: "the other side." Some philosophers believe that every object and life form was created by and is subject to God (including demons). Others wonder if there are unspeakably evil forces that had their origins in another realm outside of God's command, or at least of a place that was forsaken by God, or where the inhabitants had no respect for God at all. Such a place is the *Sitrah Akhra.*

***Get* (Hebrew):** A divorce document in Jewish religious law, which must be presented by a husband to his wife to effectuate their divorce. The essential part of the *get* is very short, and the text reads: "You are hereby permitted to all men," which means that the woman is no longer married and that the laws of adultery no longer apply. The *get* also returns to the wife the legal rights that a husband holds in regard to her in a Jewish marriage.

Notes

1 See Wang and Zhao (2011).
2 See Abend-David (2010).
3 Another important production, despite the fact that it did not receive mainstream attention, is *Romeo and Juliet in Yiddish* (2010).
4 See, among others: Berkowitz (2002), Hellerstein (2000), Norich (1995), Margolis (2006), Margolis (2009), Miller (2009), and Rosenwald (2001).
5 See, among others: Abend-David (2003), Anctil, Ravvin and Simon (2007), Miner (1990), Simon (2008), and Singerman (2002).
6 See, among others: Abend-David (2014), Bielsa and Bassnett (2008), Chiaro (2010), Díaz-Cintas (2009), Gambier and Gottlieb (2001), Luyken et. al. (1991), Nornes (2007), O'Hagan and Ashworth (2002), O'Sullivan (2011), Pérez-González (2014), and Schaeffner and Bassnett (2010).
7 See, among others: Kelman (2006), Kun (1999), Merwin (2009), Paskin and European Jewish Publications Society (1999), Schulman (1986), and Shandler (2009).
8 This type of translation is often referred to as "back translation," a term that is used in Translation Studies as well as Linguistics, Language Pedagogy, and other fields.
9 See Nornes (1999).
10 Jonathan Boyarin (2011: 381) makes a similar observation, though Stone's description is by far more amusing.
11 See for example: Shtif (1929).
12 See for example: Abend-David (2011).

13 Here, Ginsburg (2011: 358, 362) correctly connects the scene with a concept of personal responsibility, as well as the uncertainty principle that Gopnic teaches to his students.

References

2015 Chrysler 200 Commercial Japanese Quality (October 27, 2014) [TV Commercial] Producers: Wieden & Kennedy. USA: Wieden & Kennedy. Available online: https:// www.youtube.com/watch?v=j1xBaMeOs-M (accessed May 9, 2015).

A Serious Man (2009), [Film] Dir. Joel Coen and Ethan Coen, USA: Focus Features.

Abend-David D. (2003), *Scorned my Nation: A Comparison of Translations of the Merchant of Venice into German, Hebrew, and Yiddish*, New York: Peter Lang.

Abend-David, D. (2010), "Louis Zukofsky and *The West Wing*: Metaphors of mentorship, Yiddish, and translation at street level," *Forum* 8 (1): 1–35.

Abend-David, D. (2011), "Gender Benders and Unrequited Offerings: Two Hebrew Poems by Rachel Bluwstein-Sela and Dovid Hofshteyn," *Prooftexts: A Journal of Jewish Literary History*, 31: 210–228.

Abend-David, D. (ed.) 2014), *Media and Translation: An Interdisciplinary Approach*, New York: Bloomsbury Academic.

Abrams, N. (2011), *The New Jew in Film: Exploring Jewishness and Judaism in Contemporary Cinema*, New Brunswick, NJ: Rutgers University Press.

Anctil, P., N. Ravvin, and S. Simon (2007), *New Readings of Yiddish Montreal*, Ottawa: University of Ottawa Press.

Benjamin, W. (1970), "The Task of the Translator," in H. Zohn (trans.), *Illuminations*. 69–82, London: Collins (Fontana).

Berkowitz, J. (2002), *Shakespeare on the American Yiddish stage*, Iowa City: University of Iowa press.

Beygl, Beygl, Dakim BeTeamim (2011) [*Thin Crackers with Flavors*; TV Commercial] Dir. Rani Carmeli, Israel: Paradiso. November 14, 2011. Available online: https:// www.youtube.com/watch?v=-AayI6Hvkto (accessed May 9, 2015).

Bielsa, E. and S. Bassnett (eds) (2008), *Translation in Global News*, Milton Park: Routledge.

Blazing Saddles (1974), [Film] Dir. Mel Brooks, USA: Crossbow Productions.

Boyarin, D. (1997), *Unheroic Conduct: The Rise of Heterosexuality and the Invention of the Jewish Man*, Berkeley: University of California Press.

Boyarin, J. (2011). "An ugly story?" *AJS Review*, 35 (2): 377–382.

Brothers & Sisters (2006–2011), [TV Series] Creator: Jon Robin Baitz, After Portsmouth.

Chiaro, D. (2010), *Translation, Humour and the Media*, New York: Continuum.

Cohen, N.M. (2011), "A Serious Man," *Journal of Religion and Film*, 15 (2). Available online: http://digitalcommons.unomaha.edu/jrf/vol15/iss2/8/ (accessed August 7, 2017).

Díaz-Cintas, J. (ed.), (2009), *New Trends in Audiovisual Translation*, Briston: Multilingual Matters.

Delabastita, D. (2004), "If I Know the Letters and the Language: Translation as a Dramatic Device in Shakespeare's Plays," in T. Hoenselaars (ed.), *Shakespeare and the Language of Translation*, 31–52, London: Arden Shakespeare.

Delabastita, D and T. Hoenselaars (2015), "Introduction: 'If But as Well I Other Accents Borrow, that can my Speech Diffuse'—Multilingual Perspective on English Renaissance Drama," in D. Delabastita and T. Hoenselaars (eds.), *Multilingualism in the Drama of Shakespeare and his Contemporaries,"* 1–16, Netherlands: John Benjamins.

East Side Sushi (2014), [Film] Dir. Anthony Lucero, USA: Blue Sun Pictures.

Finkelstein, N. (2001), *Not One of Them in Place: Modern Poetry and Jewish American Identity*, Albany: State University of New York Press.

Fredman, S. (2001), *A Menorah for Athena: Charles Reznikoff and the Jewish Dilemmas of Objectivist Poetry*, Chicago, IL: University of Chicago Press.

Gambier, Y. and H. Gottlieb (eds.) (2001). *(Multi) Media Translation: Concepts, Practices, and* Research, Amsterdam: John Benjamins Publishing Company.

Ginsburg, S. (2011), "The Physics of being Jewish, or on Cats and Jews," *AJS Review*, 35 (2): 357–364.

Hellerstein, K. (2000), "Translating as a Feminist: Preconceiving Anna Margolin," *Prooftexts: A Journal of Jewish Literary History,* 20 (1–2): 191–208.

House M.D. (2004–2012), [TV Series] Dir. David Shore. Heel & Toe Films.

Inglourious Basterds (2009), [Film] Dir. Quentin Tarantino, USA: Universal Pictures.

Kelman, A.Y. (2006), "The Acoustic Culture of Yiddish," *Shofar*, 25 (1): 127–151.

Kilbourn, R.J.A. (2014), "(No) Voice Out of the Whirlwind: *The Book of Job* and the End of the World in *A Serious Man*, Take Shelter, and the Tree of Life," *Adaptation*, 7 (1): 25–46.

Kun, J, (1999), "The Yiddish are Coming," *American Jewish History*, 87 (4): 343–374.

Lang, A. 2011, "From Boys to Men: Gender Politics and Jewish Identity in *A Serious Man*," *AJS Review*, 35 (2): 383–391.

Lewit, I. (2009), "The Kafkaesque Cinematic Language of the Coen Brothers' *A Serious Man*," *Journal of the Kafka Society of America: New International Series*, 33–34 (4): 29–38.

Linnitt, C. (2009), "*A Serious Man*," *Journal of Religion and Film*, 13 (2). Available online: http://digitalcommons.unomaha.edu/cgi/viewcontent.cgi?article=1499&contex t=jrf (accessed August 7, 2017).

Lost in Translation (2003), [Film] Dir. Sofia Coppola, USA: Focus Features.

Luyken, G. et al. (1991), *Overcoming Language Barriers in Television Dubbing and Subtitling for the European Audience*, Manchester: European Institute for the Media.

M*A*S*H (1972–1983), [TV Series] Creator: Larry Gelbart, 20th Century Fox.

Mathews, P. (2014), "The Morality Meme: Nietzsche and *A Serious Man*," *Cultura-International Journal of Philosophy of Culture and Axiology*, 11 (1): 63–81.

Margolis, R. (2006), "Yiddish Translation in Canada: A Litmus Test for Continuity," *TTR: traduction, terminologie, redaction*, 19 (2): 149–189.

Margolis, R. (2009), "Translating Jewish Poland into Canadian Yiddish: Symcha Petrushka's Mishnayes." *TTR: traduction, terminologie, redaction*, 22 (2): 183–202.

Merwin, T. (2009), "Yiddish Radio Project [original radio broadcast; review]," *Journal of American Folklore*, 122 (2): 210–212

Miller, L. (2009), "My Approach to the Whitman Translation," *Yiddish–Modern Jewish Studies*, 16 (1–2): 184–189.

Miner, K. L. (1990), "Yiddish V/1 Declarative Clauses in Discourse," *IPrA Papers in Pragmatics*, 4 (1–2): 122–149.

Naifeh, K. (2013), "*A Serious Man* and *The Red Book*," *Jung Journal-Culture & Psyche*, 7 (3): 45–53.

Naifeh, S. (2013), "Coen Film Noir-Dark Passages: A Cultural Commentary on the Human Condition in *A Serious Man*," *Jung Journal-Culture & Psyche*, 7 (3): 25–35.

Norich, A. (1995), "Isaac Bashevis Singer in America: The Translation Problem," *Judaism: A Quarterly Journal of Jewish Life and Thought*, 44 (2): 208–218.

Nornes, A.M. (1999), "For an Abusive Subtitling," *Film quarterly*, 52 (3): 17–34.

Nornes, A.M. (2007), *Cinema Babel: Translating Global Cinema*, Minneapolis: University of Minnesota Press.

Niger, S. (1990), *Bilingualism in the History of Jewish Literature*, trans. J. Fogel, Lanham, MD: University Press of America.

O'Hagan, M. and D. Ashworth (2002), *Translation-Mediated Communication in a Digital World*, Clevedon: Multilingual Matters.

O'Sullivan, C. (2011), *Translating Popular Film*, Basingstoke: Palgrave Macmillan.

Paskin and European Jewish Publications Society (1999), *When Joseph met Molly: A Reader on Yiddish Film*, Nottingham: Five Leaves.

Pérez-González. L. (2014), *Audiovisual Translation: Theories, Methods and Issues*, Abingdon: Routledge.

Prell, R. (2011), "*A Serious Man* in situ: 'Fear and Loathing in St. Louis Park,'" *AJS Review*, 35 (2): 365–376

Primor BeYidish (2016) [Primor in Yiddish; TV Commercial], Producers: Primor. Israel: Primor. May 6, 2012. Available online: https://www.youtube.com/watch?v=JVDa5a4TzeU (accessed: May 9, 2015).

Romeo and Juliet in Yiddish (2010), [Film] Dir. Eve Annenberg, USA: Vilna City Films.

Rosenwald, L. (2001), "The Implications of a New Bergelson Translation," *Prooftexts: A Journal of Jewish Literary History*, 20 (2): 237–248.

Rubin, S.I. (2013), "*A Serious Man*: Interpretation as a Fairy Tale," *Jung Journal–Culture & Psyche*, 7 (3):36–44.

Schaeffner, C. and S. Bassnett (eds.) (2010), *Political Discourse, Media and Translation*, Newcastle upon Tyne: Cambridge Scholars Publishing.

Schulman, S. (1986), "*Yidl mitn fidl*: Yiddish Fictional Cinema," *Jump Cut: A Review of Contemporary Media*, 31: 42

Shandler, J. (2009), *Jews, God, and Videotape: Religion and Media in America*, New York: New York University Press.

Shandler J. (2011), "Serious Talk," *AJS Review*, 35 (2): 349–355.

Shtif, N. (1929), "די סאציאלע דיפערענציע אין יידיש: די העברעישע עלעמענטן אין דער שפראך [Social Differentiation in Yiddish: The Hebrew Element in the Language]." *The Yiddish Language*, 17–18: 1–22. In Yiddish.

Simon, S. (2008), "Yiddish in America, or Styles of Self-Translation," in Pym, Shlesinger and Simeoni (eds.), *Beyond Descriptive Translation Studies: Investigations in Homage to Gideon Toury*, 67–78, Netherlands: Benjamins Translation Library.

Singerman, R. (2002), *Jewish Translation History: A bibliography of bibliographies and studies*, Netherlands: Benjamins Translation Library.

Stanley, T. (2014), "*A Serious Man*," *Bible and Critical Theory*, 9 (1–2): 27–37.

Stone, A.A. (2010), "*A Serious Man*," *Psychiatric Times*, 27 (2): 32–33.

The Big Lebowski (1998), [Film] Dir. Joel Coen and Ethan Coen, USA Polygram Filmed Entertainment.

The Frisco Kid (1979), [Film] Dir. Robert Aldrich, USA: Warner Brothers. 1979.

The Interpreter (2005), [Film] Dir. Sydney Irwin Pollack, USA: Universal Pictures.

The Nanny (1993–1999), [TV Series]. Dir. Fran Drescher, CBS.

The Longest Day (1962), [Film] Dir. Ken Annakin, USA: 20th Century Fox.

Tollerton, D. (2011), "Job of Suburbia? *A Serious Man* and Viewer Perceptions of the Biblical," *Journal of Religion and Film*, 15 (2). Available online: http://digitalcommons.unomaha.edu/cgi/viewcontent.cgi?article=1052&contex t=jrf (accessed August 7, 2017).

Tyree, J.M. (2010), "No Fun: Debunking the 1960s in *Mad Men* and *A Serious Man*," *Film Quarterly*, 63 (4): 33–41.

Wang, L. and G. Zhao (2011), "Function-oriented Approaches in Commercial Advertisement Translation," *Theory and Practice in Language Studies*, 1 (15): 521–524.

West Wing (1999–2006), [TV Series] Creator: Aaron Sorkin, NBC.

Wood, M. (2005), "The Languages of Cinema," in M. Wood and S. Bermann (eds), *Nation, Language, and the Ethics of Translation*, 79–88, Princeton and Oxford: Princeton and Oxford University Press.

Yes Pirsomet Kharedim (2012) [*Ultraorthodox Commercial for Yes Satellite Television*; TV Commercial] Dir. Ifat Shlazinger, Israel: McCann-Erikson. October 17, 2012. Available online: https://www.youtube.com/watch?v=wtjDbSisRZQ (accessed May 9, 2015).

Zemmelman, S. (2013), "The Tempest Speaks: Liminality in *A Serious Man*," *Jung Journal-Culture & Psyche* 7 (3):16–24.

Zukofsky, L. (1978), *A*, Berkeley: University of California Press.

Contributors

Dror Abend-David
University of Florida

Dror Abend-David is a lecturer at the Department of Languages, Literatures and Cultures at the University of Florida. He is a scholar of Media and Translation; author of *"Scorned my nation": A Comparison of Translations of* The Merchant of Venice *into German, Hebrew and Yiddish* (Peter Lang 2003); and editor of *Media and Translation: An Interdisciplinary Approach* (Bloomsbury 2014, 2016). Dror received his doctorate in Comparative Literature from New York University (2001), and has published extensively on Translation in relation to Media, Literature, and Jewish Culture.

Chiara Bucaria
University of Bologna

Chiara Bucaria is Associate Professor of English Language and Translation at the University of Bologna's Department of Interpretation and Translation, where she teaches courses in translation from English into Italian, including audiovisual translation, subtitling, and voice-over. Her research interests include the impact of censorship and manipulation in dubbed and subtitled films and TV programs, with a specific interest in the linguistic and cultural adaptation of controversial and taboo humor. She has published journal articles and book chapters on audiovisual translation, textual manipulation in translation, translation and humor, and the cross-cultural adaptation of media paratexts. She is co-editor of the volume, *Taboo Comedy: Television and Controversial Humour* (Palgrave 2016).

Delia Chiaro
University of Bologna

Delia Chiaro is Professor of English Language and Translation at the Department of Interpretation and Translation of the University of Bologna at Forlì. She has authored over a hundred publications on diverse aspects of translation including the entry for audiovisual translation in *The Encyclopedia of Applied Linguistics* (Wiley-Blackwell 2013 and 2018). Her most recent monograph is *The Language of Jokes in the Digital Age* (Routledge 2018). She has been invited as keynote speaker at conferences worldwide.

Ying Cui
School of Translation Studies, Shandong University, Weihai, People's Republic of China

Ying Cui received her PhD from City University of Hong Kong. She is an Associate Professor at the School of Translation and Interpretation, Shandong University, Weihai. Her major research interests include translation practice and theories as well as linguistics.

Erga Heller
Kaye Academic College of Education

Erga Heller is head of the Arts Department and Literature Department at Kaye Academic College of Education, Beer Sheba, Israel. She is the chief editor of *Kolot*, a journal of education and culture published by Kaye College, in Hebrew. She received her doctorate from Tel Aviv University in Cultural Studies in 1995. Since then she published papers on translation into Hebrew in peer reviewed journals and in collections about: Hebrew food language; substandard dialects in Modern Hebrew; the aesthetics of "lower Hebrew" translations; English/Hebrew television subtitling; technical translations containing Medical Terminology; and local and foreign first names in Hebrew children's literature.

Iwona Mazur
Adam Mickiewicz University in Poznan, Poland

Iwona Mazur is a lecturer and researcher at the Department of Translation Studies, Faculty of English, Adam Mickiewicz University in Poznan, Poland. Her research focuses on audio description. She has participated in a number of Polish and international research projects, including an AD reception study: ADVERBA, Digital Television for All Project, and the ADLAB Project. Recently, she has co-authored a book on audio description (Polish title: *Audiodeskrypcja*). She serves as Executive Board member at the European Association for Studies in Screen Translation (ESIST).

Zoë Pettit
University of Greenwich

Zoë Pettit is Associate Professor and Head of the School of Humanities and Social Sciences within the Faculty of Liberal Arts and Sciences at the University of Greenwich, London. She holds a PhD in audiovisual translation (2000) from Paul Valéry University, Montpellier, France. Her research interests include interlingual subtitling and dubbing, multimodality, verbal and non-verbal communication, and multilingual film. She has published a number of journal articles and book chapters on Audiovisual Translation.

Kayoko Takeda
Rikkyo University

Kayoko Takeda is Professor of Translation and Interpreting Studies in the College of Intercultural Communication at Rikkyo University in Tokyo. Her main research areas are: translator and interpreter education; socio-cultural aspects of translating and interpreting; history of translation and interpreting; audiovisual translation; and technologies used in translating and interpreting. She is the author of *Interpreting the Tokyo War Crimes Trial* (University of Ottawa Press 2010) and a co-editor of *New Insights in the History of Interpreting* (John Benjamins 2016).

Ying Xiao
University of Florida

Ying Xiao is Associate Professor of Chinese film and media at the University of Florida. She received her PhD from the Department of Cinema Studies at New York University where she finished a dissertation on soundtrack and Chinese cinema. She has published articles on Chinese female writers, Chinese documentaries, Chinese hip-hop culture, Chinese rock 'n' roll film, and the Chinese film industry under neoliberal globalization. Before joining the University of Florida, she was involved in a series of TV and documentary productions. She has participated in the curatorship of Reel China Documentary Film Festival since 2004 and organized "DV China and Social Change" film series and workshop at the University of Florida in 2011. She is the author of *China in the Mix: Cinema, Sound, and Popular Culture in the Age of Globalization* (University Press of Mississippi 2017), and her co-authored book on the films of Jia Zhangke is forthcoming with Edinburgh University Press.

Yanli Zhao
School of Translation Studies, Shandong University, Weihai, People's Republic of China

Yanli Zhao is a lecturer of English Language and Literature at Shandong University, Weihai. Her areas of expertise include Literary Translation, Cultural Studies, and Discourse Analysis.

Index

Lightning Source UK Ltd.
Milton Keynes UK
UKHW020710311220
376184UK00003B/197